WORKHOUSES
OF WALES
AND THE
WELSH BORDERS

WORKHOUSES OF WALES AND THE WELSH BORDERS

PETER HIGGINBOTHAM

First published 2022

The History Press
97 St George's Place, Cheltenham,
Gloucestershire, GL50 3QB
www.thehistorypress.co.uk

ISBN 978 0 7509 9488 0

Typesetting and origination by The History Press
Printed and bound in Great Britain by TJ Books Limited, Padstow, Cornwall.

Trees for LYfe

CONTENTS

INTRODUCTION 7

1 ANGLESEY 44

2 BRECONSHIRE (BRECKNOCKSHIRE) 49

3 CARDIGANSHIRE 57

4 CARMARTHENSHIRE 65

5 CARNARVONSHIRE 75

6 DENBIGHSHIRE 83

7 FLINTSHIRE 88

8 GLAMORGAN 95

9 MERIONETHSHIRE 113

10 MONMOUTHSHIRE 121

11 MONTGOMERYSHIRE 135

12 PEMBROKESHIRE 143

13 RADNORSHIRE 149

14 CHESHIRE 155

15 GLOUCESTERSHIRE 179

16	HEREFORDSHIRE	216
17	SHROPSHIRE (SALOP)	231
18	WORKHOUSE RECORDS	267
19	USEFUL WEBSITES	271
20	PLACES TO VISIT	273
	NOTES	275
	BIBLIOGRAPHY	298
	INDEX OF PLACES	306

INTRODUCTION

In a roundabout way, the workhouse owes its existence to Henry VIII, whose dissolution of England's religious houses from 1536 onwards removed a major source of support for the nation's poor. Over the following decades, a variety of legislative measures were tried that gradually established the principle that the relief of the poor should come from the public purse rather than through charitable endeavours.

The 1552 Act for Provision and Relief of the Poor required that 'collectors of alms' be appointed in each parish, with every parishioner giving whatever their 'charitable devotion' suggested.[1] When the funds raised by such voluntary donations proved inadequate, compulsory contributions were instituted by the Vagabonds Act of 1572, which introduced a local property tax, the poor rate, administered by parish collectors and overseers. The money raised was to be used to relieve 'aged, poor, impotent, and decayed persons'.[2]

In 1576, the Act for Setting the Poor on Work stated a principle that was to influence the administration of poor relief for centuries to come – that the able-bodied were not to have 'any just excuse in saying that they cannot get service or work and be then without means of livelihood'.[3] To achieve this, every town was enjoined to provide 'a stock of wool, hemp, flax, or other stuff by taxation of all; so that every poor and needy person, old or young, able to work and standing in need of relief, shall not fear want of work, go abroad begging, or committing pilfering, or living in idleness.'

Further measures were included in the 1597 Act for the Relief of the Poor. The Act, which brought together elements of earlier legislation, required parishes to appoint Overseers of the Poor, whose responsibility was to collect and distribute the poor rate, to find work for the able-bodied, and to set up 'houses of dwelling' for those incapable of supporting themselves.[4] In the same year, the Hospitals for the Poor Act encouraged the founding of hospitals or 'abiding and working houses' for the poor. Accommodation for those in need through no fault of their own – often referred to as the 'impotent' or 'deserving' poor – coupled with premises and work for the able-bodied, formed the basis of what would eventually evolve into the workhouse.[5]

THE 1601 POOR RELIEF ACT

In 1601, another Act for the Relief of the Poor, essentially a slight refinement of its 1597 predecessor, formed the basis of the what became known as the Old Poor Law.[6] The main elements of the 1601 Act were: the parish being the administrative unit responsible for poor relief, with its Overseers collecting poor rates and allocating relief; the provision of materials to provide work for the able-bodied poor, those refusing to work liable to be placed in a House of Correction;[7] the relief of the impotent poor, including the provision of 'houses of dwelling'; and the setting to work and apprenticeship of pauper children.

The assistance given to the poor through the parish poor rates was predominantly dispensed as 'out-relief' – what might now be referred to as hand-outs. Out-relief could be given as a cash payment, either for one-off specific purposes, such as the purchase of clothing or shoes, or as a regular weekly pension. Alternatively, it could be dispensed in kind, most commonly in the form of bread or flour.

At the heart of all this activity was the parish's governing body, the vestry, which comprised the priest, churchwardens, and other respected householders of the parish.

THE STATUS OF WALES

Following the Acts of Union (1536–43), Wales was administered under the same laws as England. Thus, the Poor Law Acts of 1597 and 1601 and successive Poor Law legislation applied to Wales as well as England.

One Welsh county, the border county of Monmouthshire, had a peculiar status. After its name was omitted from the second Act of Union in 1543, the notion arose that it was a part of England rather than Wales. As a result,

Monmouthshire was frequently placed in the English section of directories, reports and other publications, while statutes and other legal documents often used the phrase 'Wales and Monmouthshire' to deal with the ambiguity. The situation was only fully resolved by the Local Government Act of 1972, which formally placed the county in Wales.

EARLY WORKHOUSES

Although the 1601 Act talked about 'work' and 'houses', it made no mention of the word 'workhouse' – a term that seems to have come into general use in the 1620s. These early workhouses were often non-residential establishments, more like workshops in character. Work, usually related to the production of textiles, was provided for the willing able-bodied, either on a daily basis on the premises, or taken away to be done in their own homes.

At Shrewsbury, as early as 1604, the town corporation made plans to set the poor to work in the old castle, but the scheme appears not to have come to fruition. In 1627, however, it was ordered that 'the Jersey house be made a work-house', with 'Jersey cloth' being manufactured there.[8] At around the same time, similar initiatives were taking place across the country in towns such as Reading, Taunton, Sheffield, Halifax, Leeds, Exeter, Plymouth and Cambridge.[9] Later in the century, workhouses were established at Ludlow (1676), Nantwich (1677) and Macclesfield (1698).

SETTLEMENT AND REMOVAL

The 1662 Settlement and Removal Act decreed that a parish was required to give poor relief only to those who were legally established or 'settled' there.[10] Unless they were able to rent a property for £10 a year or more, any new arrivals deemed 'likely to be chargeable' to the poor rates could be forcibly removed back to their own parish.

A child's settlement at birth was taken to be the same as that of its father. At marriage, a woman took on the same settlement as her husband. Illegitimate children were granted settlement in the place where they were born and thus became the responsibility of that parish. This sometimes led parish Overseers to try and get rid of an unmarried pregnant woman before her child was born; for example, by forcibly transporting her to another parish just before the birth, or by paying a man from another parish to marry her.

Over the years, the settlement laws were much amended. From 1691, settlement could be obtained by serving an apprenticeship in a new parish or by a year's continuous employment there. Although gradually diluted, the settlement laws governed the administration of poor relief for almost three centuries, their final remnants only being repealed in 1948.

LOCAL ACT ADMINISTRATIONS

The administrative framework laid down in 1601 did not suit everyone. This was particularly the case in towns that contained a number of small parishes. In 1696, Bristol's eighteen parishes obtained a Local Act of Parliament to create the Bristol Incorporation of the Poor. The Act enabled the incorporation to manage poor relief across the whole city, including the appointment of paid officers and the setting up of workhouses. By 1712, more than a dozen other towns had followed Bristol's example and formed civic incorporations under Local Acts. This route was taken by Hereford in 1698, Gloucester in 1702, and Chester in 1761. The workhouses set up by Local Act incorporations were usually styled 'Houses of Industry' in the expectation, often unrealised, that the labour of the inmates would make a substantial contribution to the running costs of the establishments.

Despite the considerable legal expense involved in obtaining a Local Act, parishes usually judged that the benefits would justify the cost. Things did not always turn out that way, however. Within five years of Gloucester obtaining its Local Act, the city's parishes had reverted to administering poor relief individually. Eventually, in 1764, the city obtained a second Local Act, which was successfully put into ongoing operation.

THE WORKHOUSE TEST ACT

By the start of the eighteenth century, parishes were increasingly providing residential accommodation for their poor. In most cases, these establishments – generally referred to as poorhouses – housed only the elderly and infirm, who received little or no supervision. However, the idea of the residential workhouse was gaining ground, where paupers were expected to work in return for their accommodation and maintenance. As well as the labour element, workhouses typically had a resident governor, strict rules regulating the inmates' conduct, and a plain diet. However, use of the terms 'poorhouse' and 'workhouse' was

An early 1900s view of St Peter's Hospital, Bristol – originally the city's 'Mint' workhouse, established in 1698.

An Act for the better Relief and Employment of the Poor of and belonging to the Parish of *Tewkesbury*, in the County of *Gloucester*.

Preamble.

WHEREAS the Parish of Tewkesbury, in the County of Gloucester, is large and populous, and the Poor thereof exceedingly numerous, who are maintained and supported at a great and burthensome Expence by the Inhabitants of the said Parish: And whereas the providing of a convenient House or Houses for the Reception of the Poor of the said Parish, and granting proper Powers for the Government, Regulation, and Employment of such Poor, would tend to the more effectual Relief, Assistance, and Accommodation of such as by Age, Infirmities, or Diseases, are rendered incapable of supporting themselves by their

14　E 2　　　　　　　　　　　　　　Labour,

The preamble to Tewksbury's 1792 Local Act, promoting a new workhouse to be administered by an incorporated board of 'guardians of the poor'.

not always consistent and the two words could be used almost interchange-ably, as at Mydroilyn in Cardiganshire, where the poorhouse inmates were to be 'properly employed'.[11] The character of an establishment could also change over time, as happened in 1810 at Mitcheldean in Gloucestershire, when the existing workhouse was turned over for use as a poorhouse.[12]

A major impetus to the use of parish workhouses came from the 1723 Workhouse Test Act, also known as Knatchbull's Act.[13] The Act gave a legal framework for workhouses to be set up by parishes either singly, or in com-bination with a neighbour. Premises could be hired or purchased for the purpose, and workhouse operation could be contracted out – a system known as 'farming' the poor. The Act also provided for the use of the workhouse 'test' – that the prospect of the workhouse should act as a deterrent and that poor relief could be restricted to those who were prepared to accept its regime. Parishes often hoped that offering only the workhouse to some or all of its relief applicants would reduce the number of claimants and so reduce the cost of the poor rates. If it did not fulfil these expectations, the workhouse could be closed and a return made to solely using out-relief.

Workhouses sometimes operated in existing premises that might be owned by the parish or be rented for the purpose, and their location could change

The workhouse at Sutton Lane Ends, near Macclesfield, erected in 1785.

over time. If a parish felt confident about the benefits of a workhouse, it might purchase or erect a building for the purpose. Parishes often switched to and fro between running the workhouse themselves and appointing a contractor. Contractor-run workhouses were normally located within the parish that was financing them, although other arrangements were possible. From 1748 onwards, Thomas Hazlehurst's establishment, based in Wellington, also received paupers from Newport, Little Wenlock, Wrockwardine and Berrington. In 1774, the Bromyard township of Winslow began using privately run workhouses 15 miles away in Hereford.[14] Up until 1795, Knighton employed a contractor in Ludlow.[15] In 1832, the Cheshire parish of Bostock was sending paupers to a workhouse in Middlewich.[16]

Although the 1723 Act was permissive, many parishes made use of its provisions and it led to a surge in workhouse provision. Parishes establishing workhouses in the first ten years following the passing of the Act included: Cheltenham, Chester (St John the Baptist and St Mary's on the Hill), Cirencester, Congleton, Ellesmere, Knutsford, Ledbury, Lymm, Much Wenlock, Shifnal, Stockport, Stroud and Tarporley. One of the earliest workhouses in Wales was opened at Hawarden in 1736.

THE PARISH WORKHOUSE REGIME

Parish workhouses varied in matters such as the inmates' diet and the tasks given to those able to work. A typical establishment was that at Bishop's Castle, in Shropshire, which in 1797 featured in a pioneering national survey of the poor by Sir Frederic Eden:

> The contractor has £105 a year to feed and clothe [the inmates] and defray all other expenses, except appeals. 14 paupers, chiefly old, infirm and insane, are in the house. Those who can work are employed in spinning lint or other common work, according to their age and abilities. Table of diet in the Workhouse: Breakfast—every day, broth, or milk and water gruel. Dinner—Sunday, Wednesday, hot meat and vegetables; other days, cold meat and vegetables. Supper—every day, same as at breakfast. No bread is allowed at dinner. Sometimes potatoes and milk are served for supper. The matron always gives each person a little bread and cheese after breakfast. The house is kept pretty clean: of 10 beds 6 are stuffed with feathers and 4 with chaff. Both beds and bedclothes are very old.[17]

It is clear from reports such as this that bed-sharing was the norm in work-houses of the period.

Parish workhouses often had extensive rules covering matters such as the daily routine, prohibitions on smoking or the use of distilled liquors, and punishments for behaviour such as swearing, lying, malingering or disobedience. Despite the ban on strong drink, parish workhouses frequently had their own brewhouse and served 'small' or weak beer to their inmates, including children – it was often healthier than the local water supply.

Conditions in parish workhouses could vary widely, though, and some were clearly grim. In 1835, a workhouse at Clifton, in Bristol, was 'filthy in the extreme, the appearance of the inmates dirty and wretched'.[18] In contrast, at nearby Westbury-on-Trym, inmates were provided with a good building, good food and kind treatment – one writer suggesting that 'even today it would be unlikely for an old person in a geriatric ward to receive such good treatment'.[19] Despite the potential for making the workhouse a deterrent institution, this was far from always being the case.

GILBERT'S ACT

In 1782, MP Thomas Gilbert successfully promoted his Act for the Better Relief and Employment of the Poor.[20] Gilbert viewed existing parish work-houses as 'dens of horror'.[21] The aim of his Act was to:

> have the poor well accommodated and treated with great humanity, but kept
> under a strict conformity to the rules and orders of the house; to encourage
> good behaviour, sobriety and industry, by proper rewards, and to find suitable
> and proper employment, under prudent and careful inspection, for all who
> are able to work.[22]

Under the Act, whose adoption was voluntary, the use of workhouses was to be restricted to the old, the sick and infirm, and orphan children, while able-bodied paupers were to be found employment near their own homes, with landowners, farmers and other employers receiving allowances from the poor rates to bring wages up to subsistence levels. Refusal to do such work would result in being placed in a House of Correction. The Act allowed parishes to form groups or 'unions' and operate a joint workhouse. The administration of Gilbert Unions was through a board of guardians, elected by the ratepayers

Llantrisant's former workhouse premises on Swan Street.

of each member parish, and supervised by a Visitor. The appointment of the Guardians and Visitor, the location of workhouses, and the appointment of a governor or contractor all required the approval of local magistrates.

Well over 100 Gilbert administrations were eventually established, most of which were Gilbert Unions, some comprising more than forty parishes. Motives for adopting the Act varied. Apart from any humanitarian considerations regarding the treatment of the poor, having a share in a large Gilbert Union workhouse could prove financially attractive for a parish compared to running its own institution. In some places, magistrates seem to have actively endorsed use of the Act, perhaps reflecting the greater control it bestowed on them in relation to the local operation of poor relief.[23]

Gilbert's Act proved particularly popular in Gloucestershire, where fifteen individual parishes eventually adopted its provisions.[24] No Gilbert administrations seem to have been formed in Cheshire, Herefordshire or Shropshire, and apparently just two in Wales, at Bangor and Swansea, although the Glamorgan parish of Llantrisant was clearly motivated by the Act despite not formally adopting it.

RURAL INCORPORATIONS

In the second half of the eighteenth century, a series of Local Act incorporations were formed in rural East Anglia. Fifteen were eventually established, most being based on traditional county sub-divisions known as hundreds. In 1784, Shrewsbury obtained a Local Act and its incorporation opened a large House of Industry in a building originally erected as a branch of London's Foundling Hospital. Seven years later, apparently stimulated by Shrewsbury's activities, five rural incorporations were formed in just two years in north-west Shropshire and neighbouring Montgomeryshire. The five – Atcham, Ellesmere, Oswestry, Whitchurch, and Montgomery and Pool – all closely followed Shrewsbury's model of operation and the style of its workhouse. The Montgomery and Pool Incorporation was run by a board of twenty-one directors, appointed by its constituent parishes. The incorporation spent £12,000 on erecting a House of Industry at Forden for up to 500 inmates, who were occupied in spinning, weaving, tailoring and shoemaking.

OUT-RELIEF VERSUS THE WORKHOUSE

A parliamentary survey published in 1777 revealed that there were almost 2,000 workhouses in operation in England, with around one in seven parishes operating an establishment. In total, almost 90,000 workhouse places were provided, enough to accommodate about 1.1 per cent of the population. It was rather a different picture in Wales (Monmouthshire included), however, where a mere nineteen workhouses were in use, covering about one in sixty parishes and able to house about 0.1 per cent of the population.[25] Eleven of

The Foundling Hospital building was adopted as the Shrewsbury Incorporation's House of Industry and became a model for five further establishments in the region.

these workhouses were in Pembrokeshire. In 1803, a total of 3,755 parishes in England were making use of (though not necessarily themselves operating) workhouses, while the figure for Wales was then seventy.[26]

Despite the growing use of the workhouse, out-relief was the dominant means for supporting the poor on both sides of the border – one in seven English parishes running a workhouse meant that six in seven were *not* running one. In 1802–03, across England and Wales, 956,248 paupers were relieved outside the workhouse at a cost of just over £3 million. At the same date, 83,468 paupers were maintained in workhouses, at cost of about £1 million.[27]

As the figures indicate, workhouses played very little part in parish poor relief in Wales, where out-relief was always the preferred method of providing for the poor. The main means of support were by the payment of rents out of the poor rates, by the exemption of cottages from rate assessments, by regular periodic relief, by casual or occasional assistance in money or kind, and in some parishes by establishing poorhouses where poor individuals or families could live rent-free but without any supervision.[28]

The readiness with which out-relief was provided could vary over time, however, depending on factors such as the prevailing economic conditions in the area. In the 1820s, able-bodied applicants in Shrewsbury first had to work on the town's streets. In lean times, some Shropshire coalfield parishes cut down on the numbers they supported with out-relief.[29]

THE OLD POOR LAW IN CRISIS

The early nineteenth century saw a time of increasing financial problems for the poor relief system. The national cost of poor relief rose enormously – from around £2 million in 1784 to a peak of £7.87 million in 1818.[30] The majority of that expenditure was on out-relief.

In many parts of the country, the supplementing of labourers' wages from the poor rate as advocated by Gilbert's Act had become common. The practice had become formalized in allowance systems such as that introduced in 1795 at Speenhamland in West Berkshire, which linked wage supplements to the price of bread and size of family. The Napoleonic Wars (1803–15) also contributed to an increase in the number of relief claimants, while the introduction of the Corn Laws in 1815 led to higher food prices and the cost of feeding the poor.

A few places, however, managed to buck the national trend of rising poor rates. In the early 1820s, the Nottinghamshire parish of Southwell virtually abolished out-relief and claimants were instead offered only the workhouse. The workhouse was strictly and economically run, with males and females segregated, work required of the inmates and a restricted diet imposed. As a result, the parish's poor relief expenditure fell from £1,884 in 1821–22 to £811 the following year. In 1824, a much larger workhouse run on similar lines was opened nearby by the Thurgarton Incorporation, again achieving significant financial savings.[31]

Elsewhere in the country, growing discontent among the labouring classes reached a climax in the autumn of 1830 with the so-called 'Swing' riots. Beginning in Kent and rapidly spreading across Surrey, Sussex, Middlesex and Hampshire, agricultural labourers engaged in increasingly violent protests against low wages, expensive food and the growing mechanization of farms. Attacks on workhouses featured among their activities.

A Royal Commission, appointed in 1832 to review the operation of the Poor Laws, highlighted the deficiencies of poor relief administration in many parishes. The Commission's report, published in 1834, characterized the typical parish workhouse as containing:

> a dozen or more neglected children, twenty or thirty able-bodied adults of both sexes and probably an equal number of aged and impotent persons who are proper objects of relief. Among these the mothers of bastard children and prostitutes live without shame, and associate freely with the youth, who also have the example and conversation of the inmates of the county gaol, the poacher, the vagrant, the decayed beggar, and other characters of the worst description. To these may be added a solitary blind person, one or two idiots, and not infrequently are heard, from among the rest, the incessant ravings of some neglected lunatic.[32]

A subsequent report on the Llantrisant workhouse was no better, describing it as a 'large workhouse … but it is ill-managed, the children are half naked and dirty, while the diet was as the Overseer admitted better than that of most of the small farmers of the Parish'.[33] Llantrisant's vestry, described by one writer as 'corrupt and inefficient', was not untypical of others in the region. Having to run the workhouse was a 'thorn in the flesh of the vestry' – the Overseers at one point looking after the place on a monthly rota system.[34]

The Royal Commission noted that many parishes in Monmouthshire had no workhouse or poorhouse, while most of those in Herefordshire and Shropshire did possess them. However, many Herefordshire parishes with workhouses had recently discontinued their use, believing they could maintain their poor more cheaply without them. In the north of Shropshire, the practice of parishes maintaining their poor in a common House of Industry was widespread. It was also observed that farming the poor was common in the region. In Monmouthshire, the common practice was for the contractor to be paid a gross annual sum, while in Shropshire and Herefordshire it was more usual for him to receive a weekly payment for each of the inmates in the house, with their daily diet being prescribed. In the former case, the contractor benefited from admitting as few paupers as possible, while in the latter it was in his interest to admit as many as possible.[35]

The Commission particularly criticised the use of allowance systems, said to be particularly prevalent in towns in the south of England, and also documented numerous examples of inefficiency or corruption in the local administration of poor relief. Eradicating this state of affairs was the main thrust of their report's proposals.

THE 1834 POOR LAW AMENDMENT ACT

The Royal Commission's recommendations were implemented in the 1834 Poor Law Amendment Act.[36] The Act, which formed the basis of what became known as the New Poor Law, aimed to create a national, uniform and compulsory system of poor relief administration under a new central authority, the Poor Law Commissioners (PLC). New groupings of parishes areas known as Poor Law Unions were created, each managed by a board of guardians elected by local ratepayers. Funding of the new system continued to be from local poor rates. Each union was expected to provide a workhouse, which was to be the only form of relief available to able-bodied men and their families, although out-relief would still be available in certain situations.

Although the 1834 Act had an enormous impact, it did not actually overturn existing principles of poor relief – the financial responsibility of the parish, the use of a workhouse test, the administrative grouping of parishes, local management by ratepayer-elected bodies, settlement qualifications, and plural voting had all featured in Old Poor Law legislation. What the 1834 Act did change was the administrative structure through which poor relief was dispensed. Details of exactly how the new system would operate were left for the PLC to devise.

One of the three Commissioners, George Nicholls, later noted two significant deficiencies in the Act. First, it allowed Local Act Incorporations and Gilbert Unions to continue operating if they wished to do so. The latter continued to hinder the formation of new Poor Law Unions in some areas until all remaining Gilbert Unions were abolished in 1869. Second, the PLC could not compel a union to provide a workhouse without the support of a majority of its ratepayers or its board of guardians, although the alteration or enlargement of existing workhouse premises could be demanded.[37]

THE FORMATION OF UNIONS

The creation of Poor Law Unions was supervised by Assistant Poor Law Commissioners in consultation with local parish officials and landowners in each area. Unions could vary widely in size and population, but typically comprised one or two dozen parishes, centred on the main town in the area. However, local geography and, often more importantly, local politics could play a large part in the number and make-up of the unions in each area.

The Assistant Commissioner responsible for Breconshire, Cardiganshire, Herefordshire and Radnorshire was Edmund Walker Head, who proposed placing the parishes of Radnorshire in unions based on the market towns of Builth, Hay, Kington, Knighton, Presteigne and Rhayader, all of which straddled the county's borders. Presteigne, whose member parishes had a total population of only 3,441, was the smallest by far of any union in Wales and barely viable. However, it lay between its more prosperous neighbours of Kington and Knighton, with whom it had considerable rivalry, and its formation was largely due to Presteigne's jealously guarded status as Radnorshire's county town.

In unions spanning the England–Wales border, Head's strategy was to include a majority of English parishes so as to counteract any rebellious tendencies among the Welsh members. He also believed that the Welsh guardians, mostly small tenant farmers, would have their character raised through contact with their English counterparts, who were more likely to be substantial yeoman farmers.[38]

RESISTANCE TO THE NEW POOR LAW

Apart from a few short-lived protests in Kent and Sussex, the introduction of the 1834 Act in the south of England was relatively trouble-free – unions were formed, guardians elected, and workhouses put into operation. However, the subsequent implementation of the Act in other parts of the country, notably in the manufacturing areas of the north of England and in rural central and north-west Wales, met with considerable resistance.

Poor Law Union areas in the 1880s. (By kind permission of GB Historical GIS Project)

At its mildest, this could be a letter of protest such as that from the vestry of the Merionethshire parish of Maentwrog to the Home Secretary, Lord Russell, in November 1836. The letter expressed disapproval of workhouses because they separated man and wife, provided an inadequate diet, and prevented inmates attending their usual places of Sunday worship.[39] In rather more forceful terms, in August 1839, the Bangor & Beaumaris guardians wrote to the PLC expressing their reasons for not erecting a workhouse: the union had insufficient paupers in the relevant condition to justify it, orphan children could be more cheaply maintained by out-relief, and families would be separated by it.[40]

At Macclesfield, in 1836, the guardians' plans for a new workhouse had to be shelved after intense local opposition, particularly from workers in the town's declining silk-weaving industry. The builder contracted to erect the building was abused and menaced by a mob. In May 1837, at Llanfair Caereinion (part of the Llanfyllin Union), a 400-strong mob hurled missiles at the Llanfyllin guardians and a visiting Assistant Poor Law Commissioner. In May 1838, the part-built walls of the Newtown & Llanidloes Union workhouse at Caersws were damaged by 'idly and evil disposed persons'.[41] Two months later, Llandovery's nearly completed workhouse suffered serious damage from a fire, thought to have been started deliberately. In January 1839, the new workhouse at Narberth suffered an arson attack. Workhouses were also among the targets of the 'Rebecca Rioters' who, in 1842-43, carried out a campaign of protests across South Wales, which included the storming of the Carmarthen workhouse.

The most sustained resistance came from the boards of guardians in unions, particularly those in Wales, who were opposed to the New Poor Law in general and – in a region deeply rooted in the use of out-relief – to the provision of a workhouse in particular.

One tactic was for a board to endlessly postpone discussion of the workhouse question until some future occasion. At Rhayader, in 1838, the guardians initially agreed to build a workhouse but somehow could never agree on a suitable site and the scheme went into limbo. During the 1840s, the guardians actively even appealed to the public to avoid claiming poor relief and thus the need for the establishment.[42]

Although opposition to the 1834 Act in Wales was widespread, some Welsh unions were persuaded of its potential benefits. At Aberayron – the first union in Cardiganshire to build a workhouse – the guardians saw it as a way of reducing the number of relief claimants, especially single mothers, and the expenditure on cottage rents. It would also provide a way of providing labour for the able-bodied poor.[43]

Where unions lacked a workhouse in which to relieve their able-bodied paupers, the PLC introduced the Outdoor Labour Test. This allowed such claimants to receive out-relief, half in cash and half in bread, in return for performing daily physical labour such as repairing roads, spade husbandry, and stone breaking.

In 1841, the PLC recorded seventeen out of the forty-seven Welsh unions as still 'not having efficient workhouses in operation'. This compared with nineteen out of 544 English unions lacking operational workhouses at the same date.[44] Steady pressure from the Commissioners, and their successors the Poor Law Board (PLB), gradually reduced this number, but by the late 1860s five unions in the centre of Wales (Builth, Lampeter, Presteigne, Rhayader and Tregaron) were still holding out, together with Crickhowell, which was refusing to replace its ageing and inadequate former parish workhouse. Further pressure and threats resulted in compliance from all but Rhayader and Presteigne. Finally, in 1876, the Local Government Board (LGB), which replaced the PLB in 1871, obtained new powers enabling it to dissolve any union if it deemed it necessary. In the face of this threat, Rhayader finally proceeded to build a workhouse. It received its first inmates in August 1879, making the union the last in the whole of England and Wales to provide a workhouse. Presteigne, however, stood its ground and was dissolved in 1877, with its constituent parishes being redistributed among adjacent unions.

Even when a union had a workhouse, the guardians did not necessarily make great use of it, often still preferring to support the poor through out-relief. Apart from any ideological grounds, this was usually the cheaper option. The 1841 census recorded that a year after its opening, the Pwllheli workhouse had only six inmates, the same number as the master and his family. Following the opening of three workhouses in Cardiganshire, the number of inmates was small, mostly comprising children, the chronic sick and vagrants.[45] In August 1843, the Aberystwyth Union workhouse, with accommodation for 200, had only six inmates.[46] On 1 January 1870, when the union was supporting 1,615 individuals, only fifty were in the workhouse.[47]

ENTERING THE WORKHOUSE

Although it was a lynchpin of the New Poor Law, relief claimants were not 'sent' to the workhouse, rather they resorted to it. Their initial contact with the system was usually through one of the union's relieving officers. Most unions had two or three of these officials who regularly visited each member parish, interviewed claimants, and assessed their circumstances. In the case of the able-bodied, the most likely outcome was an offer of the workhouse. Although entry into the institution was a voluntary process, a person's situation might give them little option but to accept. Families entered the workhouse together and left together. A man could not abandon his family outside while he entered the workhouse or, once they entered, leave them behind there.

On admission to a union workhouse, new inmates were given a bath, had their own clothes taken away for disinfection and storage, and were issued with workhouse clothing – the term 'uniform' was never officially used. At the Hereford workhouse in 1837, clothing purchased for the male inmates included: jackets, breeches and trousers of Fearnought cloth; strong calico shirts; shoes, hats and cloth caps. For women and girls there were grogram gowns, calico shifts, petticoats of Linsey-Woolsey material, gingham dresses, stays, stockings and shoes.[48] New entrants to the workhouse usually spent some time in a receiving or 'probationary' ward and had a medical inspection in case they were carrying any infectious disease such as smallpox.

Inmates could discharge themselves at any time – workhouses were not prisons. However, leaving the premises without permission while wearing workhouse clothing could result in a charge of stealing union property and earn a month's hard labour. A few hours' notice had to be given for an inmate's own clothes to be retrieved from storage.

CLASSIFICATION AND SEGREGATION

The operation of New Poor Law workhouses was based on a principle known as 'less eligibility' – that the regime they provided would always be less attractive than that enjoyed on the outside by even the lowliest independent labourer. Accordingly, inmates in union workhouses had plain repetitive food, were required to work according to their ability, and were separated into a number of groups or classes – the aged and infirm, the able-bodied, children aged from 7 to 15, and those under 7 years. The first three groups were further divided by gender, creating seven classes in total. Additional classes could be locally designated by the guardians, such as the 'lewd women' at the Cheltenham workhouse.

A fundamental requirement of workhouse accommodation was the segregation of the various classes of inmate. This could be achieved in two ways: by housing different groups in separate premises, or by partitioning a single building. Many English unions initially adopted the former option, making use of two or three former parish workhouse premises, but only while they erected a large, new single-site workhouse. The relative paucity of parish workhouses in Wales meant that their re-use was not an option for most Welsh unions. Very quickly, the single 'general mixed workhouse' emerged as the simplest and cheapest arrangement and became the standard style of workhouse provision.

The segregation of families as soon as they passed through the doors of a workhouse was one of the most resented aspects of the workhouse system. Husbands were separated from wives, and parents from children, only to be reunited when they left the workhouse. There were some small concessions to this requirement. A child under the age of 7 could reside in one of the female departments and its mother allowed access to it at all reasonable times. In addition, the father or mother of a child in the same workhouse could request a daily 'interview' with that child, though a weekly meeting on Sunday afternoon was the most common arrangement. From 1847, unions could allow elderly married couples, both aged over 60, to live together, so long as they were provided with their own sleeping apartment. By 1853, 297 couples in England were enjoying this privilege, with just two in Wales.[49]

Workhouses usually contained more elderly men than elderly women, usually attributed to women's greater adaptability in being able to support themselves and stay independent in their old age.

UNION WORKHOUSE ARCHITECTURE

In 1835, the PLC published a set of model plans to assist unions in the construction of new workhouse buildings, most of which were by a young architect named Sampson Kempthorne. His radial layouts, influenced by prison designs of the period, had wings for the different classes of inmates that radiated like spokes from a central polygonal hub, whose windows looked out in all directions. The wings, up to four storeys in height, could number three or four, respectively forming a 'Y' or a '+'. The space between the wings formed segregated exercise yards, which could be supervised from the hub where the master and matron had their quarters. An entrance block at the end of one of the wings contained a porter's lodge and waiting room on the ground floor, with the guardians' boardroom above. The perimeter buildings housed stores, workshops, laundry, stables, mortuary, etc. The four-wing or 'square' design (so-called because of the shape of its overall footprint) was the most popular, with typical examples at Pembroke, Hay and Northleach. A cut-down version of the 'square' design, referred to as the '200-pauper' plan, was aimed at 'less pauperised districts', with Northwich providing a good illustration of the layout. It was limited to two storeys (or just one for the parts to the rear of the centre) and lacked the polygonal hub. The rooms in all Kempthorne's designs occupied the full width of the building, with windows at each side providing light and ventilation.

Kempthorne himself designed two individual workhouses in the area covered by this volume, those at Winchcombe and Thornbury, and also gave advice on the adaptation of the existing workhouse at Tetbury. However, his model plans formed the basis of tens of designs by other architects, most notably George Wilkinson, who was responsible for a dozen workhouses in Wales, four in Herefordshire, and two in Gloucestershire.

PERSPECTIVE VIEW OF A WORKHOUSE FOR 300 PAUPERS.   Sampson Kempthorne, Architect.

A bird's-eye view of Sampson Kempthorne's model 'square' design, published by the PLC in 1835.

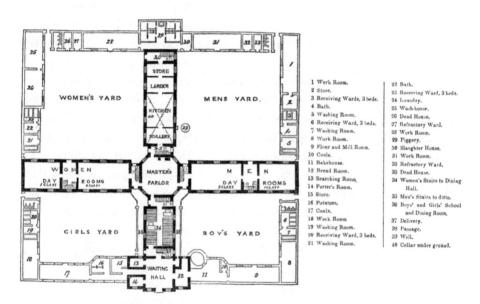

1 Work Room.
2 Store.
3 Receiving Wards, 3 beds.
4 Bath.
5 Washing Room.
6 Receiving Ward, 3 beds.
7 Washing Room.
8 Work Room.
9 Flour and Mill Room.
10 Coals.
11 Bakehouse.
12 Bread Room.
13 Searching Room.
14 Porter's Room.
15 Store.
16 Potatoes.
17 Coals.
18 Work Room.
19 Washing Room.
20 Receiving Ward, 3 beds.
21 Washing Room.

22 Bath.
23 Receiving Ward, 3 beds.
24 Laundry.
25 Wash-house.
26 Dead House.
27 Refractory Ward.
28 Work Room.
29 Piggery.
30 Slaughter House.
31 Work Room.
32 Refractory Ward.
33 Dead House.
34 Women's Stairs to Dining Hall.
35 Men's Stairs to ditto.
36 Boys' and Girls' School and Dining Room.
37 Delivery.
38 Passage.
39 Well.
40 Cellar under ground.

The ground-floor layout of the 'square' plan, of which many variations were devised.

Other prominent workhouse architects of the period included the partnership of George Gilbert Scott (previously an assistant to Kempthorne) and William Bonython Moffatt, who designed over forty workhouses and evolved their own distinctive layout, which was used at Gloucester and Chipping Sodbury. It featured a single-storey block at the front, which typically contained the porter's lodge, boardroom, receiving wards and chapel. A central entrance archway led through to an inner courtyard, either side of which were boys' and girls' yards. A long main building, running parallel to the entrance block, was typically three storeys high and again featured a central hub containing the master's quarters, with kitchens and scullery leading off behind. The male and female accommodation wings to each side contained day rooms and dining rooms on their ground floor with dormitories above and sometimes cross-wings at their outer ends. A separate infirmary was placed at the rear of the site, parallel to the main block.

Although Scott and Moffatt's later designs, such as that at Macclesfield, were more varied, their use of parallel blocks became a popular workhouse layout. Such designs increasingly featured deeper blocks where the rooms were placed off a corridor running along the centre or side of the building. Corridor-plan workhouses in the region included those at Bangor, Congleton, Ross and Wellington.

Among the many other workhouse layouts were the simple T-shape (examples at Builth and Great Boughton) and the double-courtyard design (Neath and Swansea).

THE WORKHOUSE REGIME

Daily life in a union workhouse was conducted to a fixed timetable, punctuated by the ringing of the workhouse bell. On Sundays, no work was performed except for essential domestic chores. Below is the typical routine for able-bodied inmates.[50]

	Rise	Breakfast	Start work	Dinner	End work	Supper	Bedtime
Summer	5.45 a.m.	6.30–7 a.m.	7 a.m.	12–1 p.m.	6 p.m.	6–7 p.m.	8 p.m.
Winter	6.45 a.m.	7.30–8 a.m.	8 a.m.	12–1 p.m.	6 p.m.	6–7 p.m.	8 p.m.

Communal prayers were read before breakfast and after supper every day and Divine Service was performed on Sunday, Good Friday and Christmas Day. The PLC's rules originally required that during meals 'silence, order and decorum shall be maintained', though from 1842 the word 'silence' was dropped.

The nature of the work demanded from able-bodied adults was decided by each board of guardians. Some workhouses, such as Macclesfield, had workshops for sewing, spinning and weaving or other local trades. Others, such as Chepstow and Cleobury Mortimer, had extensive vegetable gardens where inmates, particularly older boys, worked to provide produce for the workhouse. Women chiefly performed the domestic tasks of cooking, cleaning and laundry. Able-bodied men were given heavy manual work such as breaking stone (e.g. at Abergavenny and Hereford), pumping water from a well (Bangor and Newtown), turning a large corn mill (Pembroke), or picking oakum – teasing apart the fibres of old ropes, known as 'junk' (Pwllheli and Macclesfield).

Children were required to receive at least three hours a day of schooling in 'reading, writing, and in the principles of the Christian Religion; and such other instructions ... as are calculated to train them to habits of usefulness, industry and virtue'.[51] Initially, this usually took place within the workhouse but, as time went on, children increasingly went out to local schools.

Workhouse discipline distinguished two classes of offence. Conduct classed as disorderly, which included swearing, failing to wash, refusing to work, or feigning sickness, could be punished by withdrawal of foods such as cheese or tea. The more serious category of refractory conduct, such as disobeying or insulting a workhouse officer, being drunk, or damaging workhouse property, could earn a period of solitary confinement. This was often in a windowless 'dark cell' or 'black hole'. More serious misdemeanours could be referred to a magistrate. An act such as deliberately breaking a window could result in two months' hard labour.

If an inmate died, their next of kin were given the opportunity to arrange a funeral. If that did not happen, there were two possibilities. The first was a pauper burial, usually in the local parish churchyard in an unmarked multiple-occupancy grave. The second, from 1832, was for the body to be donated for use in medical training or research.

WORKHOUSE FOOD

In 1835, the PLC published a set of six model 'dietaries' or menu plans. Their intention was that the workhouse diet should on no account be 'superior or equal to the ordinary mode of subsistence of the labouring classes of the neighbourhood'.[52]

The dietaries prescribed repetitive meals of basic foods such as potatoes, bread, cheese, suet pudding, gruel and broth, with meat and vegetable dinners two or three times a week. At the Conway Union workhouse in 1859, the able-bodied men's diet was as follows:[53]

	Breakfast	Dinner	Supper
Sunday	6 oz. bread, 1½ pints gruel.	14 oz. suet pudding.	6 oz. bread, 1½ oz. cheese.
Monday	" "	4 oz. cooked meat, 1 lb. potatoes.	6 oz. bread, 1½ pints broth.
Tuesday	" "	1½ pints soup, 4 oz. bread.	As Sunday.
Wednesday	" "	6 oz. bread, 1½ pints buttermilk.	As Sunday.
Thursday	" "	1 lb. rice, 1½ pints buttermilk.	As Sunday.
Friday	" "	As Monday.	As Monday
Saturday	" "	As Tuesday.	As Sunday.

The uptake of the different dietaries by unions varied around the country and could, with the PLC's approval, be amended to reflect local preferences. At Pwllheli, in 1840, the inmates were served herrings for dinner three times a week.[54] Men received, on average, around 25 per cent more food than women. The elderly could usually enjoy a ration of butter, sugar and tea. Children under 9 were given a locally decided proportion of the adult amount. Contrary to the impression given by Charles Dickens, workhouse inmates – including children – never existed just on watery gruel.

Alcohol was prohibited in union workhouses except for medical or sacramental purposes. An exception was added in 1847, when it could be provided along with other treats on Christmas Day. Some workhouses also provided a daily ration of beer to able-bodied inmates engaged in certain types of heavy labour such as laundry or nursing work.

The standard of workhouse food gradually improved, although changes were not always well received. In 1883, in an effort to improve health, the LGB suggested that inmates receive cooked fish for dinner once a week. Although the experiment was successful in some places, such as Bristol, more typical were the reactions at Ludlow, where some inmates claimed that fish 'disagreed' with them, and at Ross, where the master reported that 'in many cases the inmates would not touch it and that on the second occasion he had cut up cheese and given it in lieu of fish'.[55]

An overhaul of workhouse food in 1900 allowed guardians to compile their own weekly dietary from a list of fifty or so dishes approved for the purpose. These included items such as Irish stew, pasties, roly-poly pudding and seed-cake, with a specially compiled cookbook issued to each workhouse to standardise the composition and preparation of the food.[56]

MEDICAL CARE

In the early 1860s, there was growing criticism of the frequently poor conditions inside the workhouses in London, many of which occupied old premises, often dating from the previous century. Medical care was a particular concern. Most nursing was carried out by elderly and often illiterate female inmates, and workhouse medical officers were usually required to bear the cost of any medicines they prescribed. A campaign for improvement attracted support from notable figures of the day, including Florence Nightingale and Charles Dickens.

Outside London, the need for improvement in workhouse conditions was being publicised by the Quaker social reformer Joseph Rowntree of Leeds, whose reports of his visits in 1864 to the workhouses of the Bala, Brecknock, Cardiff, Carmarthen, Dolgelley, Hay, Neath, and Newtown & Llanidloes Unions appeared in the letters columns of newspapers in each area. After visiting Neath, for example, he concluded that he had 'never viewed property so cramped and manifestly unsuitable in every way for the erection of a union workhouse'.[57] Perhaps because of the widespread antipathy to workhouses in Wales, it has been suggested that they were often 'squalid and badly administered'.[58]

Matters were brought to a head in 1865 after the medical journal *The Lancet* began publishing detailed reports about the frequently abysmal conditions in the capital's workhouses and their infirmaries. A few eyewitness reports were also published by the *British Medical Journal*, which visited several workhouses in Gloucestershire. At Northleach, for example, there was not a single water-closet in the entire establishment and the old men's dayroom was 'little else than a bare and stony cell'.[59]

Eventually, the campaigners' efforts bore fruit in the shape of the 1867 Metropolitan Poor Act, which aimed to take the care of London's sick poor away from individual unions and parishes. A new body, the Metropolitan Asylums Board, was set up to provide city-wide care of the poor who were suffering from infectious diseases and those who were, at the time, referred to as 'imbeciles' and 'idiots' – two increasingly serious degrees of intellectual impairment. London boards of guardians were pressed to separate the administration of their workhouses and infirmaries, which ideally would be sited at separate locations, and to employ more trained nurses.

Although only directly applying to London, the changes that followed the 1867 Act slowly percolated to unions outside the capital, with more trained staff employed and new infirmary buildings erected. Perhaps most significant was the increasing referral of paupers who were not themselves inmates of the workhouse, for treatment in its infirmary. In many places, the workhouse infirmary effectively became the local hospital for the poor. It often also became the de facto provider of accident and emergency facilities. In 1910, following a serious accident to a railway worker, the man was taken to the sick ward of Pwllheli workhouse, it being the only institution in the area for treating such cases.[60]

PAVILION PLAN BUILDINGS

New workhouse buildings erected from the 1870s onwards were increasingly based on the approach of placing different departments in separate blocks or pavilions. This concept had its roots in the principles espoused by Florence Nightingale in her 1859 *Notes on Hospitals*. What became known as 'Nightingale' wards were long and narrow, with their windows placed in opposing pairs, allowing a through-draught. Beds, typically between twenty-eight and thirty-two per ward, were placed along each wall either singly or in pairs between the windows. Sanitary facilities were placed in towers at the outer ends of the blocks, which were typically two or three storeys high.

Workhouse infirmaries incorporating 'Nightingale' wards began to appear in the mid-1860s. They usually comprised a number of men's and women's ward blocks, all linked by a corridor or covered walkway to an administrative block, which was often placed between the men's and women's sides. Unions that erected pavilion-plan infirmaries included Altrincham, Birkenhead, Merthyr Tydfil, Neath, Newport (Monmouthshire) and Stockport.

Following a PLB circular on workhouse design in 1868,[61] the first entire workhouse based on the pavilion–plan principle was erected in 1871–75 by

The Barton Regis Union's pavilion-plan workhouse at Southmead. The separate blocks are connected by covered walkways.

the Madeley Union in Shropshire. The reception, inmates' wards, chapel, infirmary and isolation wards were all in separate interlinked blocks. Later examples in the region were erected by the Newport (Monmouthshire) and Barton Regis Unions.

CASUAL WARDS

From 1837, workhouses were obliged to provide temporary overnight shelter for any destitute person at their door. At first, the 'casual' poor, as they were officially known, were often housed in stables and outhouses. Eventually, most workhouses had a purpose-built casual ward, an institution that became popularly known by tramps and vagrants as the 'spike'.

The casual ward was usually placed at the edge of the main workhouse site, often with its own separate access gate. The wards were sometimes superintended by the workhouse porter, perhaps with his wife attending the female casuals. Some spikes were in the charge of a 'Tramp Major', usually a former tramp, informally employed by the workhouse.

At opening time, usually 5 or 6 p.m., new arrivals would be admitted and searched, with any money, tobacco or alcohol confiscated. Vagrants often hid such possessions in a nearby hedge or wall before entering the spike, although the items were often at risk of being removed by local children. Contraband such as cigarettes could be smuggled in by various means. One ploy was to hide such items under the armpit, held there by sticking plaster.

Entrants were required to strip and bathe – in water that might already have been used by several others. They were then issued with a blanket and night-shirt, with their own clothes being dried and fumigated or disinfected. Each was given a supper, typically 8oz of bread and a pint of 'skilly' (gruel), before being locked up until 6 a.m. the next morning. Until the 1870s, the norm was for casual wards to have communal association dormitories where inmates either slept on the bare floor or in rows of low-slung hammocks.

The following morning, a breakfast of bread and gruel would be served. From 1842, casuals were required to work for up to four hours before being released. For male casuals, stone breaking and oakum picking were widely used. For females, labour tasks included oakum picking and domestic work such as scrubbing floors. Once vagrants had done their stint of work, they were given a lump of bread and released to go on their way. From 1882, casuals were detained for two nights, with the full day in between spent performing work. They could then be released at 9 a.m. on the second morning, allowing more time to search for work or to travel to another workhouse. From 1871, return to the casual ward of the same union was not allowed within thirty days. Tramping circuits evolved linking a progression of spikes, eventually allowing a return to the first a month later.

In the 1870s, a new form of casual ward was developed. It consisted of indi-vidual cells, much like those in a prison, usually arranged along one or both sides of a corridor. Sleeping cells contained a simple bed, while work cells were usually fitted out for stone breaking. These featured a hinged metal grille in the outside wall through which unbroken lumps of stone could be deposited in the cell. The inmate had to break the stone into lumps small enough to pass back through the holes in the grille. Sometimes sleeping cells and work cells were separated, sometimes they were paired together.

Occasionally, casual wards were erected on sites separate from the workhouse. This could be the case in larger towns such as Newport (Monmouthshire) and Cardiff, or when the workhouse was in an isolated location. As the Congleton Union workhouse was several miles from the nearest town, Sandbach, the union opened a separate casual ward in Congleton.

Casuals were generally unpopular with workhouse officials and were often provided with uncomfortable conditions to discourage them from staying.

From 1848, tramps could be required to first obtain an admission ticket from a local police station, which dissuaded many applicants. In an 1866 report, the master of the Wrexham workhouse disparaged vagrants for their 'low cunning, outward immoral conduct, obscene language, and, in many cases, barefaced lying and stealing'.[62] The same report recorded some of the graffiti left on the walls of casual wards, which acted as an informal noticeboard for leaving messages and passing on news, rather in the style of present-day social networking.[63] The graffiti often included complaints or comments about the relief provided in different unions. They contrasted the 'bare-boards' of some vagrant wards with the 'good padding' of others, and warned about the quality of the 'chuck' (food) or the treatment of 'tear-ups' – those deliberately tearing up their clothing in the hope of being given a better replacement suit. Here are some typical examples:

> Oh Sandbach, thou art no catch,
> For like heavy bread, a damned bad batch,
> A nice new suit for all tear-ups,
> And stones to crack for refractory pups.

Exterior of the Festiniog Union workhouse work cells showing the grids through which broken stone had to pass.

Beware of Ludlow – bare boards, no chuck.

Bishop's Castle Union Workhouse is a good place to be down in, but a damned bad lot of paupers about it.

Salop Jack, Glo'ster Charlie and Emma, Lank Bill was here 16th October, bound for North Wales.

CHILDREN'S ACCOMMODATION

In 1838, children under 16 formed almost half the workhouse population.[64] They were usually housed in their own section of the workhouse, although a few unions that had taken over several former parish workhouses, such Cheltenham, Macclesfield and Wellington, allocated one of them to house children – at least until they had built new, single-site premises.

That year,1838, was also the year in which Dr James Kay (later known as Sir James Kay-Shuttleworth) put forward his proposals for removing all pauper children to their own accommodation, away from what he saw as the 'polluting association' with adult workhouse inmates.[65] Kay's scheme envisaged the creation of School Districts, each serving a group of unions who would share its large District School. Kay argued that such establishments would give pauper children a much better education, together with 'industrial training' – practical skills to equip them for later life, such as manual trades for the boys and domestic training for the girls.

Eventually, around a dozen School Districts were established. One of these was the South East Shropshire School District, which was formed in 1849 and operated a school at Quatt (see page 265). As well as District Schools, some individual unions established their own separate schools. Notable among these were the establishments opened by the Newport Union at Caerleon, the Cardiff Union at Ely, and the Merthyr Tydfil Union at Trecynon.

Separate and District Schools, or 'Barrack' Schools as they were disparagingly known, became the subject of growing criticism. They were viewed as too impersonal and were also a breeding ground for infectious conditions such as ringworm and ophthalmia.

From the late 1870s, an alternative form of accommodation gained popularity. Cottage homes, as they were known, typically comprised a 'village' of small houses, often erected in a rural location. In each house, fifteen to twenty girls or boys of varying ages lived under the supervision of a house mother or house parents. As well as houses and a school, larger cottage home sites could include workshops, an infirmary, chapel, bakehouse, laundry, gymnasium, and even a swimming pool. Boys were taught practical trades such as shoemaking, tailoring and joinery, while girls learned household skills such as sewing, cooking and cleaning, to equip them for domestic service. Cottage homes often had a boys' military band, which could lead to a career as a musician in the army or navy. In contrast to the frequent Welsh resistance to erecting accommodation for adult paupers, some of the earliest Poor Law cottage homes developments were by unions in South Wales. These included Neath and Swansea (both opened in 1877) and Bridgend & Cowbridge (1878).

Cottage homes were criticised by some for isolating children from the real world, and in the 1890s another system, known as scattered homes, was pioneered by the Sheffield Union. Like cottage homes, these were based on family-style groups of children under the care of a resident house mother. Scattered homes, however, were distributed around the suburbs of a town or city and their inmates attended ordinary local schools. Unions making use of scattered homes included Cardiff, Bristol, Birkenhead and Atcham.

From 1904, to help avoid possible stigma in later life, the birth certificates for those born in a workhouse could identify the location by an anonymous-sounding street address. For example, the Merthyr Tydfil workhouse was

The Bridgend & Cowbridge cottage homes, arranged around a green. Each housed twenty boys or girls plus a house parent.

denoted as '44 Thomas Street', while Cheltenham's was recorded as 'The Elms, Swindon Road'. Not all boards of guardians took up this option, however. After some discussion, the Wrexham board decided to continue to specify the location as the workhouse.[66]

As well as institutional care, some pauper children – primarily those who were orphaned or whose parents were otherwise absent – were boarded out with foster parents. Others were emigrated, mainly to Canada.

In 1913, the LGB decreed that after 1915 no healthy child over the age of 3 should be permanently living in a workhouse.[67]

WARTIME

During the First World War, many workhouse premises were given over to war-related use. In Wales and the border counties, those taken over, entirely or in part, for use as military hospitals included: Aberayron, Atcham, Bangor, Bedwellty, Bridgend, Bristol (Southmead and Stapleton), Builth, Carmarthen, Carnarvon (Infirmary), Chester, Gloucester (Infirmary), Holywell, Knighton, Merthyr Tydfil (Trecynon), Newport, Neath (Infirmary), Pontardawe, Pontypool, Pontypridd (Llwynpia), Ross, Ruthin, Stockport (Stepping Hill), Stroud, Tetbury, Wellington and Wrexham. The Dore, Ledbury and Northleach workhouses were used to house prisoners of war.[68] Where necessary, the existing pauper inmates were usually dispersed among other workhouses in the area. Staff, however, generally stayed on to assist with the institution's new role.

At the end of the war, the military were sometimes slow in returning premises to the Poor Law authorities. At Bangor and Neath, for example, parts of the workhouses were retained as hospitals for disabled officers and men. When they were eventually handed back, there was often lengthy haggling over compensation for the state of disrepair and decoration in which the buildings had been left.

THE END OF THE WORKHOUSE

A Royal Commission set up in 1905 to examine the operation of the poor relief system was divided in its conclusions. The majority of its members recommended the creation of a new Public Assistance Authority in each county or county borough, together with the replacement of workhouses by more specialised institutions catering for separate categories of inmate such as chil-

Nurses and their military patients during the Aberayron workhouse site's use as a military hospital in 1917.

dren, the old, the unemployed, and the mentally ill. A minority group, which issued its own report, advocated the complete abolition of the Poor Laws.

Although no new legislation directly resulted from the 1905 Commission, change was in the air at a local level, especially in Wales. In some areas, unions were exploring schemes to rationalise their indoor accommodation, usually in collaboration with neighbouring unions in the same county, such as that debated by Montgomeryshire's four unions in 1912.[69] Some unions with small and underused workhouses decided to close them, as happened at Aberayron in 1914, Tregaron and Newcastle-in-Emlyn in 1915, Machynlleth in 1916, Newent in 1918 and Dolgelley in 1919. These closures were primarily on the grounds of economy rather than ideology. In each case, existing inmates were simply rehoused in the workhouses of adjacent unions. Part of the Dolgelley workhouse was retained for use as a Poor Law infirmary.

By the 1920s, the ever-growing responsibilities of local councils in public administration and service provision were making the role of the boards of guardians look increasingly anachronistic. The death knell for the guardians came in the form of the 1929 Local Government Act, which abolished them the following year. Responsibility for poor relief (or public assistance, as it then became known) was then transferred to county and borough councils. Each council set up a new Public Assistance Committee, although, perhaps unsurprisingly, its members were often former Poor Law Guardians.[70]

Most workhouse sites continued in operation as Public Assistance Institutions (PAIs), providing accommodation for a similar range of inmates except that the able-bodied were no longer received. Many casual wards also continued in use. The 1929 Act included the power for councils to 'appropriate' part or all of their former workhouse premises for use as municipal hospitals. Councils taking advantage of this option included Birkenhead, Bristol (Southmead site), Cardiff (Llandough), Cheshire (Clatterbridge), Chester, Gloucester (City General), Gloucestershire (Tetbury) and Shropshire (Berrington).

A few workhouse buildings were converted to other uses. The Bangor & Beaumaris site was sold to the Bangor Ice Company, Hawarden was converted for use as an institution for young 'mental defectives', and Cleobury Mortimer was used for several years as a youth hostel. Children's establishments taken over by local councils in 1930 mostly continued in operation with relatively little change.

In 1948, most PAIs either joined the new National Health Service (NHS) or became council-run old people's homes.

THE LONG VIEW

Today, the workhouse is usually portrayed as a relentlessly grim and inhumane institution, thanks, in no small part, to the writings of Charles Dickens. Although *Oliver Twist* was set in an early 1830s parish workhouse, it still shapes most people's view of the entire workhouse system, as if it were frozen in time, an impression reinforced by most portrayals of the institution in today's media. Over the years, however, the workhouse changed enormously.

As already noted, the food improved steadily. Christmas, of course, was always the highlight of the inmates' year. On Boxing Day at Corwen in 1864, they received a sumptuous dinner of roast beef and plum pudding, with a good supply of ale. Tobacco and snuff were provided to the adults while the juveniles were allowed out for a run about the town and up Berwyn mountain. Tea and currant cake were served at 6, followed by singing, including humorous contributions by the workhouse schoolmaster. There was then dancing until a late hour.[71]

At other times, inmates might have treats in the form of outings to local beauty spots, visits to large houses in the area, or other entertainments, usually with tea included. In July 1861, the young inmates of the Haverfordwest workhouse enjoyed a day's excursion to the seaside village of Broad Haven, where they were 'indulged in a variety of amusements' and 'regaled with refreshments of a most substantial description'.[72] In February 1868, inmates from the Merthyr Tydfil workhouse were invited to a variety performance at the local Temperance Hall.[73] At a garden party in the local rectory in 1904, Hawarden workhouse inmates played games, listened to gramophone music, and feasted on strawberries and buns.[74]

The Workhouse Visiting Society, founded by Louisa Twining in 1858, provided visitors for inmates who would otherwise have none, and its members gave readings of both religious and secular works, ran classes of instruction, and taught handicrafts such as knitting.

Workhouse inmates also benefited from the efforts of local people in providing small pleasures by putting on concerts in the workhouse or donating books and magazines. In 1890, the Cheltenham workhouse had its own library and was given magazines and newspapers 'too numerous to mention'. Such contributions varied widely, however – at the Aberystwyth workhouse, periodicals were received only occasionally and newspapers twice a week.[75] The following year, the LGB agreed that if such supplies were inadequate, they could be supplemented from the poor rates. Guardians were also encouraged to provide illustrated books and papers for the children and the sick, together with toys for the infants, and bats, balls and skipping ropes for the older children.[76]

By the 1890s at Macclesfield workhouse, the respectable aged poor had brightly decorated wards with comfortable furniture. They could wear their

Llanfyllin workhouse inmates at a celebration in one of the workhouse yards.

own clothes, retain a few of their own possessions, keep small pets, were served afternoon tea, and could go out each day and visit friends.[77]

By 1914, the older inmates at the Ross workhouse had mixed dayrooms and individual cubicles in their dormitories, and fixed mealtimes had been abandoned. Inmates even had weekly trips to the local cinema.[78] By the same date, the majority of workhouse children lived in separate accommodation and received education and training to make them employable as adults.

Workhouse inmates were not always the passive recipients of the regime imposed on them. Despite the obstacles placed in their way, the sexes could still find ways to have contact with one another. At the Ross workhouse, male inmates managed to scale the wall separating the men's and women's yards. After putting a stop to that, the guardians discovered that some resourceful female paupers had dressed themselves in men's clothing and got into the men's ward.[79] At Ludlow, the guardians were unable to prevent female inmates discharging themselves from the workhouse to attend the town fair, or other local events, then returning a few hours later to demand readmission, as they were perfectly entitled to do.[80]

Any evaluation of workhouse conditions needs to be made against those experienced by the poor of the time, rather than modern-day standards and attitudes. For many of the nation's poorest, a roof over their head and three meals a day could prove a tolerable respite from an otherwise grinding hand-to-mouth existence. And it is all too easy to judge workhouse 'uniforms', for example, as deliberately dehumanising imposition rather than as a practical solution to clothing large numbers of people who might be arriving at its door in filthy rags.

The workhouse system was not without its faults, of course. To some degree, it acted as a poverty trap. Adults leaving a workhouse rarely received any kind of help in finding accommodation or employment in order to escape from pauperism. And despite all the material improvements, the dread of entering the institution could even drive some to suicide, as was the case with 53-year-old Eliza Evans of Bishop's Castle, who in 1884 hanged herself rather than face the separation from her husband that it would bring.[81]

Perhaps the most significant legacy of the workhouse era comes from the widespread improvement in its medical facilities from the 1870s onwards, which fostered the principle of free publicly funded treatment for those in need. A large proportion of the real estate inherited by the NHS in 1948 came from former workhouse sites. It was significant, perhaps, that when Health Minister Aneurin 'Nye' Bevan officially launched the new service on 5 July 1948, the location chosen for this momentous occasion was a former workhouse infirmary.

The stigma of the workhouse was to leave a long-lasting mark, however. For decades afterwards, many elderly people adamantly refused to enter the doors of an NHS hospital that had once been a workhouse, convinced that they would only leave in a coffin. That belief was actually founded on reality. The elderly poor frequently did die in workhouses, though not because they were such terrible places, but because in their day they were generally the only source of free medical care available to those approaching the end of their life.

WORKHOUSE CATALOGUE

The rest of this book provides more detailed information on the hundreds of workhouses that existed in Wales and the English border counties of Cheshire, Gloucestershire, Herefordshire and Shropshire. County boundaries reflect those that existed at the time.

Each county's chapter has alphabetically arranged sections covering the post-1834 Poor Law Unions that it encompassed. With very few exceptions, information on parish workhouses is included under the Poor Law Union of which they later formed part. Thus, the Coleford workhouse, located in Gloucestershire parish of Newland, is referred to in the section on the Monmouth Union. A few border-county parishes that joined unions in more easterly counties, such as Staffordshire, are omitted from this volume. Conversely, Staffordshire parishes that were placed in Cheshire unions, for example, are included. All the workhouse locations mentioned in the text are referenced in the index. Welsh place-name spellings are generally the anglicised ones that were in use in the workhouse era, for example 'Dolgelley' rather than 'Dolgellau'. Except in the case of formal titles, the counties of Brecknockshire and Salop are referred to by their now more common respective names of Breconshire and Shropshire. For simplicity, the term 'parishes' sometimes includes other administrative units such as townships, hamlets, chapelries, etc., which had equivalent status for Poor Law purposes,

Where unions spanned county borders, they were assigned, for administrative and statistical purposes, to the county that contained the largest portion of their population. In the case of the Whitchurch Union, placed in Shropshire, only two of its twenty-five members were actually in that county, almost all the remainder being small townships in Cheshire. Over the years, there were many adjustments to the places included in each union.

Details for many pre-1834 workhouses are taken from parliamentary reports published in 1777 (based on data collected in 1776), 1804 (1803), 1818 (1813–15) and 1834 (1832).[82] Unless otherwise noted, references to data for these collection dates should be assumed to come from those sources. It is important to appreciate that these surveys are not always directly comparable. For example, the 1777 report recorded if each parish was operating a workhouse and how many people it could accommodate. The 1804 and 1818 surveys recorded how many actual persons in a particular year that each parish had 'permanently' relieved in *any* workhouse – not necessarily one it was running itself. The 1832 data included returns from only 10 per cent of parishes. All of these reports placed Monmouthshire in England.

Where known, building locations include a Great Britain National Grid Reference (e.g. TQ123456), which indicates the bottom left-hand corner of a 100-metre-square map area. Map websites that handle such references include the National Library of Scotland's historical maps collection (maps.nls.uk/geo) and the Old-Maps archive (old-maps.co.uk), which allow the development of workhouse sites to be tracked from the 1850s onwards.

Abbreviations used in the text:

BMJ   British Medical Journal
LGB   Local Government Board
NHS   National Health Service
PAI   Public Assistance Institution
PLB   Poor Law Board
PLC   Poor Law Commissioners

1

ANGLESEY

ANGLESEY

Anglesey Poor Law Union was formed on 1 June 1837, with fifty-three member parishes. Its board of guardians met on Wednesdays at 10.30 a.m., the venues including the Bull's Head Inn at Llanerchymedd and the Crown Inn at Bodedern. For many years, despite the efforts of central authorities, the guardians resisted the erection of a workhouse. In 1852, the union was divided, some of its parishes forming the new Holyhead Union covering the western part of the island, and a few being added to the Bangor and Beaumaris Union.

Finally, at their meeting on 6 March 1867, the Anglesey board was persuaded of the financial and other benefits of providing a workhouse and an order was signed for its construction.[1] Mr Gundry was subsequently appointed as architect but after tenders for the building of his design could not be obtained within the guardians' initial £1,800 budget, alternative plans from Mr R.G. Thomas of Menai Bridge were adopted.[2] The workhouse, for seventy inmates, was erected on Amlwch Road to the north of Llanerchymedd (SH420848) at a total cost of about £2,200.

The workhouse had a cruciform main building with an entrance block at the north-west. Unusually, the site was not divided into simple male and female halves. Instead, the boys' and men's yards respectively occupied the north and south quadrants of the workhouse, and the girls' and women's the west and east.[3] At the left of the front entrance was the guardians' boardroom, with the children's schoolroom to its rear. At the right of the entrance were the union clerk's office and a parlour, with a waiting room and the master's room to the rear. Single-storey boys' and girls' dayrooms were respectively located at the left and right ends of the block. A single-storey dining hall, flanked by the boys' and girls' yards, linked the entrance block to the now demolished main accommodation section. On its ground floor was the kitchen, with pantries and scullery behind, separating the women's and men's yards. On the male side, at the south of the kitchen, were the able-bodied and infirm men's dayrooms. A similar pattern existed on the women's side, A laundry block at the rear was accessed from the women's yard. There were dormitories on the upper floor. Around the main building were placed a vagrants' ward at the north, an infirmary at the south, and an isolation block at the east.

In 1869, Meshach Thomas, formerly schoolmaster at the Bangor workhouse, and his wife, Grace, were appointed as the first master and matron at Llanerchymedd, a post they were to hold until 1900.

In July 1906, two little girls, playing in a workhouse outhouse, removed a loose brick in the floor and found an old pincushion. Inside was a National Provincial Bank deposit note, dated December 1898, by then worth about £32 15s. The note belonged to Ann Owen, an inmate admitted in 1899 and classed as

The first master and matron at the Llanerchymedd workhouse, Meshach and Grace Thomas, and their five children. (Courtesy of Hugo Vanneck.)

weak-minded. Since her admission, the woman had cost the union over £69. It was resolved to take steps to have the money paid into union funds.[4]

The workhouse was closed in 1919 owing to the small number of inmates. Those still in residence were then boarded at the Holyhead workhouse. The Llanerchymedd premises, renamed Bryn Hafod, were later used as council offices. The buildings were left empty in the 1980s and became derelict. In around 2000, the entrance block was renovated to create residential and gallery accommodation.

HOLYHEAD

Holyhead had a parish workhouse at Black Bridge, with Lewis Roberts as its governor in 1828.[5] In 1832, it had either closed or was viewed as a poorhouse.[6] However, an 1835 directory reports it as being run by Benjamin Griffith.[7]

Holyhead Poor Law Union formed on 29 September 1852 and comprised twenty-five parishes from the western part of the existing Anglesey Union.

Following in the footsteps of Anglesey Union's board, the Holyhead guardians initially resisted the provision of a new workhouse. At a board meeting held at the Valley Inn on 22 February 1853, the benefits of the institution were depicted in glowing terms by Assistant Poor Law Commissioner Andrew Doyle.[8] On a division, four members voted for erecting a workhouse, with twenty-four against. It was not until March 1867 that a majority of the board were persuaded to support the provision of a workhouse.

The building was designed by R.G. Thomas of Menai Bridge, who was also architect of the Anglesey Union workhouse, which had similar specifications.[9] The new workhouse, for up to seventy inmates, was erected at Valley to the south-east of Holyhead (SH290794). Construction was delayed following the bankruptcy of the original building contractor.

Like the Anglesey Union's workhouse, Holyhead's had a deep entrance block linked to a cruciform central section. However, Holyhead's workhouse appears to have been slightly larger, with a higher standard of construction and decoration. An infirmary stood at the west of the main building and a casual ward at the east. The infirmary was enlarged in 1890, and by 1924 was as large as the main workhouse complex.

In October 1900, Richard Parry, the elderly parish clerk of Abberffraw, presented himself at a meeting of the guardians, asking whether he could see some of the female inmates in the house, his object being to obtain a wife. He went on a round of the wards, but none of the women at that time came up

The former Anglesey Union workhouse in 2000, at the time of its conversion to an art gallery.

The entrance block of the former Holyhead Union workhouse just prior to its demolition in 1995. (Courtesy of Anglesey Online)

to his ideal. However, he reappeared at a subsequent meeting to report that an inmate, Catherine Roberts, a widow with four children, was willing to accept him. The guardians consented and the woman was discharged from the workhouse, with 30s being subscribed by the members of the board for the bride's trousseau.[10]

After 1904, for birth registration purposes, the workhouse was identified as 'Cartref' ('Home'), Valley.[11]

In 1909, on the recommendation of the workhouse medical officer, the guardians decided to remove the pudding from the inmates' Sunday dinner as it was overloading their digestive organs. Dr Edwards told the board that it was impossible to stop some of the inmates once they had started on their Sunday roast beef. As Wednesday's dinner was the poorest of the week, he thought that the pudding might be served on that day.[12]

In 1930, the site was taken over by Anglesey Council and became a PAI, then in 1948 joined the NHS as Valley Hospital. It closed in the mid-1990s and the buildings were demolished. The housing of Garth Y Felin now covers the site.

BRECONSHIRE (BRECKNOCKSHIRE)

BRECKNOCK

Brecknock (now usually known as Brecon or Aberhonddhu) had a parish workhouse located on The Struet and linked to a House of Correction.[1]

By 1803, the parish of Llanddetty had erected a workhouse alongside the Monmouthshire and Brecon Canal, about 1.5 miles west of Llangynidr (SO135197).[2] The building is now a residential property known as the Old Workhouse.

Brecknock Poor Law Union was formed on 5 October 1836. The union initially took over the existing Brecknock workhouse, which was then used to house the mothers of bastard children; single women, or widows, who were incapable of working; and children under 14.[3]

In 1838, the PLC approved an expenditure of £2,649 on a new workhouse for 100 inmates. The building, designed by H.J. Whitling, was erected on Bailihelig Road, a mile or so to the south-west of Brecon (SO037280), and was completed by May 1839.[4] The H-shaped main section was two storeys high and plain in appearance. A small infirmary block stood at the rear.

A depressing picture of the workhouse was provided by social reformer Joseph Rowntree, who visited the establishment in 1864. The whole place was dirty and was deficient in washrooms and baths. There were no comfortable seats for those not confined to bed. The two dayrooms for the men and boys were 'lamentably dreary' and some of the boys' accommodation was said to be 'wretched'. The infirmary was 'a very poor, contracted place' and lacked any appliances for ventilating its smoky rooms. Dinner on three days each week was just soup, and much was thrown away. When boiled meat or suet pudding were served, the quantities were less than was the case in other unions. The bread, however, was of good quality and the quantity sufficient. Visits by the workhouse's paid chaplain were said to be 'few and far between', whereas a local non-conformist visited each Sunday, without payment, to read from the Bible in the infirmary and other wards. On the positive side, the union's treatment of casuals and wayfarers appeared to be better than in some other unions. A stove had been installed in the casual ward to warm the room and dry wet clothes.[5]

After 1904, for birth registration purposes, the workhouse was identified as 'Gorphwysfa' ('Resting Place').[6]

In 1930, the workhouse became a PAI, run by Brecknockshire Council, then in 1948 joined the NHS as St David's Hospital, providing care for geriatric patients. After its closure in the early 1990s, the site was taken over by the Christ College Public School for use as hall of residence.

BUILTH

Builth Poor Law Union was formed on 2 January 1837. A third of its thirty-one member parishes lay in the neighbouring county of Radnorshire.

Like several other unions in rural central Wales, the Builth guardians conducted a long-running campaign of resistance to the construction of a workhouse, preferring instead to dispense out-relief. The possibility of a workhouse was periodically discussed by the guardians, though probably with little sincerity and just playing for time.[7] In 1875, however, under the threat from the LGB to dissolve the union, a new workhouse for sixty inmates was finally opened.

The establishment was situated at the south of Builth, on the east side of the Brecon Road (SO042507). The entrance to the site at the south-west was flanked by two small blocks, a boardroom at the north, and receiving and vagrants' wards to the south. Behind these were boys' and girls' playgrounds respectively. The T-shaped main building had the master and matron's accommodation at the centre. To each side were male and female dayrooms on the ground floor and dormitories above. At the centre rear were the dining hall and kitchens, with adult yards either side. A T-shaped infirmary lay at the north-east, with fever wards and a mortuary beyond.[8]

Unfortunately, the new building turned out to be defective in its construction. In June 1875, a report on the structure by Hereford architect W.E. Martin

A view of Brecknock Union's workhouse, now known as St David's House.

A view from the west of the Builth Union workhouse, otherwise known as Victoria House. (Courtesy of Builth Wells & District Heritage Society)

declared 'the external walling to be throughout of the very worst and cheapest description of random rubble work, the foundations insufficient, the mortar a mixture of lime, limestone partly burnt, ballast, mud, small coal, and ashes, scarcely deserving the name of building.'[9]

In 1890, as was the custom in union workhouses, Christmas was a day of treats:

> Santa Claus made his usual visit in the morning with the result that each of the adult inmates found a Christmas letter, and the children toys, biscuits, and so on awaiting them upon rising from bed. Breakfast was partaken of in the dining room, which had been handsomely decorated for the occasion by Mr and Mrs Targett. It consisted of tea, cake, bread and butter, and so on. A capital dinner of roast beef, roast pork, vegetables, and plum pudding, was subsequently partaken of in the same room, and the inmates thoroughly enjoyed themselves, the men and women having an allowance of beer with their dinner and the children milk. After dinner, the men received doles of tobacco, and the women tea, and the children, apples, biscuits, sweets, etc. The adults also had apples. Afterwards Christmas Carols were rendered, accompanied by Miss Targett, who also at intervals during the evening played selections of pianoforte music. After partaking of a good supper, the inmates retired to rest well pleased with the Christmas festivities.[10]

After 1904, for birth registration purposes, the workhouse was identified as 'Victoria House, Brecon Road'.[11]

In January 1914, the inmates were treated to an afternoon performance at the local 'Kino' cinema, with the promise of further monthly trips. In the same month, gas lighting was installed at the workhouse.[12]

In August 1914, the guardians agreed to allow the women's ward to be used as a wartime Red Cross hospital, with the boardroom also employed in 1916.[13]

In November 1914, with only twenty-three paupers in residence, a proposal was made to close the workhouse and sell the building.[14] Despite periodic discussions along these lines, the workhouse continued in operation until 1930. Unlike other establishments in the county, which became council-run PAIs, the Builth workhouse was then closed. The buildings were demolished in 1943.

CRICKHOWELL

In 1817, the Llangynidr vestry resolved that 'a workhouse shall be procured towards employing and maintaining the Poor of this Parish'.[15] However, it was not until 1826 that an existing house in the village, Ty Newydd, was purchased for the purpose.[16]

In 1823, Llangattock established a House of Industry in a converted row of cottages at Danyffawydog (SO206183). The following year, the vestry agreed to admit up to fifteen paupers from Llanelly for a weekly payment of 2s 8d per head, although no pregnant woman or anyone diseased, of unsound mind, or under the age of 45 was to be admitted. Similar arrangements were agreed with Llandetty, Cwmdu, Crickhowell and Llangenny.[17]

Cwmdu also appears to have operated its own workhouse, on Darren Road, Bwlch,[18] as did Crickhowell, in premises on Castle Street.[19]

Crickhowell Poor Law Union was formed on 6 October 1836, with ten constituent parishes. Initially, the union made use of existing parish premises at Crickhowell (for female inmates) and at Llangattock (for males). In 1837, the PLC authorised the expenditure of £1,150 for the enlargement of the existing building at Llangattock. The old Crickhowell building was sold off in early 1838.

The first master at Llangattock, Samuel Mainwaring, died in 1841. His successor, William Lewis, was quickly dismissed as being unsuitable and was replaced by John Allen. In October 1841, a meeting of the Guardians' Visiting Committee heard charges against Allen of taking improper liberties with one of the female inmates and of drunkenness and irregularity. On being called before the meeting, Allen admitted the allegations and was discharged from his duties. His successor, Edward Clinton, the workhouse's fourth master that year, restored some stability to the position, which he held until his death in 1844.

The workhouse buildings and the steeply sloping Llangattock site became the subject of increasing complaint by the central authority, who viewed them as 'inconvenient and ill suited'. In 1847, an extension to the existing buildings was only approved by the guardians after an outbreak of typhus at the workhouse.[20] It was not until 1870 that the PLB was able to report that the guardians had finally agreed to erect a workhouse 'adapted to the requirements of their union'.[21]

The new workhouse, designed by W.P. James of Cardiff, occupied the existing site at Llangattock. The inmates' accommodation block ran north to south at the centre of the site, with the master's house adjoining its eastern side and a chapel linked to its northern end. An infirmary, fever ward and mortuary lay to the south, while casual ward and laundry blocks stood at the east of the site.[22]

After 1930, the site became a 105-bed PAI, run by Brecknockshire Council and known as Llanyffwddog, also referred to as Welfare House.

During the Second World War, members of the British and Free Belgian forces stationed in the area were accommodated at the workhouse. Officers were housed in the infirmary block, with lower ranks in the laundry and casual ward.

Most of the surviving buildings have now been converted to residential use, while the infirmary block is now home to the Ty Croeso B&B.

HAY

In 1803, the parish of Clifford maintained nine paupers in a workhouse, location unknown.

In 1813, workhouse relief was provided by Dorstone for sixteen paupers and by Hay-on-Wye for six.

Hay Poor Law Union was formed on 26 September 1836 and comprised twenty parishes drawn from Breconshire, Herefordshire and Radnorshire. In January 1837, the guardians invited tenders for the construction of a new

The former Crickhowell Union workhouse infirmary – now the Ty Croeso boutique B&B.

workhouse designed by George Wilkinson.[23] Its layout was based on the PLC's model 'square' layout (see page 26) and intended to accommodate 110 inmates. It was erected on a 4-acre site on the south side of St Mary's Road at the west of Hay-on-Wye (SO225420).

The workhouse was visited in November 1864 by social reformer Joseph Rowntree, who recorded that the inmates comprised thirteen men, eleven women and twenty-seven children. He found the premises generally to be clean but some of the dormitories were poorly ventilated due to their chimneys having been bricked up. More washrooms and baths were needed, together with one or two water closets. The refractory cells, where those breaking workhouse rules were placed, were damp, cold and dark, and had no seating. Men in the workhouse were allowed a fortnightly 'liberty day' for visiting their friends, while none of the women were allowed this privilege. The workhouse did not employ a teacher, and the children, who attended a local National School, gave a poor account of themselves in mental arithmetic. Rowntree suggested that the workhouse master, who was an experienced teacher, might spend a few hours a week instructing the young inmates, rather than pursuing his photographic interests, which were for his own pleasure and pecuniary benefit, in a room in the workhouse he had appropriated exclusively for the purpose. The guardians came under his fire for renting out a

The former Hay Union workhouse with the entrance block (right) and supervisory hub just visible (centre).

plot of valuable ground, opposite the workhouse, to the union's paid chaplain, who then sub-let it to several others. In Rowntree's view, the land could have been better used to provide employment for the men and boys and as recreational space for infirm, aged or imbecile inmates. Criticism was also made of a relieving officer named Powell who, contrary to regulations, did not make himself available to deal with accommodation requests from wayfarers. To assist one such individual in need of a night's shelter, Rowntree eventually tracked Powell down late in the evening at a local hostelry.[24]

One area in which the workhouse was not lacking was in its medical provision. By 1866, it had erected a detached infirmary, rated as 'pretty good' by a government inspector, while the original infirmary at the back of the workhouse was being used as foul wards for venereal cases.[25]

In 1897, new casual wards were erected to a design by Cardiff architect J.H. Phillips.

After 1904, for birth registration purposes, the workhouse was identified as '7 St Mary's Road'.[26]

In 1930, the site was taken over by Brecknockshire Council and became a PAI, later known as Cockcroft House old people's home. The surviving buildings have now been converted to residential use.

3

CARDIGANSHIRE

ABERAYRON

In 1784, the Dihewyd vestry resolved 'to build a house in the church yard wall, for the poor'.[1]

In 1790, the vestry at Llanarth agreed to build a poorhouse near Mydroilyn, where paupers were to be 'admitted and maintained, and properly employed' – making the establishment sound more like a workhouse.[2]

Aberayron Poor Law Union was formed on 8 May 1837 and comprised fourteen parishes. In 1838–39, the union erected a workhouse for 100 inmates on Princes' Street, just to the east of the town (SN461629). The architect was George Wilkinson and the construction contract, initially agreed at £1,200, was awarded to local builder William Green. The challenge of the small site was resolved by a compact T-shaped design with four small yards for the different categories of inmate, two within each arm of the 'T'.

In September 1887, on hearing that the bill of fare at the workhouse did not include potatoes, one of the guardians, David Thomas, delivered a hundredweight of potatoes to the institution. He said, 'My pigs have potatoes, why not the workhouse inmates?'[3]

In 1898, the workhouse medical officer, Dr Evans, gave a sorry picture of the building's cramped facilities. There was just one dormitory for males and one for females, and no separate place for placing sick people. Ten men occupied the small room they had at their disposal. There was great need for a proper dining room and there was no room for receiving the applicants and other visitors. As regards the vagrants, there were no separate cells for males and females and the small bath they had was never used. Male and female tramps were huddled together and the beds had wooden frames, the favourite resort of fleas. Evans also proposed that a plot of land be obtained as a garden for the inmates, instead of their being huddled together in the small space they had at their disposal.[4]

A 1901 survey of 139 workhouses in England and Wales found that Aberayron's had a mere seventeen inmates, the lowest number in the sample. Five of them had lived in the reigns of five successive monarchs, beginning with George III, who died in 1820. This was the largest proportion of such elderly inmates recorded in the survey.[5]

In 1914, the workhouse was converted into a cottage hospital, the existing pauper inmates being transferred to the Lampeter workhouse. In the latter part of the First World War, the hospital provided care for injured soldiers. The building is still in use as Aberaeron Hospital.

ABERYSTWYTH

Aberystwyth Poor Law Union was formed on 5 May 1837, and comprised thirty parishes. A union workhouse for 200 inmates was opened in 1840 on the Penglais Road, to the east of Aberystwyth (SN591818). The building, a mixture of the Elizabethan and Gothic in style, was designed by William Ritson. An 1841 report described it as follows:

The frontage of Aberaeron Hospital, once the union workhouse.

The west or principal front, looking towards the town, is upwards of 200 feet in length. It has two projecting wings, and the chapel, which is in the centre, also projects. The chapel is lighted by a large Gothic window, 15 feet high, and 8 feet wide. The interior comprises, on the ground storey, the chapel and board room, which are in the centre of the building, and divide the men's and women's apartments; on one side the master's and matron's parlour, porter's lodge, men's first and second class day rooms, and boy's schoolroom; on the other side, the clerk's office, (which opens into the board room), store rooms, women's day rooms, and girls' schoolroom. The centre building at the back consists of a large kitchen, larder, washhouse, bake-house, &c. The back wing buildings consists of the boys' and girls' dormitories, receiving, and bath rooms, refectory rooms, and other offices. On the [first floor] are the master's and matron's bed-rooms, large airy dormitories for the men and women, and rooms for the sick and infirm. Each ward has a large exercising yard, and there is a good space of ground for a garden attached to the building.[6]

A visitor in 1842 commended the workhouse. Its situation was said to be pleasanter and healthier than anywhere in the neighbourhood, its inmates a picture of cleanliness and health, and its bread superior to that eaten by the poor outside. Offered the choice between stone breaking in the workhouse and working in their own home, the able-bodied poor invariably chose the latter.[7]

An early 1900s view from the entrance of the Aberystwyth Union workhouse. (Courtesy of Ceredigion Archives, ref. ADX/817)

For many years, inmate numbers were low, with only nineteen in residence in 1851. The number had risen to seventy-eight in 1881 and included seven 'imbeciles', eight 'idiots' and six categorised as blind, deaf or dumb.

In 1870, a Poor Law Inspector described the establishment as 'the most wretched I have ever seen'; the state in which the children were kept was 'the one in which you keep dogs'; the privies were 'in every respect objectionable, and the stench emitted is awful'; and the dietary table was 'odious'.[8]

Things had improved by 1894, when the *BMJ* found the workhouse to be 'a cheerful-looking place, clean and well cared for'. The sick, too, received generally good care. The journal's recommendations included: an enlargement of the infirmary, the provision of isolation wards and separate quarters for the imbeciles and idiots, and the employment of a paid night attendant in the sick wards.[9]

After 1904, for birth registration purposes, the workhouse was identified as 'Bronglaise, Penglaise Road'.[10]

In 1930, the site became a PAI run by Cardiganshire Council, then in 1948 joined the NHS as Bronglais Hospital. Most of the old buildings were demolished in 1966 and a car park now covers the area where the workhouse stood.

The tranquil surroundings of the Cardigan Union workhouse at St Dogmaels.

CARDIGAN

In 1785, St Mary's vestry in Cardigan drew up a plan for a workhouse for its poor, together with a set of rules.[11] In 1803, the parish relieved seven paupers in a workhouse.

A tithe map of 1841 shows a field referred to as 'Workhouse and Garden' at the west side of the village of Llechryd (SN212437).[12]

An 1842 tithe map of the parish of Nevern identifies a 'Poorhouse and Garden' at the south of the B4329, a few hundred yards to the east of Brynberian (SN107349).[13]

Cardigan Poor Law Union was formed on 9 May 1837. Seventeen of its twenty-six member parishes lay across the county border in Pembrokeshire. A new workhouse, for 120 inmates, was erected in 1838–39 on an elevated site to the north of St Dogmaels (SN160467). Designed by William Owen of Haverfordwest, it adopted the model 'square' layout (see page 26), with its entrance block facing north-east. There were separate entrance doors for males and females. A shed and a piggery were erected in the front yard. Able-bodied inmates worked in the shed, which also acted as a stable for the guardians' horses during board meetings. Visits to inmates were allowed, with the permission of the master, between 9 a.m. and noon, and between 2 p.m. and 6 p.m.[14]

In 1881, to improve the warmth of the bedrooms used by the children and aged inmates, it was proposed to half-ceil the rooms. Stone-breaking cells were erected in 1884 at the south-east side of the workhouse. In 1890, the guardians advertised for tenders for erecting new ceilings and dormitories. Further improvements in 1901 included installing baths into the male and female receiving wards.[15]

After 1904, for birth registration purposes, the workhouse was identified as 'Albro Castle', named after the nearby Albro Bank.[16]

In July 1910, a 96-year-old inmate of the workhouse applied for a day's leave to look for a cottage into which he could move when the disqualification of paupers from receiving an old age pension was removed at the end of that year. The old man regularly walked 2 miles to attend church on Sundays.[17]

In 1930, the site was taken over by Cardiganshire Council and became a PAI. The establishment closed in 1935 and the remaining inmates were transferred to similar institutions in Lampeter and Aberystwyth. During the Second World War, the premises saw use by the US Army and Women's Voluntary Service. The buildings are now used as residential and holiday accommodation.

LAMPETER

Lampeter Poor Law Union was formed on 15 May 1837. Its thirteen member parishes included four in Carmarthenshire.

Like several other unions in the area, Lampeter steadily resisted the provision of a new union workhouse. In November 1845, following renewed pressure from the PLC, the chairman of the guardians put forward a proposal for the construction of a workhouse for up forty inmates, costing no more than £1,500.[18] The proposal was accepted, and by the following June a site had been found and an architect was planned to be contacted. However, various objections began to be raised and the scheme stalled. From 1850, the guardians attempted, unsuccessfully, to be allowed to board out paupers at the Aberayron workhouse.

Finally, in 1874, under the threat of the dissolution of the union by the PLB, the guardians capitulated. A new workhouse was built in 1875–76 on the south side of Pantfaen Road at the west of Lampeter (SN574481). It was designed by the partnership of Szlumper and Aldwinckle.

The T-shaped main block was three storeys high at its centre, with the master's office and sitting room and a children's dayroom on the ground floor. Above were the master's bedroom and children's dormitory on the first floor, and sick wards and a lying-in ward on the second floor. Two-storey wings to each side contained dayrooms for the able-bodied and aged, with dormitories above. At the centre rear, a single-storey wing contained the dining hall and kitchen. Females were accommodated at the east of the site and males at the west.[19] By 1904, two further blocks had been added adjacent to the road at the north.

After 1904, for birth registration purposes, the workhouse was identified as 'Temple Buildings, Temple Terrace'.[20]

In September 1913, LGB Inspector H.R. Williams began an inquiry into allegations of a feud between the workhouse master, James Evans, and matron, Hannah Lloyd, which had begun when Evans was courting his wife. Evans was also accused of having been intimate with an inmate, Charlotte Jones, said to be a certified imbecile, and of showing favouritism to several female inmates. The inquiry found the allegations by Jones to be unsubstantiated but that he and Lloyd should both resign.[21] Charlotte Jones was also a complainant in an inquiry in November 1919, when there were accusations that the then matron, Mrs Sarah Ann Lewis, had roughly handled some of the inmates. It was also alleged that on one occasion the soup served to inmates had contained maggots.[22]

In November 1926, local builder Walter Williams gave up his farm and entered the workhouse as a paying guest. At his death in 1927, he requested a pauper's grave so as to maximise the benefit for the charitable institutions to which he left his £2,000 estate.[23]

In 1930, the site became a PAI run by Cardiganshire Council. In the 1960s, the Lampeter Welfare Home, as it was then referred to, was replaced by a new care home on the same site known as 'Hafandeg' ('Fair Haven').

TREGARON

Tregaron Poor Law Union was formed on 15 May 1837, with twenty-two member parishes.

In common with the neighbouring Lampeter Union, the Tregaron guardians were opposed to the construction of a workhouse. In 1838, in order to appease the PLC, the guardians indicated an intention to build a workhouse but then used a variety of tactics to delay taking the matter forward. In March 1846, the order for the erection of a workhouse was entered in the guardians' minute book and advertisements were placed inviting builders to tender for the work.[24,25] However, further prevarication occurred, with excuses including the failure of the potato crop that year. The guardians' evasion continued for over twenty-five years, but by the end of 1873, under increasing threat of the union being dissolved by the LGB, they had committed themselves to the

The architects' proposed design for the frontage of the Lampeter Union workhouse. (Courtesy of Ceredigion Archives, ref. CDC/A/2/6)

building of a workhouse. The project crawled forward, partly due to delays in the conveyancing of the site and with bad weather also slowing construction work. The construction contract eventually overran by almost a year and the building was finally ready in the spring of 1878.

The workhouse occupied a site on Dewi Road, to the south of Tregaron (SN678593). Designed by George Jones, the building comprised two parallel ranges with by a short central connecting block. It could accommodate fifty-eight inmates.

After 1904, for birth registration purposes, the workhouse was identified as 'Brynhyfryd' ('Lovely Hill').[26]

The workhouse attracted some publicity in 1907 after the inmates were given a special dinner and tea on New Year's Day. Beer was offered, but not one of them chose to have it.

The institution closed in 1915 with its sixteen remaining inmates being transferred to Aberystwyth workhouse. The site was then taken over on a ninety-nine-year lease by the King Edward VII Welsh Memorial Association, who converted it for use as a sanatorium, known as the King Edward VII Hospital, for the treatment of tuberculosis patients.

The site is now a community hospital, although it is scheduled to close. Only the workhouse's front block now survives.

A 1930s view of what had become Tregaron's King Edward VII Hospital.

4

CARMARTHENSHIRE

CARMARTHEN

In 1758, the St Peter's vestry in Carmarthen began renting part of the Old Priory for use as a poorhouse. The inmates had to eat at a common dining table, unless declared sick by the establishment's apothecary, in which case they could then eat in their own rooms. Failure to attend Sunday worship resulted in a dinner of rice gruel. In 1785, an attempt was made to occupy the inmates in hat-making.[1] In 1788, however, prison reformer John Howard noted that 'at the work-house (or poor-house) in this town, there is no form of employment'.[2]

In 1799, St Peter's decided to erect a new poorhouse at Waundew Common. It proved an expensive project, with the parish in debt to the tune of £1,400 by the time it opened in 1805.[3] An admiring tourist in 1809 wrote that:

> the poors'-house, a short distance from the town, is so clean and well regulated, that it is a pleasure to observe so many infirm old people comfortably lodged; and by the excellent management of the matron, on the slender allowance of only fourpence a day each person, I understand, they live very well.[4]

In October 1822, the Rev. D.A. Williams, Assistant Master of Carmarthen Grammar School, was appointed Evening Lecturer to the workhouse.[5]

In 1776, Laugharne had a workhouse for up to six inmates. The following year, a workhouse was established at Llangendeirne where 'all whom refuse to come in shall not be entitled to any relief'.[6] Seven paupers were maintained there in 1803 and five in 1813. In 1803, two hamlets in the parish, Velindra and Gwempa, each had ten paupers as workhouse inmates.

Llandefeilog was employing a workhouse by 1803, when seventeen of its paupers were maintained there.

Carmarthen Poor Law Union was formed on 2 July 1836, with twenty-eight member parishes. In October 1836, tenders were sought for 'the enlarging of the present workhouse', at the west side of what is now Penlan Road (SN411206).[7] Following the expansion, the two-storey main block had a double-courtyard layout and could house 260 inmates. The existing arched gatehouse was retained. Casual wards were subsequently added at its north side and in 1845 a register office was attached at the south.

On 19 June 1843, the workhouse was stormed by 'Rebecca Rioters' who, in 1842–43, carried out a campaign of protests across South Wales, mainly against high charges at tollgates on public roads. A large crowd arrived at the workhouse, where the matron was forced to hand over her keys. The mob then entered the buildings, where they smashed furniture and broke windows. They also urged the inmates to leave with them, to which one replied, 'Why should we go along with you – you cannot better our condition.'[8] The arrival of the 4th Light Dragoons brought matters under control and sixty prisoners were taken.

In 1879, the guardians invited tenders for erecting new dayrooms and dormitories for forty-six children, and making alterations for the accommodation of tramps. George Morgan was architect for the development.[9] The children's accommodation was a two-storey block at the south of the workhouse. In 1893, tenders were invited for the construction of six stone-breaking cells and a lead cistern.[10] Advertisements for the building of a new laundry first placed in January 1901 appear not to have received a satisfactory response, as they were still being reissued in June.[11] In 1905, tenders were invited for erecting a new wood-cutting shed and for altering and improving the old laundry and old woodcutting-room.[12]

On the afternoon of 20 March 1906, a fire broke out in the master and matron's quarters in the main building. It was caused by an imbecile pauper stirring the fire during the matron's temporary absence. The fire brigade arrived quickly and the inmates were moved to the children's and other blocks of buildings, with no casualties occurring. The adults' accommodation, sick wards and master and matron's residence were completely gutted. At the time, there were 103 inmates in residence, including children and twenty certified imbeciles.[13] The main block was rebuilt in 1908 to a design by A.I. Jones at

The main building of Carmarthen workhouse following the 1906 fire.

a cost of around £9,000. The new building was three storeys high with a T-shaped layout.

After 1904, for birth registration purposes, the workhouse was identified as 1 Penlan Road, Carmarthen.[14]

During the First World War, most of the workhouse was turned over for use as an Auxiliary Military Red Cross Hospital. Troops were also quartered there during the Second World War.

After 1930, the workhouse became a PAI run by Carmarthenshire Council, continuing as an old people's home into the 1970s. In more recent times, some of the buildings were used as offices, though the site has suffered from neglect and fire damage.

By 1920, a children's cottage home known as Waterloo Cottage (now Llwyn Martin) was operating on what is now Myrddin Crescent (SN412203). By 1929, it had moved to 'Ystradwrallt' on Station Road, Nantgaredig (SN492211).

LLANDILO FAWR

The parish of Llangeler established an institution in 1764 that acted both as an almshouse and a workhouse.[15]

In 1832, Llangathen purchased an inn called The Serving Cross for the reception of the parish poor.[16]

Llandilo Fawr Poor Law Union was formed on 14 December 1836, with thirteen member parishes. At their first meeting, the guardians agreed 'to build a workhouse forthwith'. There was apparently little debate of the matter, perhaps because of prior discussions between the Assistant Commissioner, local gentry and vestry members.[17] An initial proposal to erect a joint workhouse with the neighbouring Llandovery Union came to nothing and the union erected its own workhouse in 1837–38 at Ffairfach, half a mile to the south of Llandilo (now Llandeilo, SN630215). Intended to accommodate 120 inmates, the building was based on the PLC's model 'square' (see page 26).

The architect, George Wilkinson, had hoped to introduce some variations into the model plan, but the guardians, anxious to minimise the cost, instructed him to make it identical to his design for the Pembroke workhouse. However, they subsequently imposed some of their own alterations to the layout, deciding to convert Wilkinson's planned dining room into a chapel, and the chapel into a bakehouse. In a similar vein, they opted to take possession of the building early and avoid paying for work that was 'improperly completed'. The first board meeting at the new workhouse took place in December 1838. The unfinished work included a leaking roof, which continued to cause problems for several decades.[18]

Later alterations to the building included the enlargement of the sick ward in 1845 and new dayrooms in 1883. A proposal to connect the workhouse to mains water was rejected in 1862, but it was agreed in 1880 that oil lights should replace candles. Spending was rather more enthusiastic on the provision of work facilities for the able-bodied and vagrants: a four-man rotary mill was purchased in 1843, a stone-breaking shed erected in 1863, followed by a vagrants' ward in 1867. In 1884, the boardroom was extended by 9 feet and new windows added, together with a urinal for the guardians' use. Despite this upgrade, it was decided to hold winter meetings at the Shire Hall to shorten most guardians' journey by a mile.[19]

After 1904, for birth registration purposes, the workhouse was identified as 'Abercennen'.

In 1930, the site was taken over by Carmarthenshire Council and became the Abercennen PAI. The buildings were demolished in the mid-1960s and the Awel Tywi care home now occupies the site.

An aerial view of the Llandilo Fawr Union workhouse building – a typical 'square' design. (Courtesy of Terry Norman)

LLANDOVERY

Llandovery Poor Law Union was formed on 15 December 1836. Two of its eleven member parishes lay in Breconshire.

The union erected a workhouse in 1837–38 on Llanfair Road, to the north of the Llandovery, in the parish of Llandingat (SN768349). The PLC authorised an expenditure of £3,000 on construction of the building, which was to accommodate 120 inmates. It was designed by George Wilkinson and was based on the PLC's model 'square' plan (see page 26).

At about 2 a.m. on 25 July 1838, not long before the building work was completed, a fire broke out at the workhouse. Only one wing and the outbuildings were preserved, with most of the remainder needing to be rebuilt. The fire was thought to have been started deliberately and a reward of £100 was offered by the guardians for information leading to the conviction of the offenders.[20]

The inmates received a New Year's treat in January 1899, with a dinner of roast beef, plum pudding, mince pies, beer, etc., given by the mayor, Dr Owen. After dinner, presents of 1lb sugar and ½lb tea were given to each of the females, and 4oz tobacco to each of the smokers, while oranges, sweets, etc., were given to the non–smokers, imbeciles, and children.[21]

The surviving reception block of the Llandovery Union workhouse.

In April 1902, it was noted that of the 109 vagrants visiting the workhouse over the previous fortnight, only eight were Welsh, while eighty-two were English, fourteen Irish, and five Scottish.[22]

In November 1919, when there were only fourteen inmates in residence, the guardians decided to close the workhouse, although the casual ward continued in operation. Land at the south of the workhouse was subsequently donated by the guardians for construction of the Llandovery Cottage Hospital, which opened in 1926.

In 1930, control of the site passed to Carmarthenshire Council. Most of the workhouse buildings are believed to have been demolished in 1938. However, the front block, which included the casuals' accommodation, was retained and a council depot created at its rear. After the Second World War, the front block was used for several years as a girls' home, then in 1952 became part of the cottage hospital premises.

LLANELLY

An 1844 tithe map identifies a 'Poorhouse on the Allt' above the village of Llangennech (SN554022).[23]

Llanelly Poor Law Union was formed on 24 October 1836, with ten member parishes. The union erected a workhouse in 1837–38 at the north side of Swansea Road, Llanelli (SN514008). The PLC authorised an expenditure of £2,800 on construction of the building, which was to accommodate 200 inmates. It was designed by George Wilkinson and based on the PLC's model 'square' plan (see page 26).

Troops were billeted at the workhouse during the Rebecca Riots of 1842–43 and one of the ringleaders, David Davies, was held there for interrogation before being removed to the County Goal at Carmarthen and later transported to Australia.

In January 1892, an LGB inspector found much of the workhouse to be in a 'dirty and slovenly condition'. Some of the beds had not been made by midday and the sheets were changed only fortnightly.[24] A subsequent visit by the ladies' committee found that the butter was bad and unfit for use, and the bread not much better. The suet pudding was not properly cooked, and the broth made was from fat meat only. The bed linen was extremely deficient in quantity and there was not a kitchen towel in the house.[25]

In July 1892, the guardians invited tenders for the erection of sick wards and other additions and alterations at the workhouse, to plans by W. Griffiths.[26] In 1897, tenders were sought for further alterations and additions, which

The entrance block of the Llanelly Union workhouse, now incorporated into a
residential development.

This aerial view of the Newcastle-in-Emlyn Union workhouse shows the extensive
vegetable cultivation in its grounds.

included a new boardroom.[27] Most of the new buildings were on land to the north of the workhouse.

After 1904, for birth registration purposes, the workhouse was identified as 116 Swansea Road.[28]

In May 1928, the guardians invited tenders for the erection of new kitchens, sculleries, dormitories, and master's quarters, designed by Messrs W. Griffiths and Son.[29]

In 1930, the workhouse became a PAI run by Carmarthenshire Council. In 1948, the site joined the NHS as Bryntirion Hospital and continued to provide geriatric care until its closure in 2004. The site was subsequently redeveloped for housing, which, following a local campaign, preserved the entrance and hub sections of the old building.

A T-shaped building at the west of the workhouse served as the union's children's home from around 1900, later becoming the town's register office. A campaign to also save this building proved unsuccessful and it was demolished.

NEWCASTLE-IN-EMLYN

Newcastle-in-Emlyn (or Newcastle Emlyn) Poor Law Union was formed on 31 May 1837. Its twenty constituent parishes were drawn from Cardiganshire, Carmarthenshire and Pembrokeshire.

The guardians decided to build a new workhouse to accommodate 150 inmates. The selected site, known as Pantyronnen in Aberarad, was almost a mile to the east of Newcastle-in-Emlyn, on the road to Bwlchydomen (SN315402). Plans were obtained from Thomas Rowlands, who was also appointed to superintend the building work. An estimate of £2,750 from Richard Evans was accepted for the construction of the workhouse, which was to be roofed by 1 September 1839 and completed by that Christmas.[30] By January 1839, the low buildings were complete except for the roofs. It appears that someone had forgotten to order the slates, which also meant the floors could not be completed. Construction was completed in October 1839. Rowlands's design was based on the PLC's model 'square' plan (see page 25), with its entrance block at the west of the building.

In 1841, the guardians were unable to find a schoolmistress for the workhouse. Eventually, the workhouse master agreed to teach the children for three hours a day, in return for a £15 advance of salary, while a woman was employed to instruct the girls in skills such as sewing, knitting, spinning, washing and ironing.[31]

In 1852, the master reported that a woman in the workhouse was pregnant by a boy who was also an inmate. At first, the woman denied that he was the father, but confessed after other inmates said they had witnessed the couple's 'congress' in the pigsty in the garden.[32]

In 1897, the workhouse privies were converted into water closets.[33]

In July 1902, the guardians removed coffee from the workhouse dietary after the master reported that the inmates disliked it, and in the medical officer's opinion it was injurious to the health of the aged paupers.[34]

After 1904, for birth registration purposes, the workhouse was identified as 'Foellalt Castle'.

The workhouse was closed on 30 September 1915 and the existing inmates were transferred to the Cardigan workhouse.[35] During its seventy-six years of operation it had only four masters. The first was David Davies, who held the post until his death, twenty-nine years later, in 1868. For the next two years, the house was in the charge of his son, John Richard Davies, after which Lewis Morgan was appointed. When Mr Morgan retired after thirty-three years' service, Henry Evans, the final master, was appointed, retiring in 1915 after twelve years' service.

From June to December 1918, a party of Danes was billeted at the workhouse, while they were engaged in clearing and replanting pine plantations in the area. In 1922–24, the West Wales Farmers Dairy Society rented part of the premises for cheese production. In around 1924, part of the building was converted to flats for people awaiting housing in Aberarad, and concerts and Eisteddfodau were organised. In 1931, the Cow & Gate company took over the premises for the manufacture of dried milk products. Since 1989, mozzarella cheese has been made at the site. None of the original building now survives.[36]

5

CARNARVONSHIRE

BANGOR & BEAUMARIS

In 1801, the Bangor vestry adopted Gilbert's Act but appears to have made little use, if any, of its provisions.[1] The parish had several poorhouses at a location known as Caemaesidan (or Cae Maes Idan), at the east side of the Carnarvon Road, Glan Adda (SH571709).[2]

The Bangor and Beaumaris Poor Law Union was formed on 30 May 1837. Sixteen of its twenty-one member parishes were on Anglesey.

Initially, the guardians proposed buying the Caemaesidan site and early in 1838 agreed a price of £500 with the parish. However, after the sitting tenants refused to leave, the guardians began to look elsewhere. The delay allowed opponents of the workhouse to sway the board against its construction. By the end of 1842, however, the tide had swung the other way and they revived and successfully concluded their bid for the Caemaesidan site.

The new building, designed by Messrs Weightman and Hadfield, had a long, corridor-plan main block, with narrower cross-wings at each side. To provide an adequate water supply, a new well had to be sunk, the water being raised by inmate labour to a tank in the roof of the building. The workhouse began operation on 22 September 1845, with 197 paupers 'ordered for admission'. They comprised nine orphans, five widows with eight children, two men with five children, two women without children, and seventy-seven women with their eighty-eight illegitimate children.[3] Males were housed in the southern half of the building and females at the north. The transverse block at the north contained a laundry at its east end and married couples' and receiving wards at the west. An infirmary, imbeciles' ward and infectious ward ran across the south of the site, with a vagrants' block at the south-west corner.

In 1846, the labour required to be performed by able-bodied adult males, both inmates and vagrants, was ordered to be three hours working at the pump or picking one pound of oakum fibre. Females were employed in scouring or other household duties.[4]

In December 1889, the chairman of the guardians told a meeting that he had visited the workhouse dining room and seen the inmates clawing their food with their hands, just like savages. It was agreed that a stock of knives and forks should be purchased.[5]

A former inmate, writing in 1904, characterised workhouse life as being governed by cleanliness and punctuality. In winter, the inmates rose at 6.45 a.m. and breakfast was served between 7.15 and 7.30. Work was performed from 8 a.m. until noon, when the dinner bell rang. It resumed at 1 p.m. and continued until 4.30 in winter or 5 in summer. Tea was served at 5.15. From then until 'lights out' at 8 p.m. inmates were free to do as they wished, the favourite pastimes being smoking, reading and gossiping.[6]

After 1904, for birth registration purposes, the workhouse was identified as 'Cae Maesagan'.[7]

The union opened a children's home in 1905 at Maesgarnedd, in Llanfairpwllgwyngyll on Anglesey. In 1909, it was reported to be a rather

Officers, staff and other officials at the Bangor & Beaumaris Union workhouse, early 1900s.

broken-down piece of property, which had needed a considerable sum spending on it. However, the children were very cheerful and comfortable.[8]

The same 1909 report described the workhouse as being on a rather limited site and too small. The guardians had an extension scheme under consideration but the Medical Officer and architect were advising them to instead build a new workhouse and infirmary on a different site. In 1912–13, a new ninety-bed infirmary, designed by Frank Bellis, was erected at west side of the Carnarvon Road, just north of the main workhouse (SH569710).[9] In 1914, the buildings were taken over for use as a military hospital.

After its closure in 1930, the workhouse site was sold to the Bangor Ice Company, and later housed a creamery. A supermarket now occupies the site. The union infirmary later became a maternity and children's hospital known as St David's. It closed at the beginning of 1994 and a retail park now stands on the site.

CARNARVON

In 1786, Carnarvon, in the parish of Llanbeblig, spent £360 on a building for use as a workhouse. It was in the Twthill area of the town, the site now lying beneath the tarmac of Tanrallt (SH483627). Inmates were occupied in spinning flax.[10] In 1813, thirty-seven paupers were maintained in the establishment.

In 1801, Llanrug built three cottages for the use of its parish poor at a total cost of £27. The buildings were very small, measuring 5 yards by 4½ yards and only 5 feet high.

Carnarvon Poor Law Union was formed on 1 June 1837, with five of its sixteen parishes being on Anglesey. The Carnarvon guardians were divided in their opinion as to the erection of a union workhouse and endlessly made and then reversed decisions on the matter. Eventually, in 1843, the PLC resorted to a legal order to force the matter. A new workhouse, accommodating up to 200 inmates, was finally opened in 1846 at Tyddyn Morfa, north of where Seiont Mill Road now runs (SH486615).

The entrance to the premises, at the south of the site, was flanked by single-storey blocks, which included a boardroom, porter's lodge and receiving wards. The main building was three storeys high, with short cross-wings at each end. The central portion of the main block protruded at the rear to form a supervisory hub whose windows overlooked all the inmates' yards. A single-storey wing ran back from the centre-rear of the building. A row of buildings ran along the north of the site, perhaps including the original infirmary.

The main building of the former Carnarvon Union workhouse – the right-hand entrance has been blocked up.

In October 1846, the PLC were asked whether the master, at board meetings, could provide bread and soup to the guardians, some of whom travelled up to 15 miles, direct from home. The Commissioners' answer, though sympathetic, was in the negative.[11]

In August 1855, the workhouse children, under the care of the master and others, enjoyed an outing to Chester.[12]

In the same year, the guardians advertised for tenders to build another storey on the workhouse infirmary.[13] In April 1881, tenders were invited for the erection of a new infirmary and vagrant wards. The infirmary, placed at the south-west of the workhouse, was designed by Messrs Thomas and Ingleton of Carnarvon.

After 1904, for birth registration purposes, the workhouse was identified as 'Bodfan, Carnarvon'.[14]

In January 1908, the union's medical officer, Dr Tom Roberts, gave the guardians a devastating appraisal of conditions in the workhouse infirmary. His complaints included that 'the epileptic, the imbecile, the old and the infirm are obliged to be mixed up indiscriminately, and often in the same wards as the acute cases', that 'there is no night nursing of any kind whatsoever', and that 'the percentage of bed-sores in your infirmary is a discredit to the institution'. He recommended the appointment of a fully qualified, trained nurse.

A Royal Commission report in 1909 recorded that: 'The workhouse is pleasantly situated. The wards are very well looked after. There is a very good infirmary of modern design with twenty beds. The total accommodation is 153.'[15] It is not clear whether this visit made was before or after Dr Roberts's report to the guardians. The Royal Commission also noted that 'a new chapel has been built by the unemployed – non-paupers'.[16]

In April 1914, the union formally opened a new sixty-bed hospital, named the Eryri Infirmary. Designed by Rowland Lloyd Jones, it was located at the north-east of the workhouse. Separate male and female ward pavilions were placed either side of a central administration block, all linked by corridors on the ground and first floors. In 1916, the Eryri was requisitioned for use as a military hospital.

After 1930, part of the site operated as the Bodfan Home for Mentally Defective Children, the remainder as Bodfan PAI. After 1948, the whole site was reunited as the Eryri Hospital. The workhouse main block, 1881 infirmary and Eryri Hospital buildings are still in use.

CONWAY

The parish of Llansanffraid-Glan-Conwy was employing a workhouse by 1813, when thirteen paupers were maintained there.

Conway Poor Law Union was formed on 11 April 1837. Its fifteen member parishes included several from Denbighshire. At their first meeting, a week later, the guardians agreed to a proposal from George Thomas Smith – a local JP and unelected ex officio member of the board – that the union should erect a workhouse to house 100 paupers. A site was found and plans drawn up by Thomas Penson. By the end of the year, however, opposition to the scheme among the elected guardians was hardening. Despite the efforts of the Commissioners, supported by local gentry and JPs, the scheme was put on hold – a situation that was to continue for the next fifteen years. In 1845, the union was forced to introduce an outdoor labour test, where out-relief could only be granted to those performing a prescribed amount of supervised daily labour. Finally, at their meeting on 9 March 1853, a majority of the guardians voted for a workhouse.[17]

Progress in erecting the building was slow. The first site provided by the Corporation proved too uneven and was replaced by one on the north side of the Bangor Road (SH774781), about half a mile from the town. The PLC demanded many changes to the initial plans for the building, especially to improve the segregation of inmates. When construction eventually started in 1856, there were further delays due to the many active springs on the site and the flooding sometimes caused by high tides. The workhouse finally opened in September 1859.

The buildings comprised a main block at the front, with three smaller, parallel ranges to the rear. Females were housed at the west of the site and males at the east, with children on the ground floor and able-bodied adults on the first floor. The front block was set back from the road and high-walled exercise yards were created for boys and girls at the front and for men and women at the rear. The main entrance was at the centre, where the master and matron's quarters were also placed. To the rear of the centre was the inmates' dining room, which also linked to the first parallel rear block. This contained the kitchen, larder, scullery, bathroom, etc. To its rear stood the original infirmary with the casual ward at its eastern end. A single-storey block at the north-west of the site accommodated the aged and infirm.

Major additions to the building in 1901–03, designed by T.B. Farrington, included a new dining hall at the rear of the original one, a separate laundry at the west of the site, and extensions to the male and female wards at either end of the front block. A new boardroom was subsequently added as an upper storey to the dining room and the aged block was converted to a female infirmary and lying-in ward. The building work caused significant disruption to the institution and the supervision of its residents. As a result, it was discovered

The long frontage of the former Conway Union workhouse prior to its demolition in 2004.

that three single female inmates had become pregnant during the work, the putative fathers also being inmates.[18]

A Royal Commission in 1909 noted that there were almost as many children as adults in the workhouse and that the guardians had little inclination to order indoor relief for adults, as it was considered more expensive that outdoor relief.[19]

In the same year the union established children's cottage homes in two semi-detached villas, 'Bryn Onen' and 'Bryn Conway', at Woodlands, on the Llanrwst Road (SH779771). The homes, one for boys and one for girls, were said to be the first of their kind in North Wales. Each housed thirteen children and a foster mother.[20] In 1926, a new children's home known as 'Blodwel' was erected on Broad Street, Llandudno Junction (SH794781).

In 1930, the workhouse site was taken over by Caernarvonshire Council and became Dolwaen PAI. In 1948, it joined the NHS as Conway Hospital for the Aged Sick, continuing as a local hospital until 2003. The site was then cleared and modern housing erected.

PWLLHELI

Pwllheli Poor Law Union was formed on 3 June 1837, with thirty-two constituent parishes. Unlike other unions in the county, the Pwllheli guardians quickly decided to erect a workhouse, and in September 1837 approval was given by the PLC for construction of a building to house 200 inmates. On 13 December, the board agreed to pay William Glyne Griffith 500 guineas for a site known as Llain Gam, at the north side of what is now Ala Road, Pwllheli (SH371350).[21]

The building's design was opened to competition, and early in 1838 the plans by local architect William Thomas were chosen from the five entries.[22] Thomas's design was based on the PLC's model 'square' plan (see page 26). The guardians held their first meeting at the new workhouse in September 1839, but it took until the following February for the fitting-out to be fully completed and allow the first inmates to be admitted. There was not an immediate rush, however. The 1841 census records only six inmates, the same number as the master and his family.

Picking oakum was the favoured task to be given to able-bodied adult inmates. In 1843, the daily amount to be picked was set at 5lb for men and 3lb for women.[23]

The inmates' diet was typically plain. For men, breakfast and supper each day was 7oz oatmeal boiled with a pint of buttermilk. Midday dinner on Sunday

The entrance block (left) and central hub (right of centre) of the former Pwllheli workhouse, now Pwllheli Hospital.

was 4oz boiled meat with 1lb boiled potatoes. For the rest of the week, dinner on three days was a herring with 2½lb potatoes; one day was 1½ pints of soup and 7oz bread; one day was 1oz cheese and 6oz bread; and one day was 'lobscouse'.[24] Women received an ounce less oatmeal for breakfast and supper and an ounce less bread on soup days. In 1856, to reduce the food bill, the Sunday meat ration was cut by an ounce, with an extra ounce of bread given on soup days.[25]

After 1904, for birth registration purposes, the workhouse was identified as 'Cartrefle' ('Homestead').[26]

In 1909, the workhouse was certified to accommodate 180 inmates but then had only 70 in residence, including several 'noisy harmless lunatics'.[27]

A chapel located at the south-east corner of the site appears to be a twentieth-century addition. In January 1928, a box belonging to a woman of 82, who had been an inmate for four years, was found to contain £72. The money was claimed by the board of guardians.[28] In September of that year, the death was reported of a man aged 70, who had been in the workhouse for sixty-three years, at a cost to the ratepayers of almost £2,000.[29]

In 1930, the site was taken over by Caernarvonshire Council and became a PAI. After 1948, it joined the NHS as Pwllheli Hospital. Most of the former workhouse buildings survive, still occupied by medical facilities.

DENBIGHSHIRE

LLANRWST

In 1813, Llanrwst relieved 135 paupers in a workhouse. In the same year, thirty-two from Eglwys-Fach (now Eglwysbach) were supported in a similar manner.

Llanrwst Poor Law Union was formed on 26 April 1837. Its seventeen constituent parishes were drawn from Denbighshire and Carnarvonshire.

Like a number of unions in central and north-west Wales, Llanrwst held out for some years against providing a union workhouse. In April 1846, however, the guardians invited tenders for erection of a new workhouse, based on plans from a Mr Griffith of Penissardre, Llanrwst.[1] The architect appears to have been William Griffith, a local solicitor, who was also the union's clerk. In June 1848, with the building nearing completion, advertisements were placed for the post of master and matron, who were to be a married couple, preferably without 'incumbrances' – a common euphemism for 'children'. The master was required to be able to speak Welsh. His salary was set at £35, while the matron received £15.[2]

The workhouse was located at the west side of Station Road, Llanrwst (SH795622). Its design followed the PLC's model 'square' plan (see page 26) and could accommodate sixty inmates.

On 31 January 1849, the workhouse inmates were treated to a special dinner and supper, provided at the request of Mrs Humphreys Jones of Glan Conway, to celebrate her daughter's wedding that day.

In February 1865, 29-year-old William Jones and his wife Margaret were appointed master and matron of the workhouse. They were to hold the post for over forty years until forced to resign through old age and ill health in January 1906.

In 1889, indicating the continuing antipathy to the strictures of the New Poor Law among the some of the guardians, the board agreed to a proposal that the minutes of their previous meeting, although required to be recorded in English, should in future be read out in Welsh.[3]

In 1909, the workhouse had no nurse but the guardians subscribed ten guineas to the Llanrwst District Nursing Association, in return for which the district nurse attended upon indoor and outdoor paupers when required. There was no isolation hospital in the district, but there were isolation wards in the workhouse.[4]

In 1910, the startling announcement was made to the board of guardians by a recent entrant to the workhouse, 'that there was a reference in the Bible to the Llanrwst workhouse, and that was why he entered it, depending upon its high reputation to be a true home of refuge to the weary'.[5] In June 1917, an old-age pensioner seeking admission to the workhouse was found to have £53 in banknotes in his pocket.

In 1930, the establishment was taken over by Denbighshire Council and became a PAI, later an old people's home. After it closed in about 1964, the buildings were demolished and housing and workshops now occupy the site.

Former Ruthin Union workhouse south yard showing (left to right) south-west wing, central hub and boiler house, *c.*1965.

RUTHIN

Ruthin Poor Law Union was formed on 1 March 1837, with twenty-one constituent parishes. A workhouse was erected in 1838 on Llanrhydd Street, Ruthin (SJ128581). The building, for 250 inmates, was designed by Thomas Penson[6] and followed the PLC's model 'square' plan (see page 26).

The workhouse employed its own schoolmaster and schoolmistress. After a visit in 1848, the government's Inspector of Workhouse Schools reported that: 'The boys are ill taught, and know very little. The girls are entirely uninstructed.' He recommended the adoption of spade husbandry for the boys, and the purchase of four dozen lesson books produced by the Irish Society and blackboards for teaching arithmetic.[7]

In May 1848, the guardians advertised for tenders for the building of fever wards at the workhouse, for which the architect was Richard Cash of Llanbedr.[8]

In 1878, the guardians debated a proposal to construct six cages, each 6 feet square, into which vagrants could be placed for stone-breaking purposes. It was said that such measures had lowered the numbers of tramps calling at other workhouses in the area.[9] At their next meeting, the master reported that after requiring vagrants to perform a certain amount of work before receiving supper, their numbers had already fallen. His request to buy twelve hammers to be used for stone breaking was approved.[10] In 1894, the tramp ward was converted into separate sleeping and stone-breaking cells.

After 1904, for birth registration purposes, the workhouse adopted the name 'Gorphwysfa' ('Resting Place'). In 1907, following a complaint from the owner of a similarly named house in the area, the name Rhyddfan ('Place of Redemption') was used instead.[11]

In 1909, it was reported that the workhouse was very old, but kept in a good state of repair. The sick wards were very comfortable and the patients well attended to. However, the children's quarters were overcrowded and guardians were encouraged to remove them to a house outside, which could be cheaply hired since Ruthin was 'a decaying town'.[12]

A new infirmary was erected at the south-east of the workhouse in 1914–15. The single-storey building, designed by F.A. Roberts, cost around £5,400.[13] On its completion, it was lent for use as an auxiliary military Red Cross hospital.

In 1930, the site was taken over by Denbighshire Council and became a PAI, continuing as an old people's home until its closure and demolition in the late 1960s. The 1915 infirmary became Ruthin Hospital and is still in operation.

WREXHAM

There was a workhouse in Wrexham by 1737. Funded by subscription, it was located at Wrexham Green, on the east side of Salop Road (SJ337499).[14] The building was enlarged or rebuilt in 1757 and spinning wheels and looms installed.[15] In 1776, the establishment could house seventy paupers. In 1797, it was reported that:

> There are 46 persons in the house, chiefly old persons or young children, or the blind, lame or insane. The master agreed to supply such Poor as the parish should send with meat, drink and fuel for 2s. a week each, and their earnings, but none of the present inmates can work. The parish provides the house, clothes, beds and bedding, and other furniture. Bill of fare: Breakfast – every day, broth or milk. Dinner – Sunday, Tuesday, Thursday, meat and vegetables; other days, bread and butter or cheese. Supper – every day, bread and milk.[16]

In June 1814, in celebration of a peace treaty with France, the Wrexham inmates were provided with a good dinner by W. Lloyd of Plas Power.[17] In that year, fourteen paupers were maintained in the workhouse.

Several other parishes and townships in the area made limited use of workhouses: Pickhill with two permanent inmates in 1803; Bangor one in 1803 and one in 1813; Marchwiel one in 1813; and Sesswick one in 1815.

Wrexham Poor Law Union was formed on 30 March 1837, with its fifty-six constituent parishes coming from Flintshire, Denbighshire and Cheshire. In 1838, the union erected a workhouse for twenty-five inmates on Watery Road, at the west of Wrexham (SJ328504). Its design, by John Welch, was based on the model 'square' layout (see page 26), with females housed at the north of the site and males at the south.

In 1842, it was reported that forty-two out of forty-nine single mothers in the Wrexham workhouse were there because of the prevailing practice, in agricultural areas of the union, of allowing young men to pay night-time visits to female servants.[18]

From 1857 to 1863, the workhouse master was William Bragger, a former army sergeant. Contrary to the usual stereotype, Bragger appears to have been a generous and indulgent master. It was said that paupers preferred to enter the workhouse rather than take jobs, as they then received a better diet, fewer onerous tasks, and other 'comforts'. Bragger also avoided giving the inmates punishments and allowed them to dress differently from one another, rather than wearing identical uniforms. It was said that he rarely returned from market without gifts of tobacco and snuff for male inmates, and toys and cakes for the children.[19]

The workhouse at that time was an unhealthy place, with the establishment's raw sewage being fed into the adjacent mill race and resulting in an outbreak of typhus. On 2 July 1863, two of the guardians visited the workhouse and found Bragger 'in a very dangerous state', while the porter, Morris, was 'dying on his legs' and unable to perform any duty. The matron was prostrate with grief and the inmates had descended into complete disorder. The schoolmaster was ordered to take over the running of the establishment.[20] Bragger died two days later and was given a military funeral.

New vagrant wards were erected in 1873.[21] In 1887, a new chapel, designed by A.C. Baugh, was built at the east of the main building.[22]

In 1877, it was decided to appoint a bandmaster at the workhouse schools.[23]

In 1894, a report by the *BMJ* noted that 'the tone and management of this house impressed us very favourably; the officers seemed to regard their charges as human beings to be cared and planned for.' Nevertheless, some improvements were recommended. These included an increased staff of nurses for the sick, the employment of a night nurse, and an end to the use of pauper help in the actual nursing.[24]

In 1902, overcrowding in the workhouse led to the boardroom being taken over for use as a sick ward. An inspection in around 1907 found the institution still to be very much overcrowded, with the sick wards being badly ventilated and ill-adapted for their purpose.[25] The situation was finally remedied in October 1908 when a new infirmary was opened at the north-west of the workhouse. Its eight wards housed a total of 150 beds, with male and female sections placed either side of a central administrative block.

In 1930, the workhouse became a PAI run by Denbighshire Council. In July 1934, Lloyd George reopened the establishment, renamed Plas Maelor, which had been rebuilt and enlarged at a cost of £100,000. In 1948, the site joined the NHS as Maelor General Hospital, now Wrexham Maelor Hospital.

7

FLINTSHIRE

HAWARDEN

The parish of Hawarden, which included fourteen townships, erected a work-house in 1736 at a cost of £114, 'borrowed' from various small legacies to the poor and never repaid.[1]

A new establishment, for up to ninety inmates, was opened in March 1830. It occupied a former mansion, rented along with 22 acres of land, close to coal pits near the Hawarden to Chester road, and about 3 miles from each town. In 1834, the workhouse was the subject of a broadly complimentary report, which noted that its regime included separation of the sexes by night, regularity in hours, and forced labour. For the able-bodied, this was the cultivation of the land by spade husbandry, while the less able were set to pick oakum and spin. Breakfast and supper consisted of milk gruel, with 7oz of wheaten bread. The dinners included meat in some form five times a week. Each inmate received a daily half a pint of beer. On Sundays, the adults were restricted to 6oz of dressed meat at dinner; but there was no limit on the other days. The over-60s received a weekly ration of half an ounce of tobacco or snuff, and females over 70 received a little tea, sugar and butter. Pregnant single women, and mothers of illegitimate children, had separate sleeping quarters, but associated with other females during the day. The children attended the local National School for six or seven hours a day.[2]

When Hawarden joined the Great Boughton Union in 1837, its old work-house was closed, in line with the union's opposition to the New Poor Law. In the years that followed, Great Boughton's unwieldy size, Hawarden's discontent with its treatment by the union, and the efforts of the LGB to bring the union into line eventually resulted in the creation of a new Hawarden Union. It was formed on 1 February 1853 and encompassed the western part of the original Great Boughton Union.

The new union erected a workhouse in 1853–54 at the south-east corner of the junction of Chester Road and Broughton Hall Road, Broughton (SJ345640). The building, designed by James Harrison of Chester, accommodated eighty inmates. Males were housed at the west of the site and females at the east. A reception block at the north, facing onto the Chester Road, was linked by an arcade to a central hub, which contained the master and matron's quarters. To each side were the male and female infirmaries. At the rear of the hub, the dining hall linked to the main accommodation block, which included a laundry on the women's side. Outbuildings on the men's side included a carpenter's shop, stables and pigsty.[3]

In 1893, the guardians invited tenders for the construction of three stone-breaking cells at the workhouse.[4] In 1895, contractors were sought for construction of a new bathroom and the laying on of hot water to all the existing baths.[5] A stable was added in 1896.[6]

At a guardians' meeting in April 1895, it was proposed 'that in future the bills for beer for the use of the master, matron and assistant matron be not allowed

Hawarden workhouse inmates on an outing at the Hawarden Rectory in 1904. (Courtesy of North East Wales Archives, ref. PH/28G/1)

as a beverage, as it is not a necessary of life'. It was finally decided to allow the master and matron £10 a year in lieu of beer.[7]

In July 1904, the old people and children from the Hawarden workhouse attended a garden party at the Hawarden Rectory, where they played games such as Aunt Sally, bowls and football, while the less mobile sat among the flowers and listened to a music box and gramophone. After tea, games were resumed before the guests were provided with strawberries and buns. The old women each also received a ¼lb packet of tea, the old men an ounce of tobacco, and the children a packet of sweets.[8]

From 1919, the workhouse adopted the name Laburnum House for birth and death registration purposes.

In 1933, the premises were converted for use as an institution for young 'mental defectives', later known as Broughton Hospital, which finally closed in 1994. The buildings have all now been demolished and replaced by a housing estate.

HOLYWELL

In September 1739, the Holywell vestry authorised money to set up a work-house or poorhouse. The building was erected over the course of the next few months at Castle Hill, Holywell, near St Winifred's Well. Its capacity was ini-tially limited to six inmates. The first master was a Mr Phillips and the inmates were employed in making clothing for other paupers in the parish. Between 1766 and 1768 the workhouse was 'farmed' by Thomas Hughes, but it was then closed.[9] A new poorhouse was opened in 1779, but closed in 1784 after it was judged not to be cost effective.[10]

Holywell Poor Law Union was formed on 25 February 1837, with four-teen constituent parishes. A new workhouse, designed by John Welch, was erected in 1838–40 on Old Chester Road, Holywell (SJ189749). Housing 400 inmates, its layout was broadly based on the PLC's model 'square' plan (see page 26). The imposing entrance and administrative block was three storeys high at its centre, with two-storey wings at each side. Unusually, the work-house was not divided into simple male and female halves. Instead, the boys' and men's yards respectively occupied the north and south quadrants of the workhouse, and the girls' and women's the east and west.[11] The central hub had the kitchen on its ground floor, connecting to the dining hall and chapel in the south-west wing. The workhouse laundry was in the outer corner of the women's yard at the west of the site.

Additions to the buildings in 1867 included new vagrant wards, infectious wards, and a washhouse and laundry. The outdoor earth closet privies were also replaced by water closets. The architect for the work was Thomas Hughes of Holywell.[12]

In 1883, the guardians sought tenders for the erection of a new school chapel at the north of the entrance block and a block of vagrants' sleeping and stone-breaking cells to its south, both designed by John Douglas.[13] A large infirmary, designed by J.H. Davies and Son, was added at the south of the workhouse in 1913.[14] Electricity was installed in 1912 to replace the old paraffin oil lamps.

From August 1917, the workhouse infirmary provided beds for military patients, with almost 500 having being treated when the last of them departed in January 1919.[15]

In 1930, the site became a PAI run by Flintshire Council. In 1948, it joined the NHS as Lluesty General Hospital. After it closed in 2008, the site was sold for redevelopment as a care home. After the scheme fell through, the building stood empty and increasingly derelict. In 2018, a new owner planned to develop the site for housing and conserve the old buildings.

In 1895–96, the union erected a twenty-five-bed children's home just to the north of the workhouse (SJ189750). The building no longer exists.

ST ASAPH

In 1813, St Asaph maintained forty-eight paupers in a workhouse. In the same year, Betws-yn-Rhos provided similar support to twenty-two individuals.

St Asaph Poor Law Union was formed on 10 April 1837, with sixteen constituent parishes. In 1838–39, a workhouse for 300 inmates was erected on a 3-acre site known as Ysgubor-y-Coed ('Barn in the Woods') at the east side of the Denbigh Road to the south of St Asaph (SJ043738). Initial designs for the building were produced by Thomas Penson, with the work being completed by John Welch.[16] The building was based on the model 'square' layout (see page 26). Males were housed at the north-west side of the building and females at the south-east. The boys' and girls' yards were at the front of the building and the adults' at the rear.

The elegant frontage of the building, with arcades at each side, was originally to be built in red brick but it was decided to use Anglesey 'marble' instead. Rooms to the left of its central entrance hall included the boardroom, a strong-room and a surgery. To the right were porter's and relieving officer's

The former Holywell workhouse entrance block and one of its inmate yards.

Front block of the former St Asaph workhouse and (inset) a plaque commemorating former inmate H.M. Stanley.

room, a tramps' room, potato store and workroom. The upper floor of the front block housed sleeping quarters for children, schoolmaster and schoolmistress. The rear of the hall connected to the hub by a range containing a schoolroom on its ground floor. The main kitchen was on the ground floor of the hub, and connected at its rear to the dining room. Adult inmates were accommodated to the right and left of the hub, with dayrooms on the ground floor and dormitories above. The female side included a room for mothers and babies and a nursery above. The north-east side of the workhouse included a laundry, bakehouse, mortuary and refractory cells, where miscreants could be placed.[17]

In 1847, 5-year-old orphan John Rowlands entered the workhouse. In later life in the USA, Rowlands adopted the name Henry Morton Stanley and, as a *New York Herald* journalist, tracked down the missing explorer Dr David Livingstone. Stanley later recalled his time in the workhouse:

> At six in the morning [the inmates] are all roused from sleep; and at 8 o'clock at night they are penned up in their dormitories. Bread, gruel, rice, and potatoes compose principally their fare, after being nicely weighed and measured. On Saturdays each person must undergo a thorough scrubbing, and on Sundays they must submit to two sermons, which treat of things never practised, and patiently kneel during a prayer as long as a sermon, in the evening.[18]

The scourge of the workhouse was James Francis, a one-handed schoolmaster, whose cruelty seemed to know no bounds. In May 1856, after none of the boys would own up to scratching a new table, Francis began to cane the whole class. When it was Stanley's turn, he knocked Francis unconscious. Terrified of the consequences, Stanley absconded over the workhouse wall and subsequently ran away to sea.

In 1890, a chapel was erected adjacent to the dining hall. It was designed by Robert Jones, the master of the workhouse from 1878 to 1911.[19]

After 1904, for birth registration purposes, the workhouse adopted the name 'Cartrefle' ('Homestead').[20]

In 1903–05, a new infirmary was erected at the rear of the workhouse. At its centre was a three-storey administrative block, and on either side, two storeys high, were male and female ward blocks. Each ward contained twelve beds, with ground-floor wards having a veranda, and the first-floor wards a balcony. The architect was James Hughes of Denbigh.[21]

In April 1906, the local MP, Howell Idris, spent several days in the new infirmary after being involved in a serious car accident nearby. Pleased with the attention he received, he subsequently sent a cheque to the union clerk for his maintenance and £10 to the master to be spent on the inmates at the master's discretion.[22]

In 1912, vagrant cells were constructed adjacent to the chapel using inmate labour.[23] A separate vagrants' block was erected in 1923 at the north of the site, together with an additional infirmary.[24]

After 1930, the workhouse became St Asaph PAI. In 1948, it joined the NHS as the H.M. Stanley Hospital, finally closing in 2012. The building has now been converted to residential use.

In 1913, the union opened cottage homes for fifteen boys and fifteen girls on The Roe, St Asaph, immediately south of the Plough Hotel (SJ033744).[25]

8

GLAMORGAN

BRIDGEND AND COWBRIDGE

Cowbridge had a workhouse by 1787, which incorporated three cottages at Pwll-y-Buts (Butts Pool), at the west end of what is now The Butts (SS991746). Twelve paupers were maintained there in 1803, and fifteen in 1813. In 1830, it moved to a new building at the west side of Church Street, later the site of a police station (SS993746).[1]

In 1803, workhouses were also in use by St Brides Major, Newton Nottage and Pencoed. The latter two had ceased use by 1813, at which date Ewenny, Lampha and Southerndown had begun using workhouses. By 1834, poorhouses or workhouses were operating at Cowbridge, Bridgend, Llantwit Major, Newton Nottage, St Athan, and St Brides Major.[2]

Bridgend and Cowbridge Poor Law Union was formed on 10 October 1836, with fifty-two member parishes. None of the old parish premises was considered suitable for use by the union, so the guardians decided to erect a new workhouse to accommodate 200 inmates.

A site at the east side of Quarella Road, to the north of Bridgend (SS905803), was purchased from Sir Digby Mackworth. The new building, based on the PLC's model 'square' plan (see page 26), was designed by George Wilkinson in his favoured Elizabethan style. Males were housed in the west half of the building and females in the east. The building was ready for use in February 1839.[3] In April 1842, the walls around the yards were wired to prevent the inmates from scaling them so easily.

On 14 April 1855, the guardians heard that the union's clerk, William Edmondes, had died suddenly. A few weeks later, it emerged that he had committed suicide. It further transpired that the union's payments to the lunatic asylum in Briton Ferry had not been received, even though the necessary cheques had been signed by the chairman of the board. An auditing of the union's accounts revealed that Edmondes had embezzled many hundreds of pounds.[4]

In 1905, a sixty-four-bed infirmary was erected at the rear of the workhouse, together with a new porter's lodge and casual wards alongside Quarella Road.[5] The architect for the additions was P.J. Thomas of Bridgend, who also designed the union's new boardroom and offices erected at the south of the workhouse in 1910–11.[6]

After Glamorgan County Council took over the site in 1930, the medical facilities at the north end became Bridgend County Hospital, while the original workhouse buildings were used as a PAI. From 1948, the whole site became Bridgend General Hospital. The workhouse section was sold off in 1985 and converted to private housing.

In 1877–78, the union erected children's cottage homes on Merthyr Mawr Road, Bridgend (SS901787). The scheme, designed by Henry C. Harris of Cardiff, initially included six homes, each housing twenty children, together with school and schoolmaster's residence, all set around a 'village green'.[7] One cottage was used as a nursery and another housed Roman Catholic children. The houses are now in private residential use.

The frontage of the former Bridgend and Cowbridge workhouse, now sheltered housing.

CARDIFF

In September 1740, the Llandaff vestry ordered that:

> every person who receives relief from the parish shall be lodged in the alms
> house till the same is full, upon pain of having their allowances withdrawn
> and for their better accommodation the Overseers are to putt the said house
> in good repair and cause a bog house to be built there in the most conveni-
> ent place.[8]

In 1776, the Cardiff parish of St John the Baptist and St Mary had a workhouse
for 200 inmates. It stood on the west side of St Mary Street, at the north end
of where Hodge House now stands (ST181763). The building, which had a
courtyard and extensive garden, was given to the poor of Cardiff in 1753 by
the Earl of Windsor, as noted on a tablet above its door.[9]

In May 1784, Llantrisant opened a workhouse in a row of four cottages on
Swan Street (ST046834). The establishment was clearly prompted by Gilbert's
Act of 1782 – the preamble to the workhouse's rules referred to the Act and
also echoed Gilbert's intention of the more humane treatment of the poor.
However, the parish does not appears to have formally adopted the Act – it did
not appoint a Visitor and able-bodied paupers were initially admitted, although
they were subsequently barred from residence. Inmates were required to wear
an upper garment badged with the letters L.P. (Llantrisant Parish) in red. They
were employed in spinning wool and worked from 6 a.m. to 7 p.m. in summer
and 7 a.m. to 6 p.m. in winter. To encourage industry, workers received 1*d* per
pound of wool made into yarn. No smoking was allowed in the bedrooms.[10]

Following a dispute between the Llantrisant vestry and the Rev. Gervase
Powell, who had lent the money to erect the workhouse, the Swan Street
premises were closed in 1799.[11] A second workhouse was subsequently opened
in part of the Black Cock pub on Yr Allt. In 1836, Llantrisant's establishment
was described as a 'large workhouse … but it is ill-managed, the children are
half naked and dirty, while the diet was as the Overseer admitted better than
that of most of the small farmers of the Parish.'[12]

In 1801, the parish of Llantwit Fardre made an agreement to rent a house
for use as a workhouse.[13] In 1803, Eglwysilan (encompassing Caerphilly)
relieved seventeen paupers in a workhouse. In 1813, Roath maintained four
paupers in workhouse accommodation.

A property on or near College Road, Whitchurch, is identified as the Old
Workhouse in the 1881 census.[14]

Cardiff Poor Law Union was formed on 13 September 1836, with forty-four constituent parishes. The guardians were divided as to whether to adapt the St Mary Street workhouse to serve the union, or to erect a new building. The latter course was eventually adopted and a new workhouse, designed by George Wilkinson, was built on a 2-acre site on Cowbridge Road in the Canton district of the city (ST173765). The building, opened in 1838, was based on the PLC's model 'square' plan (see page 26) and accommodated 260 inmates,

In 1855, a 'house of refuge' was erected at the north-west of the workhouse. Originally intended for the isolation of cholera victims, it was subsequently used to accommodate 'vagrants, Irish removal cases, and unfortunate girls suffering from disease'.[15]

Between 1801 and 1901, Cardiff's population increased almost a hundred-fold and the new workhouse quickly proved inadequate. Numbers seeking relief were also swelled during the Irish famine of 1845–50. On one occasion, in 1848, more than 200 Irish paupers from Cork landed on Penarth beach and proceeded to demand relief. They were housed in the old workhouse, but on hearing they were to be returned to Ireland, several of the men scaled the walls and deserted their wives and children.[16] Their brief stay in Cardiff and return passage cost the union more than £200. The accommodation situation was eased in 1862 with the moving of the workhouse's child inmates to the union's new Ely Industrial Schools (see below). A 164-bed infirmary was added at the west of the workhouse in 1872.

A significant increase in capacity came with a major rebuilding of the main workhouse on the existing site in 1879–81, designed by Edwin Seward. It had an imposing administrative block, facing the street, whose clock tower rose to a height of 76 feet. The ground floor of the block included master's and porter's rooms, waiting and searching rooms, bathrooms, and a clothing store, while the upper floor contained offices and bedrooms. At the rear, a corridor led to the master's house and servants' rooms. Next was the kitchen, measuring 40 feet by 30 feet, and the dining hall, 85 feet by 43 feet. Corridors to each side connected to the separate men's and women's blocks, both three storeys in height, with dayrooms on the ground floor and dormitories above. On the female side there was a block for old and bedridden women. Another block contained twelve 'cottages' for elderly married couples and included a veranda and balcony overlooking a grassed area. The laundry block, 180 feet long, included a making and mending room, a washhouse with twenty-one washing troughs and three boilers, and a drying room, where the clothes were dried by hot air. The same block included an oakum-picking room, a smithy, carpenter's, tailor's and shoemaker's shops, and other outbuildings. The buildings, all lit by gas, provided accommodation, including the house of refuge, for a total of 830 persons.[17] A further wing was added in 1890 at a cost of £9,000. By 1908, the total capacity of the workhouse was 1,020 places.

In 1912, the guardians purchased land at Llandough (ST165729), with the intention of erecting a new union hospital. However, with the onset of the First World War and other delays, the foundation stone of the 340-bed hospital was not laid until 1928 and construction work only completed in 1933.

In 1930, Cardiff Council took over the Cowbridge Road site, which became City Lodge PAI. In 1948, it joined the new NHS as St David's Hospital. After St David's closed in 1995, most of the buildings were demolished for redevelopment of the site. Only the front block now survives, converted to residential use. The council also appropriated the Llandough site for use as a municipal hospital.

In 1862, the union established an industrial school for 240 pauper children at Ely (ST142764). As well as basic education, the children were given training to help make them employable in later life. For the girls this included laundry work, housework and needlework, while the boys learned trades such as carpentry, tailoring and shoemaking. By 1901, the buildings had been extended and a separate hospital block erected at the south-west of the

The stylish entrance and administrative block of Cardiff's revamped workhouse, opened in 1881.

site. The schools were closed in 1903 and the buildings extended to provide additional workhouse accommodation for adults, primarily the aged and infirm, and mild lunatics.

After 1930, the Ely site became Ely Lodge PAI. After 1948, as Ely Hospital, it was used for mental patients and as a hospice, finally closing in 1996.

From the early 1900s, the union increasingly placed children in scattered homes around the city, with a receiving home at 103 Cowbridge Road West, adjacent to the Ely site.

GOWER

The rapid growth in Swansea's population led, in 1857, to eighteen parishes on and around the Gower peninsula separating to form the new Gower Poor Law Union.

In 1861–62, a union workhouse to accommodate fifty inmates was erected on an elevated site at Penmaen, just west of the parish church (SS530887). The builders, John and William Williams of Llanrhidian, were required to sign a contractors' bond in the sum of £6,000, undertaking to complete the work within eighteen months from 1 January 1861. As well as segregated accommodation for men, women, boys and girls, the specification required the provision of detached sick and infectious wards, a lying-in ward, detached receiving wards with a bathroom, detached vagrant wards, a dining hall and dayroom for adults, a boardroom for thirty guardians, a clerk's office and strong room, and accommodation for a master and matron. The building was to be constructed in native stone of the neighbourhood. The total cost of the scheme, including the making of a new access road, was £3,866.[18]

The main building faced to the south and had a T-shaped layout. Other facilities were placed in a long block running along the north of the site.

In 1866, the guardians leased a field opposite Penmaen School to provide the inmates with a garden.[19]

After 1904, for birth registration purposes, the workhouse was identified as 'Hill House, Penmaen'.[20]

In 1930, the site became a PAI run by Glamorgan Council. New wings were added to the building in 1939. The premises, known after 1948 as Glan-y-Mor ('Seaside'), are now occupied by the Three Cliffs care home.

The master and matron, William and Rose Williams, and their son Donald, outside the Gower Union workhouse in 1913. (Courtesy of Veronica McKenzie)

Part of the entrance building (left) and the north wing of the main block (right) of the former Merthyr Tydfil Union workhouse.

MERTHYR TYDFIL

In 1803, the parish of Llanfabon provided three paupers with permanent workhouse relief.

In February 1833, the Merthyr Tydfil vestry made plans to apply for a Local Act, whose provisions included the erection of a workhouse in the parish.[21] However, the proposal was superseded by the passing of the 1834 Poor Law Amendment Act.

Merthyr Tydfil Poor Law Union was formed on 3 November 1836, with nine constituent parishes. The union was one of the areas in Wales that showed considerable resistance to the New Poor Law and, in contrast to the vestry, to the erection of a workhouse. For many years, some member parishes declined to return a guardian. The union, contrary to the wishes of the PLC, also persisted in giving out-relief entirely in cash. Eventually, in 1848, growing concern at the terrible conditions experienced by pauper children, and the lack of provision in the town for dealing with outbreaks of diseases such as typhus and smallpox, persuaded the guardians to undertake the building of a workhouse.

A site was acquired at the east side of Thomas Street, Merthyr (SO051064), and advertisements placed for plans for a building to hold 500 inmates and costing £10,000. The chosen design was by Aickin and Capes of Holborn. In June 1851, the original building contractor, Mr Hamlyn of Bristol, withdrew, and the Cardiff-based firm of Henry Norris and Daniel Thomas took over. The workhouse eventually opened in September 1853.

The two-storey entrance block at the west of the site contained a porter's room, laundry and girls' school. The main block was three storeys high and had a cruciform layout. Men were housed at the west and women at the east, with dayrooms on the ground floor and dormitories on the first floor. A dining hall, also used as a chapel, was in the south wing. The north wing contained boys' and girls' schoolrooms on the ground floor, women's wards on the first floor, and children's dormitories, separated by a lying-in ward, on the second floor. In the basement of the building were kitchens, a bakery and stores.[22] A separate T-shaped infirmary was placed at the north-east of the main building.

In the 1870s, wage cuts during a depression in the coal and iron industries resulted in strikes by workers. In February 1875, the Merthyr guardians decided that single men on strike would only be relieved through admission to the workhouse. On 27 February, when 900 single, able-bodied men converged on the workhouse demanding relief, the master admitted as many as there was room for, then turned away the rest. Those who had been admitted tried to overthrow workhouse discipline and four policemen were moved in to keep order. By May, the workers had been starved out and the strike collapsed.[23]

In 1900, a new infirmary was erected at the north of the workhouse. The pavilion-plan design, by E.A. Johnson, was built in Ebbw Vale yellow brick. The central administrative block was four storeys high. On its ground floor were staff rooms, a kitchen and an operating theatre. Lying-in and labour wards occupied the first floor, and nurses' bedrooms the second. To its left, a two-storey women's ward block provided forty-six beds, while the men's pavilion on the right had seventy beds. A roofed open corridor linked the blocks.[24]

After 1904, for birth registration purposes, the workhouse location was recorded as 44 Thomas Street.

In 1930, the site was taken over by Glamorgan Council and redesignated as Tydfil Lodge PAI, later becoming St Tydfil's Hospital. After the hospital's closure in 2012, the site was sold for redevelopment. Most of the buildings were demolished in 2015, although the workhouse entrance block is now a listed building.

In 1871, the union erected an infirmary at Llewelyn Street, Trecynon, Aberdare (SN990038). However, the premises proved unsatisfactory, and in 1877 the site was converted to an industrial training school for 124 children. In 1904, four cottage homes were erected nearby. In 1912, the school premises were converted for use as a branch workhouse. The site later became the Tegfan Hostel. It is now occupied by various facilities for the elderly.

From around 1909, further cottage homes were erected at Cefnpennar Road, Cwmbach; Hirwaun; Beech Terrace, Abercwmboi; Bargoed; and Glannant Street, Aberdare. Each had a foster mother looking after a small group of children. A receiving home for children was built in Trecynon, adjacent to the industrial training school. A site at Corner House Street, Llwydcoed, near Aberdare, was also developed as cottage homes. The Llwydcoed Homes site was later taken over by Glamorgan Council and became known as Penybryn.[25]

The union established two institutions for the elderly. By 1912, Pantyscallog House on Pant Road in Dowlais accommodated elderly and infirm women. In 1920, Windsor House, an institution for men, was erected at the east side of the Trecynon workhouse site.[26] During the First World War, Windsor House was used as a military hospital. Only Windsor House now survives on the Trecynon site, as part of Tegfan Resource Centre.

In 1913, the union erected a sanatorium near Pontsarn, in the parish of Vaynor (SO047094). Only its central section survives, now converted to residential use.

NEATH

In October 1809, a meeting was held in Neath to discuss the adoption of Gilbert's Act and the building of a workhouse in the town.[27] The Act appears not to have been adopted, but a workhouse was subsequently established on a site between Water Street and Orchard Street (SS754975). In 1832, the fifteen inmates included one female lunatic, aged 38, and two former seamen. At its sale in 1838, the property was described as having a spacious garden and courts.[28]

Neath Poor Law Union was formed on 2 September 1836, with twenty-nine member parishes. In 1837–38, the union erected a workhouse on a narrow site at the north side of Llantwit Road, backing onto the Neath Canal (SS758979). It was designed by George Wilkinson and had a compact double-courtyard layout, with males housed at the west of the site and females at the east. The front range had two entrance doors, the right-hand one leading to the guardians' boardroom, the other to the main entrance hall, committee room, porter's room and receiving wards. Beyond the boardroom were a schoolroom, master's room and women's dayroom. At the rear of the hall, a short central range containing the kitchen, scullery, larder and stores, linked to the rear range running parallel to the canal. At its centre was the dining hall, which also served as a chapel. Men's dayrooms were placed on its west side and an imbecile ward and women's dayrooms at the east.[29]

In 1864, social reformer Joseph Rowntree visited the workhouse. Its sixty inmates comprised forty-three adults, thirteen children and four infants, including thirteen male and female imbeciles. He described the workhouse as being dirty and badly ventilated, and the beds and bedding as 'exceedingly deficient'. The lack of gas lighting resulted in early bedtimes for the inmates and curtailed their reading of the scriptures and other books. The forms in the hospital lacked backs. The inmates' dietary was 'much below par' and the succession of broth dinners and suppers, which included twice-weekly pea soup served without bread, was 'unknown in other unions'. The light wire fencing adjoining the canal was judged as insufficient to prevent accidents or suicides. In summary, Rowntree had 'never viewed property so cramped and manifestly unsuitable in every way for the erection of a union workhouse'.[30]

In 1869, the original washhouse and laundry, at the east side of the women's yard, were replaced by a separate single-storey building erected to the east of the workhouse.[31]

The workhouse had severe problems with its water supply. Although there was a well in one of the yards, some water had to be fetched in buckets from a

The entrance and right-hand section of the frontage of the former Neath Union workhouse.

spring in Gnoll Woods. In 1870, the situation was so bad some of the cooking was being done in canal water.[32]

In 1918, the name 'Lletty Nedd' ('Neath Lodgings') was adopted for the workhouse.

In 1922, the workhouse matron, Mrs Mills, died after forty-nine years working in the Poor Law system. She was succeeded as matron by her daughter, Miss Edith Mills.

The workhouse closed in 1924 and the remaining inmates were transferred to the union infirmary (see below). In 1930, the workhouse site was taken over by Glamorgan Council and became a PAI. After the Second World War, it continued in use until around 1959 as a hostel for homeless families. The eastern part of the building survives, now a mixture of residential and commercial use.

In August 1875, the union invited plans for three children's 'industrial cottage homes' at Bryncoch (SN744004).[33] Designed by W. D. Blessley, they opened in July 1877 and could claim to be Britain's first Poor Law cottage homes. Their facilities included a bakery and laundry. In 1881, the residents comprised the master, matron, two female industrial trainers, a general servant and fifty-two children aged from 5 to 14 years. In 1918, by then greatly extended, the site adopted the name 'Gwynfryn' ('White Hill'). Only one of the houses now survives.

In 1911–12, the union erected an infirmary on Briton Ferry Road, Neath (SS744958). The pavilion-plan scheme was designed by J. Cook Rees.[34] During the First World War, the infirmary became a military hospital. In the 1930s, it was known as Penrhiwtyn Infirmary, then in 1948 joined the NHS as Neath General Hospital, finally closing in 2003. Modern housing now covers the site.

PONTARDAWE

On 26 March 1875, a new union was formed based at Pontardawe. Its creation was in response to a rapid increase in the population of the Swansea and Neath Unions, which together contributed a total of seven parishes to the new union.

In November 1876, a ninety-nine-year lease was taken out on land for a new workhouse on a sloping site above the Brecon Road, half a mile to the north-east of Pontardawe (SN727047). The building contract specified that any stones on the land could be taken free of expense, and that a daily average of 12 gallons of water per head could also be taken.[35] A year later, the union invited tenders for the erection of the workhouse to plans by J.B. Fowler.[36] In January 1880, advertisements were placed for a master and matron, with respective salaries of £50 and £30, plus rations, washing and apartments in the house. Candidates were to be a man and wife, preferably 'without encumbrance'.[37]

The workhouse buildings comprised two small blocks flanking the entrance, one containing the porter's lodge and receiving wards, the other the guardians' boardroom. The main building had a typical T-shaped layout, with the master's rooms at the centre and the dining hall and kitchens to the rear. Males were accommodated at one side and females at the other. A separate block to the rear housed the workhouse infirmary.

In 1881, the union advertised for a schoolmistress to teach the workhouse children.[38] From 1889, however, the children went out to local schools.[39]

After 1904, for birth registration purposes, the workhouse was identified as 84 Brecon Road, Pontardawe.

In 1910, a new twenty-five-bed infirmary and a children's home were opened at the workhouse site, to designs by Charles S. Thomas. The new infirmary was a conversion of an existing school block, while the children's home occupied the workhouse's old infirmary.[40] In 1913, the union erected a new boardroom and offices in Holly Street, Pontardawe.[41] Designed by John Morgan, the building is now home to the town library.

In July 1916, following a request from the St John's Ambulance Association to use the workhouse infirmary for the treatment of wounded soldiers, the House Committee reported that the inmates quarters could be arranged to allow twenty-five beds to be offered.[42]

In 1930, the workhouse site was taken over by Glamorgan County Council and redesignated as a PAI. In 1948, the premises became the Dan-y-Bryn Hostel, which finally closed in 1988. The building was demolished shortly afterwards and a care home now occupies the site.

PONTYPRIDD

In response to a rapid increase in population in the industrial areas of South Wales, a new union centred on Pontypridd was formed on 27 December 1862. It comprised six parishes from outlying areas of the existing Cardiff and Merthyr Tydfil unions.

In 1863, the union paid £600 for a 2-acre site for a workhouse at the south side of Court House Street, Pontypridd (ST070897). Construction of the building was delayed several times by the slow delivery of the required quantities of stone. Even when the building was complete, the opening of the workhouse was further delayed by the late delivery of furniture and other articles. Finally, in November 1865, the first inmates could be admitted.

An early 1900s view of the Pontardawe Union workhouse on its elevated site above the River Tawe.

The workhouse was designed by George Edward Robinson of Cardiff and could accommodate 234 inmates.[43] The main building was T-shaped with its entrance range facing to the north. Males were housed at the west of the site and women at the east. On the ground floor, a porter's lodge was placed inside the front entrance, with the guardians' boardroom to the left and the dining room to the right. On the female side, there were then the kitchen, scullery, larder and girls' dayroom. On the male side were the clerk's office, a waiting room, boys' dayroom and a refractory cell in which wrongdoers could be placed for a time. On the upper floors were dormitories, with that for married couples at the centre. On the ground floor in the stem of the 'T' were adult dayrooms, laundry and bakehouse, again with dormitories above. A small block at the rear of the workhouse contained stores and workshops. In the same month that the building was completed, the guardians invited tenders for the erection of infectious and foul wards.[44]

Water for the workhouse was originally planned to be obtained by sinking a well. However, this proved to be unsatisfactory and a mains supply was arranged. The workhouse also had gas lighting, although only thirty-two lamps were fitted in the whole building.[45]

Subsequent additions to the premises included new receiving wards in 1877, and a children's block at the south of the workhouse in 1884.[46] They were followed by a new laundry and washhouse in 1889 and infectious and tramps' wards in 1890, both designed by Seward and Thomas.[47]

In 1890, the same architects also provided the plans for children's cottage homes at Church Village, Llantwit Fardre (ST084860).[48] The homes, which opened in August 1882, comprised six houses and a school block, arranged along two sides of a 'village green'. Each house accommodated a 'family' of sixteen boys and girls aged between 3 and 13 years, together with a house-mother or married couple as house parents.

Following the opening of the homes, the workhouse children's block was converted into an infirmary. At the same time, a master's residence was erected at the north of the site.[49] A reception and nursery home was established on Maes-y-Coed Road, about a third of a mile north-west of the workhouse (ST066899). In 1913, the union erected offices opposite the workhouse entrance on Court House Street.

By 1914, the workhouse was known as the Central Homes. From 1930, the site was run by Glamorgan County Council, then joined the NHS as Graig Hospital for the chronic sick. The original buildings, apart from the union offices, were demolished in the mid-1960s and the new Dewi Sant Hospital was built on the site.

An aerial view of the former Pontypridd workhouse (then Graig Hospital) during demolition in 1965. The original workhouse building is left of centre. (Courtesy of Keith Jones)

In 1900–03, a subsidiary workhouse for the aged poor, known as the Llwynypia Homes, was built at Llwynypia in the Rhondda (SS999942). An infirmary was added in 1909. In 1927, the site became Llwynypia Hospital, now demolished after its closure in 2010.

SWANSEA

In 1750, a workhouse was established in the Great Hall of Swansea Castle, at the east side of Castle Bailey Street (SS657930). In 1776, the establishment could house 100 inmates. The accommodation comprised 'a large room, with slight partitions as bedchambers, amounting scarcely to separations ... into which persons of both sexes and of all ages and characters were promiscuously sent'.[50] By 1817, the room 'was crowded to such a degree, that they lay seven in a bed, in a state of wretchedness and filth impossible to be described'.[51]

In the same year, subscriptions raised following a public meeting in the town enabled the purchase of the former Bathing House on the Swansea Burrows, just to the west of the present-day civic centre (SS651924), for use as a House of Industry and Infirmary. Following its conversion, the establishment could house 180 paupers and provided:

rooms for picking oakum, making baskets, spinning, sewing, and a school, together with a garden of nearly two acres ... and a field of the same dimensions for planting potatoes ... the house has distinct apartments for poor persons of rather a better order, and two large dormitories, one for boys, and the other for girls, and each capable of containing thirty-two, allowing for their sleeping two in a bed: the rooms for the men and women are on different sides of the house, and except in the sick rooms, and in very particular cases, they sleep two in a bed.[52]

The town adopted Gilbert's Act, placing the management of poor relief in the hands of a Visitor, Guardian and Governor. From 1818 to 1832, the Visitor was Henry Sockett. He recorded that the inmates had a meat dinner two or three times a week, and soups, fish and vegetables on other days. The breakfasts were water gruel with bread, with a piece of fat meat occasionally thrown in; the suppers were the same, alternating with bread and cheese.[53]

In 1790, Llandeilo Talybont set up a workhouse in a rented farmhouse and garden called Cefn-arda at Tir-y-Brenin (SS592996), about 6 miles northwest of Swansea. David Mathew was contracted to provide 'the maintenance, washing, fireing and all other necessaries' for those coming into house, at the weekly rate of 2s per head.[54]

In 1803, the parishes of Higher and Lower Clase, Oystermouth, Higher Penderry, Pennard and Port Eynon relieved paupers in workhouses, although all except Higher and Lower Clase had ceased by 1813. Higher Llanrhidian was using a workhouse by 1813.

The former school building on School Lane at Middleton, Rhossili, now a youth hostel, occupies the site of the parish's former workhouse (SS424880).[55]

Swansea Poor Law Union was formed on 23 October 1836, with twenty-seven constituent parishes. The union took over the existing workhouse on Swansea Burrows and made alterations and enlarged it to provide 200 places. However, conditions in the building, with its many small rooms and low ceilings, were regularly criticised as being unsatisfactory. Resistance to erecting a new building came mainly from guardians in the rural Gower area. This situation was resolved in 1857, when the Gower parishes separated to form the new Gower Union.

A site for a new workhouse was purchased at Poppithill, Mount Pleasant (SS651936), and construction began in 1860. Progress was hampered by the bankruptcy of the original contractors but the building was eventually ready for occupation in March 1863. The existing able-bodied inmates at Swansea Burrows walked to their new quarters, while the others were transported by a local livery stable owner. Some of the old furniture was also transferred to the new premises, although seventy-two new iron bedsteads were purchased. The total cost of the whole scheme was £15,860.[56] The architect of the new building was William Fynone Richards.[57] An entrance and administrative block lay to the south of the site. To its rear, the main building had a double-courtyard layout. An infirmary block lay at the north of the site.

Almost as soon as the workhouse was finished, there were complaints about the building. In August 1863, Lunacy Commissioner James Wilkes found much to criticise after inspecting the premises. There was no special accommodation for those of unsound mind. The dayrooms were poorly furnished and the beds and pillows were filled with straw. Baths other than those in the infirmary were only supplied with cold water.[58] In 1866, PLB Inspector Mr J.T. Graves recorded that the shortage of wards for cases of itch and scaldhead resulted in their being placed in the married couples' wards.[59] Initially, the site lacked mains water and gas connections, although the latter was remedied in 1865.

In 1884–86, the workhouse buildings were extended to the north-east. The additions, designed by Messrs Blessley and Aspinall, cost £30,000. A new entrance, receiving wards, etc. were also erected on Terrace Road. By 1895, the workhouse could hold 584 inmates, including 300 infirmary beds.[60]

In 1902–03, several new buildings were erected at the south of the site, involving the demolition of the old administrative existing block. The most significant addition was a large female infirmary, which was formally opened on 13 January 1904. The scheme was designed by local architect Herbert W. Wills and cost over £17,000.[61]

In 1930, the site was taken over by Swansea Council and became Tawe Lodge PAI, then joining the NHS in 1948 as Mount Pleasant Hospital. After its closure in 1995, the site was used as student accommodation. A residential redevelopment scheme in 2000 incorporated several of the old buildings.

In November 1877, the union opened a group of cottage homes on a 10-acre site at the west side of Cockett Road, Cockett (SS629948), one of the first such developments for Poor Law children. The homes were extended in 1879 and then comprised five plain stone buildings accommodating up to 120 children.[62] From 1900, boys from the homes spent several weeks at camp each summer alongside boys from Swansea Boys' Industrial School. The homes no longer exist and the site is now occupied by local social services.

A group of elderly male inmates, accompanied by a nurse, at the Swansea Union workhouse.

The entrance to the former Swansea Union workhouse on Mount Pleasant in 2000, now converted to housing.

9

MERIONETHSHIRE

BALA

In 1776, a parish workhouse was in operation at Llandderfel with accommodation for up to eight inmates.

Bala Poor Law Union was formed on 10 January 1837, with five member parishes. A workhouse for eighty inmates was erected in 1839–41 at the south side of Bala High Street (SH925358). The building, designed by Jones of Chester, had a T-shaped entrance block facing onto the High Street.[1] Linked at the rear was a two-storey octagonal hub with male and female accommodation wings to either side.

In 1864, the workhouse was visited by social reformer Joseph Rowntree, who was surprised to find it devoid of inmates. None of the walls in the paupers' accommodation had been plastered so that the bed and day wards, with damp floors in the latter, were very comfortless. There were no water closets or baths in the building, which had no piped water supply. No warm clothing was supplied to the inmates in winter. The gruel and broth were of very poor quality, and no suet pudding was served. Unlike the usual case elsewhere, the elderly were not generally allowed tea, sugar, and bread and butter for their breakfast and supper. Rowntree suggested that extra-large-type New Testaments, Psalms and spectacles should be provided for the inmates.[2]

A solution to the union's maintaining a workhouse that was much too big for its needs came in a proposal in 1866 to sell the building to the county militia for use as a barracks, and to use the proceeds to build a smaller and more efficient establishment at a new site. The sale took place in 1869 and elderly inmates were subsequently housed in temporary premises, while children were boarded out at Ruthin workhouse. In 1871, the PLB approved an expenditure of £2,000 for a new building to accommodate forty inmates.[3] In May 1873, architects were invited to submit plans for the new workhouse, which was to be erected at the east side of Mount Lane (SH928360). The chosen design was by W.H. Spaull of Oswestry, and the building contract for £2,250 was placed with Robert Roberts, mason, and Robert Roberts, joiner, of Bala.[4] The contract specified the construction of a workhouse, boardroom and vagrants' wards.[5] The new building was ready for occupation towards the end of 1877. Males were housed at the east of the site and females at the west, with boys' and girls' yards in front of the main block, and women's and men's behind, the latter two separated by the dining room and kitchen. A washhouse and laundry ran across the rear of the women's yard and connected to a vagrants' block at its west end.[6]

After 1904, for birth registration purposes, the workhouse was identified as 2 Mount Lane, Bala.[7]

In 1930, the site was taken over by Merionethshire Council, and until the Second World War operated as a PAI known as 'Hafan Bala' ('Bala Haven'). By the 1960s, the building had been demolished, with some of the stonework re-used in the construction of the medical centre that now stands on the site.

The High Street building was later variously used as a factory for bottled mineral water, for biscuits, and for clothing. The main block is now used as a guest house.

CORWEN

A workhouse was built in Llangollen in 1786 at a cost of £200.[8] It was perhaps in the vicinity of what was once known as Workhouse Field, to the south of Vicarage Road (SJ212417).[9] A workhouse was still in operation in the town in 1835.[10]

Corwen Poor Law Union was formed on 7 January 1837, its fourteen member parishes drawn from Denbighshire and Merionethshire. A workhouse to accommodate 150 inmates was erected on a 1-acre site known as Ty Hiont Yr Aber situated on London Road, at the east of Corwen (SJ080433). Prior to its completion, the guardians held their fortnightly meetings in a room at The Eagles Inn. Plans for the new building, by Jones of Chester, were approved by the PLC in June 1837. However, problems in completing the purchase of the land delayed the completion of construction until April 1840. In August 1839, the building contractor, John Boyle of Chester, was paid £10 towards the cost of 'moving the building several feet back towards the mountain'.[11]

The main building, clearly based on the PLC's model 'square' layout (see page 26), had a cruciform layout with its entrance at the north facing onto the road. Its central supervisory hub contained windows giving a view of all parts of the inmates' yards.

On 25 April 1842, the guardians refused to obey a directive from the PLC that the workhouse should purchase its bread from a particular local baker.

The frontage and central section of Bala's former High Street workhouse, photographed in 2000.

W.H. Spaull's 1874 design for the Bala Union's new workhouse on Mount Lane.

A free supply of 'heath' collected on the mountainside by the workhouse children and used as fuel for the ovens meant that they could bake their own bread more cheaply. Buying in bread was, they considered, 'a waste of this free child labour'.[12]

In 1864, the workhouse was visited by social reformer by Joseph Rowntree. The thirty-seven inmates comprised seven infirm men, fifteen females, eight of whom were imbecile, and fifteen children, thirteen of whom attended the local National School. Rowntree regretted that no teacher was employed in the workhouse to provide the children with attention and training outside of school. As a Quaker, he was, however, pleased to learn that no paid minister was engaged and that dissenting ministers volunteered their services to visit the inmates, read the Bible and hold a weekly prayer meeting in the hospital ward. Inmates could attend their own place of worship in the town on Sunday, and the children went to Sunday schools. The inmates were also allowed a weekly visit to their friends.[13]

In 1894, a vagrants' block, now home to a supermarket, was erected on the opposite side of London Road to the workhouse.

After 1904, for birth registration purposes, the workhouse was identified simply as 'London Road, Corwen'.[14]

In 1930, the site became a PAI run by Denbighshire Council. It closed in the 1930s, although the vagrant wards continued in use into the 1940s. The site was sold off in 1946, its subsequent uses including a factory for engineering, for seed production and for shirt-making. After falling into dilapidation, the building was restored in the early 1980s and now houses a café and craft shop.

DOLGELLEY

Dolgelley Poor Law Union was formed on 12 January 1837 and included parishes from Merionethshire and Montgomeryshire.

Like several other unions in central Wales, Dolgelley dragged its feet over building a workhouse. However, an establishment for up to sixty inmates was eventually erected in 1856–57 on a sloping site on Arran Road, to the east of Dolgelley (SH733177). The two-storey, H-shaped building comprised two parallel ranges running east to west, linked by a short range at the centre. The central part of the north range, where the master and matron had their quarters, had the workhouse main entrance on its north side, while the south side had canted windows providing a view over the inmates' exercise yards.

In February 1858, the guardians invited applications for the posts of master and matron, who were required to be a 'married and without incumbrance', between 30 and 50 years of age, and with a competent knowledge of English and Welsh. Their respective salaries were £25 and £15.[15]

In 1864, social reformer Joseph Rowntree visited the workhouse, which then had thirty-nine paupers in residence. He noted that 'the situation of the house is very desirable and commands splendid views'. However, the sanitation left much to be desired. The men's yard was 'in a state calculated to foster epidemics and fevers'. The nearby men's 'refractory dark cell' was damp, cold, unventilated, and without a seat. The workhouse mattresses and pillows were filled with wheat chaff or husks of oats and not suitable for the aged, the sick, and bedridden cases. The inmates' diet appeared reasonable in quantity and fair in quality, and the recently introduced suet and currant pudding was of good quality. However, cutlery was not provided and the old men had to eat with their fingers. The workhouse had just one bath, a portable one. Rowntree suggested that a small room containing a boiler, on the ground floor, could be converted into a bathroom for the inmates in turns on alternate weeks.[16]

New infectious wards were erected in 1874.[17] A new female vagrant ward was added in 1903.[18]

After 1904, for birth registration purposes, the workhouse was identified as 'Llwyn View'.[19]

The well-preserved Corwen Union workhouse, now known as Corwen Manor.

In August 1919, when the number of inmates had fallen to sixteen, the Ministry of Health gave its consent for the workhouse to change its role to that of a Poor Law infirmary.[20] In 1923, the establishment's casual wards reopened after being closed for seven years.[21]

In 1930, the site was taken over by Merionethshire Council and became a PAI, then later as Llwyn View Hospital provided care for what were classed as the 'mentally subnormal'. The building has now been converted to residential use.

FESTINIOG

Festiniog Poor Law Union was formed on 8 May 1837, with fifteen constituent parishes drawn from Merionethshire and Carnvarvonshire. The union erected a workhouse in 1838–39 at Minffordd, near Penrhyndeudraeth, to the east of Porthmadog (SH603386). Intended to accommodate 150 inmates, it was designed by James Spooner of Morfa Lodge, Tremadog.[22]

The building broadly followed the PLC's model 'square' plan (see page 26). Its two-storey entrance and administrative block was later enlarged by single-storey extensions at each side. A mortuary was located at the north-east of the site. The workhouse had a piggery where pigs were fattened with waste food and then sold.

In 1875, several additions were made to the building including infectious, vagrant and receiving wards, and an able-bodied men's dormitory, the architect for the scheme being Owen Morris Roberts of Portmadoc.[23] The vagrants' accommodation included seven combined sleeping/work cells where inmates slept on wire metal beds without a mattress. The work cells were used for stone breaking and had metal grids at the outside through which broken stone was passed when the pieces were small enough.

In 1894, a *BMJ* report on the workhouse highlighted the fact that the sole staff employed in the workhouse were the master and matron, who had to govern the establishment, nurse the sick, oversee the able-bodied, care for the children, admit the tramps, etc. There was no separate infirmary – the sick were housed in cramped quarters within the main workhouse building. There was also a general lack of toilet and washing facilities. The report strongly recommended the appointment of more staff: a trained nurse, who would also be qualified as a midwife, a night nurse, a porter, and responsible attendants for the infants and the children. The report also advised the provision of separate

The former Dolgelley Union workhouse at the time of its refurbishment for residential use in 2000.

A view of the former Festiniog Union workhouse during its later role as Bron y Garth Hospital.

accommodation for the sick, better sanitary facilities, dayrooms for the infirm, and an improved lying-in ward.[24]

In 1902, a new porter was appointed at the workhouse. Because his surname, Jones, was such a common one, the guardians decided to address him by his first name, Gittins.[25]

After 1904, for birth registration purposes, the workhouse was identified as 'Llys Ednyfed' ('Ednyfed Court').[26]

In May 1918, the inmates' daily 3 p.m. tea was suspended due to wartime rationing. In the same year, part of the workhouse was allocated to house adult 'mental deficients'.[27]

In 1930, the workhouse became a PAI run by Merionethshire Council. It joined the NHS in 1948 as Bron y Garth Hospital. After its closure in 2009, the site was sold for redevelopment but the proposed scheme stalled due to planning hurdles. In 2020, its new owners applied to turn the building into a luxury hotel.

10

MONMOUTHSHIRE

ABERGAVENNY

Abergavenny had a workhouse prior to 1790, in which there was an attempt to set up a woollen manufactory. However, it was unsuccessful and for a period the establishment became an unsupervised poorhouse. In 1832, the local Board of Health directed that part of the workhouse be set apart for use as a cholera hospital, in case of an outbreak of the disease in the town.[1] In the same year, the inmates comprised nine old and infirm men, five old women, two young women, nine boys and six girls. In 1835, the workhouse, located on Mill Street, had Richard Cross as its governor.[2]

In about 1820, Tredegar (then a chapelry in the parish of Bedwellty) erected a workhouse, known as 'Twyn y Ddraenen' ('Thorn Hill'), on what became Queen Square (SO140089). A free school was opened in part of the building, where both pauper and non-pauper children were instructed.[3]

In 1830, the parish of Llantilio Pertholey advertised for a person to undertake the management of its workhouse and also serve the office of Perpetual Overseer.[4]

A property near the parish church in Blaina, in the parish of Aberystruth, is identified as the Old Workhouse in the 1861 census.[5]

Abergavenny Poor Law Union was formed on 31 May 1836, with twenty-eight constituent parishes. Initially, the union took over existing workhouses at Abergavenny and Tredegar. A new union workhouse, for 150 inmates, was built in 1837–38 at the east side of what became Union Road, Abergavenny (SO291143). The architect was George Wilkinson, whose design was based on the PLC's model 'square' plan (see page 26). Males were housed at the south of the site and females at the north. The porter's lodge and female receiving and vagrant wards stood at the left of the entrance gate, and male receiving and vagrant wards at the right. The front part of the main building, containing the guardians' boardroom, adopted a plain Elizabethan style, typical of Wilkinson's designs. To its rear, linking to a central hub, were the master and matron's quarters. The ground floor of the hub originally contained the kitchen, with boys and able-bodied men housed in the south wing, and girls and able-bodied women in the north. At the rear of the hub, the dining hall linked to wings for sick and infirm men and women.

The old Tredegar premises ceased use as a union workhouse after 1838 but continued to be used by the Tredegar vestry to house its parish poor.[6]

In 1849, a rapid increase in the union's population led to the separation of the parishes of Bedwellty and Aberystruth to form the new Bedwellty Union.

In 1855, the guardians advertised for a labour superintendent, who had to 'understand plain gardening' and supervise the paupers' stone breaking, oakum picking, etc.[7]

In 1871, tenders were invited for the erection of infirmaries, fever wards and other additions and alterations at the workhouse, for which the architect was Joseph Nevill.[8] A fever ward and separate smallpox ward were placed at the north of the workhouse site.

The Tudor-style frontage of the former Abergavenny Union workhouse, one of many in Wales designed by George Wilkinson.

In 1902, the poor condition of the workhouse led the LGB to demand either major improvements to the buildings or the erection of a new workhouse at a new site. Despite local opposition, the guardians agreed to the latter course but no further progress took place. Eventually, in 1914, the guardians accepted an offer by Lord Abergavenny to sell them land for a new building at Llanfoist, while he purchased the old workhouse for £3,000. His plan was to transform it into cottages for working people.[9] The First World War and the Marquis's death in December 1915 intervened and the guardians re-purchased the workhouse in 1918.

After 1904, for birth registration purposes, the workhouse was identified as 'Hatherleigh Place'.

In 1930, the site briefly became a PAI, run by Monmouthshire Council. By 1934, however, only the casual ward remained in operation. The surviving buildings are now a mix of residential and small business premises.

BEDWELLTY

Bedwellty Poor Law Union was created on 26 March 1849. It resulted from a substantial increase in the population of the Abergavenny Union, especially in the parishes of Bedwellty and Aberystruth, which separated to form the new union.

In 1850–52, a workhouse for 260 inmates was erected on an elevated site at Whitworth Terrace, Tredegar (SO151080). The south-facing stone building, designed by D.J. Humphris of Cheltenham, was a foreshortened version of the model 'square' design (see page 26).[10] Instead of the usual entrance range, there was just a wall, presumably with an entrance gate giving access to the workhouse via a narrow yard between two inmates' exercise yards. By 1901, a new block, probably an infirmary, had been erected at the north of the workhouse, together with a variety of small outbuildings.

Increasing overcrowding led to the workhouse being substantially enlarged in 1905–08, taking its capacity to 440 places. A new administrative block was erected in the southern entrance yard. It contained the master's and officers' apartments, inmates' dining room, kitchen, scullery, laundry, workshops, and electricity-generating equipment. A porter's lodge was also added at the south-west of the workhouse. A new infirmary, designed by Messrs James and Morgan, was opened in March 1908 at the south of the workhouse.[11] On its ground floor were wards with forty-nine beds, an operating theatre and dispensary. On the first floor were wards with fifty-one beds, and, on the second floor, nurses' bedrooms.[12] Later that year, it was decided to provide an isolation hospital at the site.

On 10 June 1908, the workhouse master, William Thomas disappeared after £43 he had received from a local butcher could not be accounted for. He was later reported to have been seen leaving the town by train. Mrs Thomas, the matron, was apparently in the dark about her husband's behaviour.[13] A new master and matron were appointed the following month.

In January 1909, the guardians discussed a proposal to allow the workhouse dining hall to be used by the staff to hold occasional dances. The proposer suggested that a refusal to give their officers this freedom might drive them into drinking dens. The proposal was nonetheless rejected.[14]

In February 1910, to deal with overcrowding at the workhouse, the guardians erected temporary corrugated-iron buildings to accommodate an additional fifty inmates.

In 1914, the King Edward VII Memorial Fund provided seven outdoor shelters to be erected in the workhouse grounds for the use of tuberculosis patients.

In April 1918, the workhouse was commandeered for use as a 500-bed military hospital for wounded soldiers. The existing 200 inmates were transferred to other buildings and neighbouring union workhouses.[15]

In May 1926, the union was badly affected by the closure of local collieries, resulting from the miners' dispute with pit owners over reductions in wages.

The dramatic hillside location of the Bedwellty Union workhouse. (Courtesy of Rowland Topping)

The Bedwellty guardians, the majority of whom were Labour Party members, were generous in their out-relief provision, and by the start of 1927 the union was over £1 million in debt. As a result, the board was 'superseded', its role temporarily taken over by government officials.

After 1930, the former workhouse became Ty Bryn PAI, then joined the NHS as St James' Hospital. The buildings were demolished in the late 1970s and a housing development now occupies the site.

In 1905, the union erected cottage homes for seventy-five children at Park Row, Tredegar, adjoining Bedwellty Park (SO141084). The scheme, designed by W. Beddoe Rees, cost £8,000. A boys' house lay at one side and a girls' house at the other, with the superintendent's quarters and offices in a smaller block at the centre. In 1930, the homes were taken over by Monmouthshire Education Committee. After their closure in 1962, the premises were used to house evicted families. The property is now used as sheltered housing.

CHEPSTOW

In 1803, Chapel Hill maintained four paupers in a workhouse, with Itton doing the same for two individuals in 1813–15.

In December 1829, following the death from exposure of a wandering Irish woman, her three children were placed in the care of the workhouse at Matherne.[16]

In May 1830, the Chepstow Overseers advertised for 'persons to contract for maintenance of the poor'. The contractor and his wife (or a man and woman to be approved of by the vestry) were required to reside in the workhouse.[17]

In 1832, Portskewett's workhouse had ten inmates: three above 60 years; two between 30 and 40, and deformed; and five under 20 years. There were seven males and three females.

Chepstow Poor Law Union was formed on 16 May 1836, with thirty-two constituent parishes. Initially, the union made use of existing workhouses at Chepstow and Matherne, the latter being used to house children. A new workhouse was erected in 1837–38 at the north side of Mounton Road, Chepstow (ST531937). Designed by George Wilkinson, it could hold 150 inmates and was an unusual variation on the PLC's model 'square' plan (see page 26). The east-facing entrance block housed receiving wards and a clerk's office. To the rear, linking to the three-storey central hub, were the boardroom and a dining hall/schoolroom, with children's dormitories above. The hub contained a kitchen on the ground floor, with the master's and matron's quarters above.

From the hub, accommodation for females was in the wing to the south and for males to the north, with a single-storey laundry and washhouse to the west. The male and female wings were unusually long, allowing four yards to be created in the space either side of them, rather than the normal two. A small isolation block was placed at the north of the site.[18]

In 1857, the front of the building was extended.[19] A major enlargement scheme in 1877 included a new block containing a boardroom, schoolroom, clerk's and relieving officer's offices, waiting room and lavatory; a block containing a boiler house washhouse, laundry, drying closet and coal shed; a new two-storey block; a new broad staircase to the men's infirmary; and a new mortuary.[20] The additions increased the capacity of the workhouse to 175 places. The children later went out to the local board school and the schoolroom was then used as a chapel for the inmates.[21] New vagrant wards, designed by Mr B. Laurence of Newport, were erected in 1895.[22]

In May 1918, the workhouse was taken over by the military to house shipyard workers, the pauper inmates being transferred to the Cardiff workhouse.[23] When they returned in July 1921, the Chepstow workhouse adopted the name Regent House.[24]

A 1929 aerial view of Chepstow workhouse from the south-east. There were extensive vegetable gardens at the rear of the building. (Reproduced with permission of RCAHMW)

In 1930, the site was taken over by Monmouthshire Council and became a PAI. The buildings have all been demolished except for the 1877 board-room and schoolroom block at the south-east corner of the site, now used as a nursery.

In 1899, the union established a home for thirty children at what is now 7–10 The Terrace, Sudbrook Road, Sudbrook. The property is now in private residential use.

MONMOUTH

In 1743, the Monmouth Overseers purchased several houses in Back Lane (now St John's Street, SO507127) 'for the building of a Workhouse for the Benefit of this Parish'. Overmonnow, the part of Monmouth to the west of the river Monnow, had one even earlier, immediately to the south of St Thomas's Church (SO504124).[25] In 1761, a workhouse for all the town's poor was established on Weirhead Street, where Monmouth School for Boys now stands (SO510127). In 1776, the rented premises could house forty inmates, who were occupied in spinning.[26] In 1797, the establishment had twenty-four inmates (three children under 7, twelve between 7 and 30, and nine between 30 and 79), who were chiefly employed in making linen and woollen clothes for the house. The beds were said to be good, and furnished with coarse sheets but no blankets. On four days a week, breakfast was milk pottage, on other days broth. Dinner on three days was meat and vegetables, on other days bread and cheese. Supper every day was bread and beer.[27]

In November 1819, a committee of investigation was appointed to examine the affairs of the Monmouth workhouse, which were alleged to be being improperly conducted. One of the committee, named Williams, was subsequently fined 20*s* for assaulting another member, a local ironmonger named Shale, during a meeting. In 1832, the workhouse had thirty-three inmates, aged from 1 month to 96 years of age, mostly males. The females were employed in sewing and cleaning the house, and the males in agricultural work.

In the early eighteenth century, the church house on English Bicknor's main street (SO581157) was used as a poorhouse. By 1813, a new workhouse had been built next to it.[28]

In the mid-1780s, the Gloucestershire parish of Newland opened a work-house in Coleford, at the corner of St John and Bank Streets (SO574108).[29] By 1821, the parish had adopted Gilbert's Act.[30] In 1830, tenders were sought for a contractor to manage the workhouse.[31]

In 1803, Llantilio Crossenny maintained three paupers in a workhouse. It had none in 1813, by which date Dingestow and Ragland were supporting small numbers in the same way.

In April 1835, an auction was held for the sale of a property 'known by the name of George's, or the Workhouse', at Whitebrook, in the parish of Llandogo.[32] A plot of land and to the south of the village is known as the Workhouse Piece (SO536064).[33]

The 1881 census identifies a property in the Herefordshire parish of Garway as the Old Workhouse.[34]

When Assistant Poor Law Commissioner George Clive visited the area in 1836, prior to forming the Monmouth Union, he uncovered numerous malpractices and poor conditions:

> In Coleford poorhouse I found an idiot, who had been there 48 years; during all this time, winter and summer, this poor wretch had had no other covering than a canvass shirt, no shoes even or stockings. At night he was, as the master expressed it, 'ticed' or forced into an out-house, a place unfit even for an animal; a hole in the wall was the only window; there he slept in some damp straw on the bare ground.[35]

Clive also visited the Llantilio Crosseny workhouse, where meat was served every day. Otherwise, the contractor suggested, local farmers would claim he was cheating the parish and starving the poor.[36]

Monmouth Poor Law Union was formed on 11 July 1836. Its thirty-one constituent parishes were drawn from Monmouthshire, Gloucestershire and Herefordshire. The union took over the Weirhead Street workhouse, which was altered and enlarged, with G. V. Maddox as architect for the work.[37]

In December 1836, a local newspaper reported that a false rumour had been circulating that a child in the workhouse had died from cruelty and neglect and that its body had been partially devoured by rats. It also noted that no able-bodied pauper had been admitted since the formation of the union.[38]

In 1868, the guardians advertised for plans for a new workhouse to be erected at the west side of the Old Hereford Road (SO509136).[39] The chosen design was by G.C. Haddon and could accommodate 200 inmates. There were four blocks of buildings: the lodge, receiving building, main building and infirmary. The receiving building contained wards for probationers and vagrants. The main building, at the centre of its ground floor, contained apartments for the master and matron, stores and general administrative rooms. Wings to the right and left had a central corridor, off which were dayrooms, dormitories, bathrooms, lavatories, staircases and airing courts. In the centre rear of building were a chapel and dining hall, with a lift communicating with the kitchen in the basement. On the same level were covered playgrounds for the children, as well as workrooms on the able-bodied men's side, and a washhouse, laundry and drying closet on the able-bodied women's side. The infirmary building contained nurses' apartments at its centre, and in wings to right and left were convalescent and sick wards for each sex, as well as bathrooms, and spacious airing grounds. There was a detached block at the rear for infectious cases. At the west of the site was a line of buildings containing workrooms, washhouse and laundry.[40]

The well supplying the new workhouse was soon found to be inadequate and additional water had to be obtained from a neighbouring property and by collecting rainwater.

After 1904, for birth registration purposes, the workhouse was identified as 'Union Place, Monmouth'.[41]

In 1930, the site became Hill House PAI, run by Monmouthshire Council. In 1934, it was decided to house 120 'high grade female mental defectives' there.[42] The buildings were later acquired by Haberdashers' Monmouth School for Girls.

NEWPORT

The parish of St Woolos, which encompassed the western portion of Newport, erected a workhouse in about 1820.[43] An 1836 map identifies a workhouse at the south end of Commercial Street, at its junction with what is now Kingsway (ST323875).[44] Its mistress at that date was Elizabeth Morgan.[45]

In 1803, in the parish of Monythusloine (now Mynyddislwyn), the hamlets of Clawrplwyff, Mynydd Maen and Penmaen each maintained ten paupers in a workhouse. In 1832, the parish's workhouse averaged thirty-six inmates: fifteen adults and twenty-one children. Parish poorhouses also existed at Bassaleg, Rogerstone and Bedwas.[46]

In 1836, Assistant Poor Law Commissioner George Clive visited existing poorhouses in the Newport area and was not impressed by what he found:

> In only one or two of these houses is there any attempt at a dietary or employment, in none classification, in the generality every kind of abuse. In Monythusloine poorhouse the contractor keeps a shop; different families have apartments in the house; the whole is filthy to the last degree. In one room was a woman who has had nine bastard children, the last confessedly

born in the house; and from the time she had been resident there, doubtless many more.[47]

At Newport, Clive observed 'the inmates going in and out for work or pleasure, the whole being enlivened by a lunatic in rags, who was running about where he pleased'.[48]

Newport Poor Law Union was formed on 1 August 1836, with forty constituent parishes. Initially, the union took over the existing St Woolos workhouse, and purchased twenty-four wrought-iron bedsteads, measuring 6 feet 4 inches by 2 feet 6 inches.[49]

A new workhouse, for up to 200 inmates, was erected in 1837–38 at the south side of Stow Hill, Newport (ST306875), on land donated by Sir Charles Morgan. It was designed by Thomas Henry Wyatt and based on the PLC's model 'square' plan (see page 26). The entrance was at the east side of the building. Males were housed at the north of the site and females at the south. The workhouse was ready for use in February 1839. Three months later, it provided accommodation for 120 troops who had been drafted in to keep order during disturbances by Chartist agitators.[50]

Inspections of the workhouse by the PLB in 1865–66 found that the sick wards were small and sometimes crowded, concluding that 'the workhouse is not adequate to the wants of the union'. They noted that an order had been issued for enlarging the workhouse, but many of the guardians wished to postpone the additional building due to the expense.[51] The guardians soon fell in line, however, and the workhouse was enlarged in 1868–69 at a cost of £10,000, increasing its capacity to 500. The extensions, designed by A.O. Watkins, included a new infirmary, hospital and other wards on additional land purchased at the west of the site.[52] Other additions included a large chapel at the west of the workhouse and a new boardroom, which was attached to the south-east frontage of the main building. The old boardroom then became home to the town's register office.

The union's tramps' ward was separate from the workhouse and located at 67–69 Stow Hill, now the site of a car park.

In 1900–03, the workhouse was almost entirely rebuilt with only the 1869 infirmary, hospital and chapel surviving. The new buildings, designed by Messrs B. Lawrence and Son, adopted the pavilion-plan principle, with the various blocks connected by passageways. A new boardroom and union offices were also opened on Queen's Hill.

After 1904, for birth registration purposes, the workhouse was identified as 'Woolaston House, Stow Hill'.[53]

The Monmouth Union workhouse, opened in 1871. The main building is left of centre and the infirmary at the right.

The entrance to the former Newport Union workhouse, erected as part of the 1900–03 reconstruction.

In 1915, the workhouse was adopted as a military hospital and the existing inmates temporarily accommodated by other unions in the region.

In 1930, the site was taken over by Newport Council, with part then operating as a PAI, while the medical section became Woolaston House Hospital. The establishment joined the NHS as St Woolos Hospital and has since been considerably redeveloped. Some of the older buildings still stand alongside Stow Hill.

In 1859, the union opened a residential industrial school in a conversion of premises known as the Skin-yard, on Mill Street, Caerleon (ST342908).[54] Initially housing 118 children, it was enlarged in 1861 to hold 200. The staff included the superintendent and matron, a female industrial trainer, a farmer, a bailiff and a porter. As well as basic reading, writing and arithmetic, the children were taught singing. The boys received physical training, played football and cricket, and could join the school's fife and flute band. The girls learned needlework and all the girls' clothing and boys' shirts were made on the premises. The school's 14 acres were cultivated under the supervision of the bailiff. Cows were kept and some of the girls could milk and churn.[55] With a move towards other forms of children's accommodation, such as scattered homes, the school closed in 1902. The building no longer exists.

In 1917, a children's home was opened at 108 Stow Hill, also known as the Court House. Young children were also accommodated at Stelvio House on Bassaleg Road.

PONTYPOOL

By 1800, a workhouse had been jointly established by the parishes of Goytrey (now Goetre), Lower Llanover, and the hamlet of Monkswood. A resident governor and his wife cared for the inmates, who were chiefly the aged and infirm. The workhouse also admitted paupers from Llanwenarth Ultra, Aberystwith (Aberystruth) and 'Denwiston'.[56] The establishment may have originally been attached to 'Pelleney House' in Penperlleni. In 1808, it reopened at the north of the village as 'Nyth Catty', on a site now occupied by Penwern Cottages (SO328053).[57]

In Panteg, a group of cottages at Penyrheol were used to house the parish's poor.[58]

In August 1823, the Pontypool vestry advertised for a governor for its workhouse, preferably a married man without children.[59] In 1835, the governor was William Jenkins.[60]

Pontypool Poor Law Union was formed on 23 May 1836, with twenty-two constituent parishes. The following month, the county's Lord Lieutenant, Capel Hanbury Leigh, donated a 2-acre site for the construction of a new workhouse, on what is now Coedygric Road, Griffithstown (ST291995). Joshua Daniels of Crickhowell was originally named as architect[61] but the guardians subsequently adopted plans by Oxford-base architect George Wilkinson. His design was based on the PLC's model '200-pauper' plan (see page 26). Its entrance block, facing to the east, contained the boardroom and receiving ward. To the rear, four wings radiated from a central hub, Separate accommodation for males and females was placed in the north and south wings. The west wing, probably containing a chapel/dining room on its ground floor, led to a row of facilities across the back of the building containing a laundry and infectious wards. A small separate block at the west of the main building may have housed 'idiots'.

Mr and Mrs Lewis Thomas were appointed as first master and matron and took up their duties in January 1838, though had to resign when Lewis was taken ill in March. They were succeeded by Thomas Bright as master and Mary Meredith as matron. Over the following years, there were a growing number of complaints against Bright. These included the excessive corporal punishment of one of the boys, and the stopping of inmate Mary Smith's supper for misconduct – as she was suckling a young child, this was not a permissible punishment. His nailing-up of a window in the men's sick ward, after several paupers had tried to escape through it at night, led to his forced resignation.[62]

The guardians first discussed building children's cottage homes in 1875, but it was not until the autumn of 1880 that construction began at the north-west of the workhouse site. A boys' home and a girls' home, each housing thirty-two children, were placed either side of a school block. The scheme, which also included the erection of a porter's lodge and vagrants' wards, was designed by local architect J.F. Williams.[63] Unusually, no porter had been employed before this date. In return for their night's accommodation, vagrants were required to break 4cwt of stone.

Further additions to the buildings in 1884 included a new laundry, boardroom, dayroom and dormitories. In 1888, an infectious block was erected at the north-west of the workhouse. In 1895, a sixty-five-bed, two-storey infirmary, designed by E.A. Lansdowne, was built to the east of the infectious block.[64]

Between 1897 and 1901, the workhouse was substantially rebuilt with a major redevelopment of the main building and the addition of a new steam laundry, infectious disease hospital, mortuary and aged couples' home. The architects for the work were Messrs Lansdowne and Griggs.[65] The workhouse main entrance was moved to its south-west, where a new boardroom was erected. In 1923–24, new guardians' offices, designed by C.J.F. Wilton, were erected on Hanbury Road, Pontypool.[66]

Along with the new buildings came a softening of the workhouse regime. The inmates' tea was brewed stronger, and cocoa was served with bread and cheese dinners. Visitors were permitted to bring in items such as tea, sugar, fruit, cakes and sweets for inmates. The work done by vagrants changed from stone breaking to wood chopping and their plank beds were replaced by hammocks. By the late 1920s, Friday dinner comprised Irish stew and fruit pudding, with cooked bacon for breakfast once a week.[67]

From August 1916 to March 1919, most of the workhouse was given over for use as a military hospital.

In 1930, the site was taken over by Monmouthshire Council and became a PAI. In 1948, it joined the NHS as Panteg County Hospital. Many of the later workhouse buildings survive in the present-day community hospital.

An atmospheric early 1900s view of the Pontypool workhouse from the Coedygric Road railway bridge.

11

MONTGOMERYSHIRE

LLANFYLLIN

The parish of Meifod had a workhouse by 1758.[1] In 1776, it could house eight inmates. In 1813, just two paupers were maintained there, and it had closed by 1832.

In 1776, a workhouse at Llanfyllin had ten places. In 1813, the parish maintained two paupers in a workhouse. A half-timbered building on Coed Llan Lane, now a private residence, was once home to the establishment (SJ140194).

At Llanrhaiadr-yn-Mochnant in 1755, wool was delivered each week to each poor person for spinning and brought back at the end of the week for sale in a market.[2] In 1766, the parish established a residential workhouse whose inmates worked in spinning wool, hemp and flax, and dined on bread and cheese 'and other suppings'.[3]

Guilsfield once operated a workhouse in Chestnut House, 33 High Street, Welshpool, where Jehu Road now runs (SJ222076).[4] In the same parish, an 1846 tithe map indicates a 'workhouse and garden' on the north side of Broniarth Isaf, Groes-lwyd (SJ207113).[5]

Llanfyllin Poor Law Union was formed on 15 February 1837, with twenty-three member parishes. One of these, Llanfair Caereinion, was a centre of opposition to the new Poor Law. On 13 May 1837, the Assistant Poor Law Commissioner for the area, William Day, together with a small group of guardians, including their chairman, Martin Williams, visited the parish to examine a complaint that a relieving officer had been assaulted there. They were met by a 400-strong mob who began pelting Williams (who had been mistaken for

Day) with a variety of missiles. The party managed to make their escape and the cavalry and police were brought in to keep order.[6]

In 1838, construction began on a new workhouse at the south-east of Llanfyllin (SJ150186). The building, for up to 250 inmates, was designed by the County Surveyor, Thomas Penson.[7] Its layout was based on the PLC's model 'square' plan (see page 26). However, its round-headed doors, Venetian windows and other classical detail in its rather grand, town-facing façade may reflect the influence of guardians' chairman Martin Williams – plantation buildings in his native Jamaica were built in a similar style.[8] These flourishes also pushed up the cost, especially when the poor quality of the stone from local suppliers led to it having to be transported from more distant quarries. There were two entrance doors, one leading to the main workhouse, one directly into the boardroom. Across the road from the workhouse was a burial ground, in which many deceased inmates were buried.

In December 1841, there were 133 inmates in the workhouse, of whom 87 were children. Of the adults, twenty-seven were classed as able-bodied, eleven of whom were single mothers, with forty of the children recorded as illegitimate. The union's firm policy was that single mothers should only be relieved through admission to the workhouse.

In November 1844. Richard Edwards, a former innkeeper, was appointed workhouse master with his wife Sarah as matron. In 1847, it emerged that

The former Llanfyllin workhouse standing empty in 2000. The building now houses a museum and small businesses.

Edwards had defrauded the union out of a total of £225 and had also misman-aged the workhouse in a number of respects, including serving the inmates inadequate food, resulting in thirty-seven children suffering from scurvy. Edwards's successor, Joseph Jones, another former publican, also proved unsat-isfactory. His deficient bookkeeping, poor mismanagement of workhouse stores, and frequent late-night visits into the town eventually led to his forced resignation in November 1852.[9]

In 1894, the guardians invited tenders for the erection of new vagrants' wards at the workhouse.[10] The building comprised six sleeping cells and six stone-breaking cells, the latter fitted with metal grilles through which the broken stone was fed to the outside once the pieces were small enough.[11]

Electric lighting was installed in 1919 and the telephone in 1924. Other changes included giving the inmates an extra weekly meat dinner, and supply-ing the women with cups and saucers instead of mugs.[12]

In 1930, the premises, by then known as 'Y Dolydd' ('The Meadows') was taken over by Montgomeryshire Council and became a PAI, later an old people's home, which closed in 1982. The building is now part workhouse museum and part small business centre.

MACHYNLLETH

Machynlleth Poor Law Union was formed on 16 January 1837, its eleven member parishes drawn from Montgomeryshire, Merionethshire and Cardiganshire.

Machynlleth was one of the areas of Wales that was strongly opposed to the New Poor Law and the guardians endlessly prevaricated in the matter of erecting a workhouse. In 1854, however, under the PLB's threat of dissolving the union, the board quickly agreed to proceed with a building.[13] Due to dif-ficulties in finding a site and raising the required finance, things were slow to advance. In April 1858, the guardians invited plans for a building to accom-modate fifteen each of men, women, boys and girls, together with sick wards for four males and four females, the total cost not to exceed £1,500. In April 1860, a lack of further progress caused the PLB to repeat its threat of dissolving the union.

In October 1861, the posts of workhouse master and matron were adver-tised. A man and wife without children were preferred, and a knowledge of Welsh was 'indispensable'. A joint salary of £40 was offered plus rations and residence.[14]

The workhouse was designed by York-based architect John Edwin Oates and erected at the east end of Maengwyn Street (SH750009).[15] The T-shaped main building faced onto the road at the south. A female infectious ward was added in 1869.[16]

In April 1870, an afternoon tea party for the inmates, provided each year by Dr Lloyd, took place at the workhouse. Plum cake, buns and other treats were followed by tobacco for the men, while the women and children received books, toys, oranges and sweets. There was also a supply of ginger wine.[17] By way of contrast, in 1894 the guardians proposed altering the formula for the inmates' tea by reducing the amount of tea from one and a half ounces per ten pints of water to one ounce. The LGB vetoed the idea.[18]

New tramp wards, designed by Mr Hipkiss, were erected at the west of the workhouse main building in 1898.[19]

After 1904, for birth registration purposes, the workhouse was recorded as 'Gorphwysle' ('Place of Rest').[20]

Following a decline in the number of admissions, the workhouse closed in March 1916 and the inmates were transferred to the Newtown and Llanidloes institution at Caersws.[21]

In 1920, the site was leased by the King Edward VII Welsh Memorial Association, who converted it for the treatment of tuberculosis patients, under the name of the King Edward VII Hospital. The site was later known as Machynlleth Chest Hospital and in more recent times became Bro Ddyfi Community Hospital.

In the mid-1920s, the union purchased 'Newlands', a property at the west of Machynlleth (SH755010), for use as a casual ward. It continued operating until the Second World War. The building no longer exists.

MONTGOMERY AND POOL (FORDEN)

Pool (renamed Welshpool in 1835 to distinguish it from the English town of Poole) had a workhouse by 1766. An inventory of the establishment in 1767 included seven bedsteads and cords, six flock beds and bolsters, ten blankets, three sheets, two hand towels, thirty trenchers (wooden plates), twenty-four spoons and a 'large lock on the pantry'.[22] In 1771, it appears that the old Red Lyon Inn was used as a workhouse. In 1779, a parish meeting agreed that a 'proper workhouse' should be taken. By 1795, the workhouse occupied a thatched house forming part of Sergeant's Row, near the present-day Powysland Museum (SJ226073).[23]

The front façade of the former Machynlleth workhouse, now a local community hospital.

By 1776, Worthen had a workhouse half a mile north-east of the village (SJ332051). It included a separate cottage for the master, later home to the Plough Inn.[24] In recent times, the buildings have been lying empty.

Chirbury's workhouse, originally an almshouse, was at the west of the village, on the Montgomery Road (SO257984). In recent times, the property became known as Workhouse Cottages.[25]

In 1792, Montgomery, Pool and fourteen other places – including Worthen and Chirbury in Shropshire – were incorporated under a Local Act.[26] In 1794–95, the incorporation erected a workhouse a mile to the south-west of Forden village. Designed by Joseph Bromfield, its construction cost about £12,000 and it could hold 500 paupers, though was rarely full.[27] Additional land leased by the incorporation included the 140 acres of Munlin Farm.

The workhouse main building was a shallow U-shaped block, three storeys high and constructed in red brick. A small mortuary stood immediately north of the main building. One of the other outbuildings at the north of the site had partitioned yards at its rear. A chapel was located south of the main building.

The workhouse inmates were chiefly employed in making shoes, linen and 'flannel of inferior wool', in household duties , and in working in the garden and on the farm. About 40 acres of farmland were sown with wheat and other cereals, and a herd of twenty cows was kept to supply the workhouse with milk.[28] Later occupations included spinning, weaving, tailoring and straw-bonnet making.

The former Forden Union workhouse, originally opened in 1795 by the
Montgomery and Pool Incorporation to house up to 500 paupers.

In 1795, a schoolmaster was appointed at an annual salary of ten guineas.
He could earn an extra four guineas by cutting the children's hair and shaving
the adult inmates.[29]

Punishments for misbehaving inmates were severe, with the lash, scold's
bridle and stocks regularly being deployed, as the institution's records show:

> 4 Jany., 1797. Mary Preynald for embezzling bread, cheese, beef and candles,
> to be publicly whipped in the hall before dinner next Wednesday.
> 2 Sep., 1801. Elizth. Williams to be punished by a whipping for embezzling
> wearing apparel, & other misconduct in the house.
> 12 May, 1802. Anne Davies to be placed in stocks with scolding bridle for
> 2 hours at dinner time to-morrow, & Mary Nicholas stocks, same time for
> disorderly behaviour.
> 4 Sepr., 1811. That Joseph Heath, who deserted the house on 4 July last, be
> flogged on Wedy. next immediately before dinner, & to be put & kept in the
> stocks during dinner.[30]

In 1805, during the war with France, the difficulty in selling the goods
produced by the inmates led to spinning, weaving and shoe-making being
abandoned. After the war, straw-plaiting was introduced and the woollen
industry was briefly revived in 1819.[31]

The incorporation's Local Act status exempted it from most of the provisions of the 1834 Poor Law Amendment Act and it continued in operation until 1870, when it was replaced by the new Forden Union.

After 1930, the workhouse became a PAI run by Montgomeryshire Council. It joined the NHS as Brynhyfryd Hospital, mainly providing care for the elderly. The building has now been converted to flats.

NEWTOWN AND LLANIDLOES

Newtown had a workhouse by 1752, when it was receiving paupers from the adjacent parish of Kerry.[32] In 1815, Newtown maintained twenty paupers in a workhouse.

In 1758, Kerry advertised for 'a proper person to be Master of a Workhouse'. George Morres of Shifnal was appointed to the post for a term of three years. In 1780, the vestry agreed to erect a new workhouse 'within a convenient distance of the parish Church ... on a Common called Kefen-y-Vastrey, in the Township of Cloddiau'. It also specified that 60 acres of land should adjoin the house for the benefit of the parish poor. In 1817, a workhouse was established in the village by connecting two houses rented from R. Pryce.[33] In 1828, the parish had a poorhouse near the church. At that date, it typically contained twenty-six inmates, including sixteen children.[34]

A property near the corner of Mount Lane and New Street in Llanidloes is identified in the 1881 census as the Old Workhouse.[35]

Newtown and Llanidloes Poor Law Union was formed on 13 February 1837, with seventeen constituent parishes. A new workhouse, designed by Thomas Penson to hold 350 inmates, was erected in 1837–40 at Caersws, midway between Newtown and Llanidloes (SO036924).[36]

In the late 1830s, Newtown was the centre of Chartist resistance to the 1834 Poor Law Act and the partly built workhouse became a focus of opposition. In May 1838, some of the walls were knocked down by what were described as 'idly and evil disposed persons'. In December of that year, a detachment of the Montgomeryshire Volunteer Regiment was briefly stationed in a field next to the workhouse in case of attack over the Christmas period.[37]

Construction of the building was also delayed by problems with the contractors. To save money, it had been decided that bricks for the workhouse could be manufactured on site using brick clay dug in the vicinity, for which William Bullock was appointed as contractor. However, the quantity and quality of the bricks proved inadequate, and in April 1838, Bullock withdrew. There were also problems obtaining a sufficient supply of stone from Penstrowed Quarry. A further setback was caused when the sewer contractor, Edward Jones, absconded taking all his tools and equipment with him.[38]

The workhouse building finally opened on 1 September 1840, almost three years after construction work had begun. Its layout was based on the PLC's model 'square' plan (see page 26). Unusually, the entrance was at the rear of the site, furthest from the road.

In 1864, the workhouse was visited by social reformer Joseph Rowntree. Its 148 inmates comprised twenty-four men, forty-three women, thirty-one boys, twenty-nine girls, and twenty-one infants, and included thirteen imbeciles and lunatics – unusually, the children outnumbered the adults. Rowntree was unimpressed by the children's classroom performance after giving them a few easy mental arithmetic questions. In one ward, fifteen young women were nursing their children. Rowntree was dismayed that they had received virtually no attention from local ministers or other Christians. The 'dark cells', used for the short-term confinement of miscreants, also received his criticism as they were below ground level and so were cold and damp. Water at the workhouse, pumped up by inmate labour, was in short supply owing to a period of dry weather. Contrary to the usual practice, the inmates were not permitted to attend chapels on Sunday or to make monthly visits to their friends and relations.[39]

In 1930, the site became a PAI run by Montgomeryshire Council. In 1948, it joined the NHS as Llys Maldwyn Hospital, initially as a children's hospital and subsequently providing care for patients with learning difficulties. The hospital closed in around 1999 and the building has been converted to residential use.

An early 1900s view of the Newtown and Llanidloes Union workhouse.

12

PEMBROKESHIRE

HAVERFORDWEST

By 1761, a workhouse existed on Shoemakers (now Market) Street in the Haverfordwest parish of St Mary.[1] The parish was still operating a workhouse in the 1830s.

In 1776, parish workhouses existed at Camrose, housing up to ten inmates, and at Llanwnda, for up to three inmates. Neither continued in use into the nineteenth century.

In 1803, the parishes of Johnston, Letterston, St Edrens and West Walton were making use of workhouses. Of these, only Johnston was still doing so in 1813. By that date, Hubberston and Haverfordwest St Martin were placing paupers in workhouses, with Haverfordwest St Thomas joining them the following year.

Haverfordwest Poor Law Union was formed on 6 January 1837, with sixty-three member parishes. The union erected a workhouse in 1837–39 at the south of Haverfordwest on an elevated site above the old priory (SM955151). The PLC authorised an expenditure of £4,000 for the new building, which was to accommodate around 150 inmates. The building, designed by local architect William Owen, was based on the PLC's model 'square' design (see page 26) but lacked the polygonal hub. The front block at the north-east had two entrance doors, one leading into the main workhouse, the other to the relief office and boardroom.

In 1894, a report on the workhouse by the *BMJ* found much to criticise. The infirmary wards were small, dirty, and lacked hot water and adequate ventilation and heating; most of the patients slept on low plank beds; the toilet facilities indoors consisted of a few commodes, with one on each land-ing for night-time use; the water closets, all located outdoors, were described as 'simply cesspools, and some were very unpleasant'. The report concluded that the workhouse infirmary 'is unsuitable for its purpose, and the system on which it is worked is faulty in every particular'.[2]

In 1896–97, a two-storey, L-shaped children's building was erected on land purchased at the west of the workhouse. It was followed in 1898 by a new cel-lular casual ward, designed by local architect D. Edward Thomas.[3]

After 1904, for birth registration purposes, the workhouse was identified as 'The Priory'.[4]

In 1930, the workhouse site was taken over by Pembrokeshire Council and became a PAI known as Priory Mount. From the onset of the Second World War it served as a hospital, then joined the NHS as St Thomas's Hospital. It closed in 1978 and was converted into flats in 1982.

NARBERTH

In 1776, parish workhouses existed at North Narberth (for up to ten inmates), Begelly (three), Llys-y-Fran (four), Lampeter Velfrey (six) and Jeffreyston (five). All but the last of these appear to have ceased operation by 1803, while the parishes of Loveston, Ludchurch and St Issells had by then started making use of workhouses. In 1814, Llanglydwen was relieving seven paupers in a workhouse.

In 1832, the St Issells workhouse had five inmates: a man aged 67; two women aged 34 and 45; and two children aged 3 and 2. North Narberth then had a workhouse with ten inmates: four males aged from 11 to 70 years, and six females, aged 8 to 71 years. South Narberth had a workhouse for the aged poor, though there were seldom more than three or four inmates, those being infirm.

Narberth Poor Law Union was formed on 6 January 1837, its forty-six member parishes coming from Pembrokeshire and Carmarthenshire. Initially, three existing parish workhouses within the union continued to be used. A new building to house 150 inmates was erected in 1838–39 at Narberth Mountain, a mile or so to the south of Narberth (SN112133).

Completion of the new workhouse was delayed after opponents of the New Poor Law attempted to burn it down in January 1839.[5] Special consta-bles were then brought in to protect the site. The guardians also had financial disputes with the builder. After he was dismissed in April 1839, leaving the perimeter walls unfinished, they had to be completed by another contractor.

A bird's-eye view of the former Haverfordwest workhouse. Its L-shaped children's home stands at the left.

On 10 June 1839, the guardians had their first meeting in the boardroom at the new workhouse.

The new building, designed by William Owen, was based on the PLC's model 'square' plan (see page 26) though lacked an octagonal hub. It was constructed from a local stone in a simple Tudor style. Males were housed at the north side and females at the south. The entrance range, at the north, had two doors: the right-hand one leading to the relief office and boardroom, the left-hand one to the main workhouse. To the left were the schoolmistress's room, receiving ward, bathroom and a 'foul ward' for venereal cases. Right of the boardroom were the windowless 'black hole', for confining miscreants, and the girls' dayroom. At the centre rear, a laundry and pantry linked to the central dining room, with inmates' accommodation to the east and west. The range running south housed the kitchen, bakehouse, and master and matron's quarters. East to west along the south side of the building were a washhouse, casual ward, able-bodied women's dayroom, nursery and old women's dayroom. Dormitories and sick rooms occupied the upper floor. A small lodge stood at the entrance to the site.[6]

In July 1843, the workhouse was under threat from several hundred 'Rebecca Rioters', who were protesting against the introduction of road tolls. For a time, the Castle Martin Yeomanry were quartered in the workhouse to keep the rioters at bay.

The Narberth Union workhouse was very similar in design to that of its neighbour at Haverfordwest, both being designed by William Owen.

In the 1860s, the conditions in the casual ward sometimes led vagrants to tear up their workhouse clothing in order to obtain a transfer to the county gaol, where the accommodation and food were better. In 1869, the guardians became embroiled in a lengthy dispute with the PLB after a local magistrate complained that such cases were being clothed only in corn sacks before making the 8-mile walk, often in the rain, to be brought before him.[7]

In 1930, the workhouse site was taken over by Pembrokeshire Council and redesignated as a PAI, known as Narberth Lodge Hospital. After 1948, it became Allensbank old people's home. It was sold into private ownership in 1965 and finally closed in 1972. The buildings are now used as holiday and local business accommodation.

PEMBROKE

In 1776, parish workhouses were in use at: St Florence (for up to five inmates), Lawrenny (two), Manorbier (twenty) and Monkton, or Pembroke St Nicolas (twenty-six). Of these, only St Florence was still active in 1803, but the parishes of Angle, Carew, Hodgeston, Penally and Redberth had begun employing workhouses at that date.

In 1821, St Mary's parish in Pembroke established a workhouse in Long Entry, Westgate (SM982014). It comprised twenty-four one-room, lean-to cottages.[8]

In 1832, Llanstadwell had a workhouse but it was reported to have few inmates except for occasional mothers of illegitimate children.

Pembroke Poor Law Union was formed on 6 January 1837, with twenty-nine member parishes. Initially, use was made of existing premises, including the accommodation on Long Entry. A new workhouse for 180 inmates was erected on what is now Woodbine Terrace, at the north side of Pembroke River (SM986016). The first inmates moved in on 24 December 1838, although the building was not completed until the following year.

The building, based on the PLC's model 'square' plan (see page 26), was designed by George Wilkinson in his favoured Elizabethan style. The front block contained two entrances, the one at the west leading inside the workhouse, the one at the east accessing the boardroom and the relieving officer. The dining hall was placed in the central hub and, unusually, the range running north from the hub contained a dedicated chapel – the dining hall normally served this purpose. Males were housed at the east side of the workhouse and females at the west. In the row of utility rooms along the north side of the main building there were laundry facilities on the women's side. At the centre, to the north of the chapel, was a mill room, where the men ground corn. An infectious ward block was placed on the men's side. A separate block at the rear housed male and female idiot wards, each with a small enclosed yard.[9]

The first master and matron were Mr and Mrs J. Large, appointed at a joint salary of £70. A porter was appointed at £15 and a female cook at £10. A nurse, Mary Lewis, was taken on in July 1839 at 2s a week – she was later reprimanded for being drunk.

A porter's lodge stood inside the main gate and a vagrants' ward was added nearby in around 1850. The workhouse had its own piggery, which continued in use until the 1950s. In 1840, a boundary wall was erected and garden laid out where potatoes were grown. Water for the workhouse was piped from a spring at Cold Well Field, near Golden Hill.[10]

Work done by male inmates include oakum picking. As well as domestic chores, the women had spinning wheels, knitting needles and wool to knit stockings. The workhouse clothing for men included fustian coats and waistcoats, corduroy trousers, and clogs.[11]

An inspection of the workhouse school in 1848 found that the schoolroom was airy and well lit, and that the reading and spelling of the children was good, as was their discipline. Few of the children had stockings, and one had no shoes, despite the snow on the ground. The schoolmaster was Edward Shaw, a former soldier from Worcestershire, who had the boys marching around the yard, saluting him as they passed.[12]

In 1902–03, a large new infirmary, designed by E.H. Lingen Barker of Hereford, was erected at the north of the site, replacing the old idiot wards.

In April 1930, the site became a PAI run by Pembrokeshire Council. The infirmary acquired a separate identity as Woodbine House Hospital and during the Second World War provided care for war casualties.

In 1948, the site joined the NHS as Riverside Hospital. A major remodelling of the buildings began in 1960 with the demolition of much of the old workhouse. In more recent times it has served as a council-run hostel for the homeless.

In 1912, the union purchased the nearby Croft House, on The Green, as a home for up to forty children aged from 5 upwards. They received instruction in gardening, household duties and cooking from two industrial teachers.[13]

The entrance to the Pembroke Union workhouse, another of George Wilkinson's Tudor-style designs.

RADNORSHIRE

KNIGHTON

Prior to 1795, Knighton's poor were farmed by a contractor in Ludlow. A workhouse was then established, but in 1797 was said to a very rough place. Its governess was 'perfectly incompetent to enforce obedience ... the poor seldom obey and often beat her, and even among themselves they have continual disputes'. Breakfast in the workhouse was milk or broth, dinner mostly meat and vegetables, supper bread and cheese or milk.[1] In 1803, twenty-one paupers were maintained in the workhouse, and eleven in 1813.

The parish of Llanfair Waterdine had a workhouse 3 miles north-west of Knighton (SO261756). In recent times, the property adopted the name 'The Workhouse'.

Knighton Poor Law Union was formed on 9 November 1836, its twenty member parishes drawn from Radnorshire, Herefordshire and Shropshire. In 1837–38, the union erected a workhouse at the south side of Ffrydd Lane (later Ffrydd Road), Knighton (SO286720). The building, housing 120 inmates, was designed by H.J. Whitling.[2] An 1840 tithe map indicates that it had a typical cruciform layout of the period.[3]

In March 1870, the guardians invited tenders for the erection of 'school room, sick ward, officers' bed and sitting rooms, laundry, drying room, lavatories, water tank etc.'[4]

By the 1880s, the buildings had become dilapidated and inadequate, and the workhouse was rebuilt in 1886 to a design by Edward Jones of Newtown. The new administrative block at the north-west of the site had a waiting room, relieving officer's and clerk's offices on its ground floor, and the boardroom and committee room above. To its east, an infirmary building, with four octagonal sanitary towers, contained two sick wards and a dayroom on both the men's and women's sides, together with water closets, baths and nurses' rooms. At its rear, the three-storey main block had the master and matron's quarters at its centre. It also included men's and women's dayrooms, dormitories, bathrooms and lavatories, the latter connected to the main building by small lobbies. The general dining room, at right angles to the main building, connected to the kitchen block, which comprised the kitchen, scullery, bread store, pantry, laundry, drying room and washhouse. At the west end of the kitchen range was the boys' dayroom and lavatory, with water closets at the rear and storeroom over. At the south of the site, an extra storey was added to the existing school building and a new wing built at its south end. Its ground floor now consisted of a boys' and girls' schoolroom, play sheds, girls' dayrooms, schoolmistress's sitting room, lavatories and water closets. The first floor was occupied by the girls' dormitory and schoolmistress's bedroom, while the second floor housed the boys' dormitory. After the rebuilding, the workhouse capacity was almost unchanged at 119 places.[5]

In an 1885 survey of workhouse alcohol consumption, Knighton's average annual expenditure of 8*s* 10*d* per head was the largest of any union in Wales.

A view of the Knighton Union workhouse during its First World War use as a Red Cross Hospital.

On average, each inmate had consumed 1.65 pints (0.94 litres) of spirits and 28.1 pints (16 litres) of 'malt liquor'.[6]

After 1904, for birth registration purposes, the workhouse first adopted the name 'The Ffrydd'. However, after it was learned that the local MP's residence had the same name, 'Offa's Lodge' was used instead.[7]

On the morning of 12 December 1907, an explosion in the administrative block killed the workhouse master, Richard Morgan Butler, who was investigating a gas leak with the aid of a lit candle. There were no other casualties but the block was severely damaged.[8]

In June 1917, the workhouse was given over for use as a wartime Red Cross hospital. The existing inmates were housed in the Rhayader and Kington workhouses and in temporary premises on Victoria Road.[9]

In 1930, the workhouse became a PAI run by Radnorshire Council. After 1948, it joined the NHS as Knighton Hospital. The hospital is still in operation, with most of the old buildings now replaced.

PRESTEIGNE

An assessment of Presteigne's township workhouse in 1797 was rather mixed, with bed-sharing clearly in evidence:

> The Poor have been farmed by the same person for the last 8 years … there are 19 persons in the house at present … the house stands in a fine situation, but is a most wretched hovel. [The farmer] has 9 beds of chaff and flocks. He often gives the Poor three and sometimes five meat dinners in a week, and the other dinners are milk and potatoes mashed. The breakfasts are milk, or broth and bread. The suppers bread and cheese.[10]

Presteigne township provided workhouse relief for twenty-four paupers in 1803 and twenty-five in 1813. In 1814, the townships of Rodd, Nash and Little Brampton, also in the parish of Presteigne, jointly gave workhouse relief to eighteen paupers.

Presteigne Poor Law Union was formed on 8 November 1836, its sixteen member parishes coming from Radnorshire and Herefordshire. It had the smallest population of any union in Wales and its existence was largely due to its status as Radnorshire's county town. It lay between its more prosperous neighbours of Kington and Knighton, with which it had considerable rivalry.[11]

The union prepared plans for a new workhouse housing up to sixty inmates and in June 1837 advertised for tenders for construction of the building.[12] However, the project stalled after the owner of the proposed site decided not to sell. The Assistant Poor Law Commissioner for the area, Edmund Walker Head, was not unduly concerned and expected that the union – despite the bad terms that existed with its neighbours – would eventually arrange to board out its indoor at the adjacent Knighton or Kington workhouses. Although this failed to happen, Presteigne never erected its own workhouse and its paupers never experienced the workhouse regime.[13]

In November 1874, the union's relieving officer, Henry James, was fined £2 for trying to offload the support of a woman and her child to the neighbouring union of Knighton. The woman had been deserted by her husband, who had settlement in Presteigne, and was put on a bus by James, who had paid her fare to Knighton and told her to seek relief there.[14]

Eventually, under new powers in the 1876, the LGB dissolved the union on 25 March 1877, with its constituent parishes being reassigned to the Knighton and Kington unions. A public inquiry prior to the dissolution heard relatively little opposition to the proposal, the main objections being the practical difficulties for paupers if they needed to travel to their new union's centre. Ironically, there were suggestions that this could be eased by establishing a new workhouse in a former militia barracks in Presteigne.[15]

RHAYADER

Rhayader Poor Law Union was formed on 10 October 1836, with ten member parishes. Like several other unions in central Wales, Rhayader was hostile to the New Poor Law and was especially opposed to the construction of a workhouse and the expenditure involved in its erection and maintenance. Nonetheless, in 1838, the guardians apparently conceded to the PLC and made preparations for a building to accommodate sixty inmates. Early in 1839, advertisements were placed for builders to erect the workhouse, to plans by H.J. Whitling.[16] However, the guardians found that they could not reach agreement on a suitable site and the scheme went into limbo. During the 1840s, the guardians actively campaigned against the provision of a workhouse, even appealing to the public to avoid claiming poor relief and so avoid the need for the establishment.[17]

It was to be several decades before a workhouse was built. In the 1870s, under increasing pressure from the central authorities, the guardians eventually

Rhayader's former workhouse now offers residents rather more comfortable accommodation. Its stone-breaking cells also survive.

agreed to its construction, but even then, still prevaricated over such matters as the choice of site and the capacity of the building. Originally intended to accommodate sixty inmates, they successfully petitioned for this to be reduced to forty.[18]

The new workhouse was finally erected in 1877–79 on the north side of the Builth road about half a mile to the south-east of Rhayader (SN978676). Designed by Stephen William Williams, the Radnorshire County Surveyor, its construction cost about £4,000. It had a T-shaped layout, the three-storey front block having a single-storey rear central wing.

The guardians originally appointed as master and matron a local farmer and his wife, Mr and Mrs Hamer of Bryncennarth, St Harmon. However, the LGB blocked the Hamers' appointment because of their lack of experience in running a workhouse. Samuel Rose and his wife Sarah, who had previously held the posts at the Belford Union workhouse, were appointed in their place, the master receiving a salary of £40 per annum and the matron £20, plus food and accommodation.[19]

The first inmates were admitted in August 1879, making Rhayader the last union in England and Wales to begin providing workhouse accommodation.

The only significant further addition to the building was in 1893, when vagrants' stone-breaking cells were erected at the east of the site.[20]

In 1930, the site was taken over by Radnorshire Council and became Brynafon PAI. When the Royal Cambrian School for the Deaf was evacuated from Swansea in 1941, the boys' section initially relocated to Dolgerddon Hall, Rhayader, and then in 1946 transferred to the old workhouse. They remained there until the opening of the Llandrindod Wells School for the Deaf in 1950. The building was later used as a factory and as a local fire-drill site. In 1989, it was converted to become a country house hotel.

CHESHIRE

ALTRINCHAM (BUCKLOW)

In May 1728, the Nether Knutsford Overseers obtained ten square roods of land on the Lower Town Heath, on the west side of Great Moss Lake, on which to build a workhouse.[1] In 1776, the establishment could house twenty inmates. In 1813, the parish maintained four paupers in a workhouse.

A workhouse was erected at Lymm in about 1733.[2] In 1739, George Drinkwater was given a three-year appointment as its governor.[3] A new workhouse was built in 1803.[4] The parish still had a workhouse in 1831.[5]

A workhouse existed at Rostherne from around 1739.[6] In 1813, the parish provided permanent workhouse relief to just one pauper.

In 1755, the Earl of Warrington gave Altrincham a 4-acre site at Broadheath on which to build a workhouse. The establishment, at the east end of what is now Atlantic Street (SJ766891), opened the following year and in 1776 could house fifty inmates. There were periodic complaints about the workhouse's lax management. On one occasion, an investigation revealed that the inmates enjoyed butcher's meat three times a week and that its quality was very good, as was that of the bread and butter.[7] In 1822, five looms were purchased for employing the inmates at weaving. The workhouse building later became known as Duke's Cottages.

Pownal Fee, a township in the parish of Wilmslow, erected a workhouse in 1772 at the east of Lindow Common (SJ835812).[8] In 1813, fourteen paupers were relieved there.

In 1776, a workhouse at Mobberley could accommodate thirty paupers.

By the 1820s, townships making use of the workhouse at Church Street, Warrington, included Ashton-upon-Mersey, Bollington, Carrington, Dunham, High Leigh, Lymm, Millington, Partington, Sale, Timperley and Warburton.[9]

Altrincham Poor Law Union was formed on 25 August 1836, with forty member parishes. Initially, the guardians held their meetings at Altrincham, which was considered the most central and convenient location. However, the site for a new workhouse was instead chosen at Knutsford, at the north side of Bexton Road (SJ748784). In July 1838, tenders were invited for construction of the building, which was designed by Mr Clayton to house 250 inmates.[10] The layout of the workhouse was a variation on the model 'square' plan (see page 26).

In August 1841, the guardians advertised for staff for the institution. A joint salary of £70, plus meals, coals and candles, was offered for the master and matron, with preference given to a brother and sister or a married couple without children. The schoolmistress, with a salary of £20, was to be a single woman without children, and would be required to teach the children reading and writing, and instruct the girls in knitting and plain sewing. The duties of the porter, salary £20, were to include the teaching of a trade such as shoe-making or tailoring.

In May 1846, a pregnant inmate named Ann Yates claimed that the work-house master, Mr Read, was the father of her child. An official inquiry found the charge unproven, but after Read was reprimanded for some other irregu-larities, his resignation was accepted.

In 1881–82, a pavilion-plan infirmary, designed by Messrs Tate and Popplewell, was erected at the north of the workhouse site.[11] A casual ward, able to accommodate about eighty persons, was erected on Heath Side.

A lengthy programme of extending and remodelling the workhouse began in 1892. Designed by R.J. McBeath, the scheme included a new dining hall, chapel, kitchens, laundry, water tower, engine room, covered walkways, master's house, boys' quarters, and a stone-breaking shed, together with the demolition of portions of the old buildings.[12] In 1897, new union offices were erected at the east corner of the site.

In 1894, the union was renamed Bucklow. An earlier proposal to change it to Knutsford was dropped because of potential confusion with other Knutsford bodies.[13]

After 1930, the site was taken over by Cheshire Council and became Bucklow PAI. It subsequently joined the NHS as Cranford Lodge Hospital. Now Knutsford Community Hospital, a few of the old buildings are still in use.

In 1909, the union adopted the scattered homes system. In 1911, a reception home, known as Racefield, was opened on what is now Westfield Drive (SJ746784). By 1929, boys' and girls' homes on Mobberley Road had been replaced by 'Kilrie', a large property on Northwich Road (SJ745786).[14]

BIRKENHEAD

Birkenhead and its neighbouring parishes at the north of the Wirral peninsula originally formed part of the Wirral Poor Law Union. The increasing population and importance of the port of Birkenhead led to the formation on 2 March 1861 of the new Birkenhead Union to cover the area.

Initially, the new union continued to house its paupers at the Wirral Union's workhouse at Clatterbridge. After some difficulty and delay, the Birkenhead guardians obtained a 12-acre site for a new workhouse on Church Road, Higher Tranmere (SJ318875). After the cost of the proposed building and its impact on the rates aroused some controversy, it was decided to phase the construction work over a longer period and to reduce the cost, for example by omitting the provision of a basement. The foundation stone for the main block was laid on 25 August 1862, and a bottle containing a newspaper and coins of the day were placed behind the stone.[15] The official opening of the

Some of the surviving buildings of the Altrincham/Bucklow Union workhouse at Knutsford.

Staff stand on the entrance steps of the Birkenhead Union workhouse at Tranmere in about 1906.

establishment took place on 4 January 1864, although children continued to be boarded at Clatterbridge for several more years.

The building, designed by Thomas Layland of Liverpool, was constructed in red brick. It initially housed up to 230 inmates, though was planned to be capable of enlargement. The T-shaped main block, facing towards Church Road, had a tower at its centre, 60 feet in height. A tank in the upper part of the tower was connected by pipes to every corridor in the building, to provide water in case of a fire.[16] The three-storey central portion contained administrative functions and the master and matron's quarters. The wings to each side, housing female inmates at the north and males at the south, were originally two storeys high, though later increased to three. At the rear, the stem of the 'T' contained a 400-seat dining hall, which also served as a chapel, together with a large kitchen, sculleries and storerooms. Behind the main building, the western edge of the site was lined by a bakehouse, laundry and washhouses.

In 1864, the guardians invited tenders for the construction of a new hospital at the south-west of the workhouse, and in 1867 for the construction of residential schools at the north of the site, both buildings again designed by Thomas Layland.[17] In 1881, the schools had around 200 children in residence. In 1903, the union began housing its children in scattered homes at Birkenhead, Wallasey and Rock Ferry, with a central home for new admissions at 47–49 Church Street, Birkenhead.[18] The old schools building was then converted for use as a sanatorium.

In the 1890s, new pavilion ward blocks were added at the south-east of the main block. In 1911–12, the 1860s hospital was replaced by a new pavilion-plan building.

After 1904, for birth registration purposes, the workhouse adopted the address of 56 Church Road, Tranmere.

In 1930, the site was taken over by Birkenhead Council and became a PAI, although from 1933 the medical departments operated as Birkenhead Municipal Hospital. In 1948, the whole site joined the NHS as St Catherine's Hospital. The workhouse main block was demolished in 2010, with the other old buildings gone by the end of 2012.

CHESTER

The Chester parish of St John the Baptist opened a workhouse in 1724.[19] By 1730, another was operating at Handbridge, in the parish of St Mary's on the Hill.[20] In 1751, Chester Cathedral opened a poorhouse modelled on one already operating in St Oswald's parish. In 1758–59, a House of Industry for use by all the city's poor was erected at the south end of Kitchen Street (SJ399662), at the north-west corner of the Roodee – a flat, low-lying expanse at the south-west of the old city walls.

In 1761, Chester's nine city parishes were incorporated under a Local Act to provide better management of poor relief across the city by a committee of Guardians of the Poor. The Act also gave the incorporation control of the Roodee workhouse for a period of ninety-nine years.[21]

At 2 a.m. on 24 February 1767, a disastrous fire broke out at the Roodee workhouse. The building, which then housed 200 children in addition to the adults, was completely destroyed. The fatalities included sixty children, twelve men and five women. One report recounted horrifying scenes of inmates running naked from the building, while others jumped from windows and the roof. A party of thirty men was employed to dig out the bones and dead bodies, but without success – it was assumed they had all burned to ashes.[22] The workhouse was rebuilt on the same site and in 1775 could house 300 inmates.

In 1797, it was reported that, despite the original intention, very little work was done by the inmates. The rooms were said to be large and well aired, with around fifteen beds in a room, made of chaff or straw, and infested with bugs. The were no small apartments for married people. The inmates were chiefly aged persons and children. Old women were occupied in spinning flax and picking oakum. Children at 10 years of age were sent as apprentices to Manchester and other places. On three days a week breakfast was broth and bread, and on the other days milk gruel and bread. Dinner on three days a week was beef, potatoes, etc.; on other days it was either beef, soup and potatoes, or oatmeal hasty pudding. Supper on three days a week was bread and butter, and on other days milk, gruel and bread. A pint of beer a day was allowed and buttermilk was served on potato and hasty pudding days.[23]

The building was extended in 1819 by the addition at its west side of a block of twenty-four apartments for pauper lunatics. In 1821, a warm bath was installed in the main house. A school for fifty infant paupers was added in 1823. In 1831, the workhouse's internal management was said to be 'truly excellent'. The food of the inmates was 'good and nutritious' and their treatment 'gentle and humane'.[24] In 1832, male inmates aged over 50 were each allowed half an ounce of tobacco every week, while the women each received half an ounce of tea and four ounces of sugar. Several of the old paupers also had half a pint of ale a day. Some were even allowed gin.[25]

Following the 1834 Act, the Assistant Poor Law Commissioner for the area, Richard Digby Neave, urged the incorporation to convert to a Poor Law

Union, which would include all the townships within 7 miles. Otherwise, he threatened to detach those parishes that had been paying to board their paupers in the incorporation's workhouse. The guardians rejected the proposal, as it would have required the considerable expense of having to purchase the workhouse premises from the city council.[26] The Roodee workhouse continued in use, with offices and a boys' school located at 34 Bridge Street.

In 1869, following prolonged pressure from the PLB and severe overcrowding at the workhouse, the guardians agreed for Chester to form a Poor Law Union. It came into being on 30 September 1869, initially comprising the nine city parishes. In 1871, the union absorbed a further forty-four parishes from the Great Boughton Union, the remainder then continuing as the Tarvin Union.

A new workhouse for up to 850 inmates was erected in 1874–78 at 57 Hoole Lane, Chester (SJ420670), at a cost of about £30,000. Designed by William Perkin and Sons, it comprised a variety of separate buildings constructed in red brick. They included an entrance and administrative block, a three-storey T-shaped main block, an infirmary, and a school building housing up to 150 children. A chapel, dedicated to St James the Less, was erected alongside Hoole Lane and consecrated in 1880.

The old Roodee workhouse was subsequently used as a confectionery works by the Cheshire Preserving Company. It was demolished in the early 1900s.

In 1917, the Tranmere workhouse was handed over to the Army Council for use as a military hospital. The existing inmates were temporarily housed in the workhouses at Prescot and Hawarden.[27]

In 1930, the site was taken over by Chester Council and the central section became a PAI. The medical facilities became St James' Hospital, subsequently known as Chester City Hospital, under which name the whole site joined the NHS in 1948. After the hospital closed in 1991, the buildings were demolished apart from the chapel.

In 1900, the union erected a central children's home on Wrexham Road, with smaller cottage homes at Upton Heath, Saughall and Dodleston. All four buildings still exist.

CONGLETON

In 1730, a workhouse was established in the old Lower Chapel, at the Rood Hill entrance to the Dane Bridge in Congleton (SJ858633). In addition, the Mill Backside and the Byflatt were enclosed for the inmates' use. In 1752, this workhouse garden became the site of the town's first silk mill.[28] By 1810, the

The main block of the Chester Union workhouse, shortly before its demolition in 1994. (Courtesy of Chester Photographic Survey)

workhouse had fallen into a poor condition and a new building was erected on a leased site on Biddulph Road, High Town (sometimes referred to as Mossley, SJ872621). It cost about £3,000 and could accommodate 100 paupers. The 'commodious brick structure' had nineteen rooms, and measured 108 feet by 30 feet by 24 feet high.[29] The building is now occupied by an animal feed store.

The Staffordshire parish of Biddulph erected a workhouse in 1735 at Marshfield Lane, Gillow Heath (SJ882588). Its construction employed 17,800 bricks and 720 sheaves of straw for the roof. There were also 59 feet of glazing. In 1776, the building could house 100 inmates but had ceased use by 1803. The building is now home to the Staffordshire Knot pub.[30]

In 1776, Brereton-cum-Smethwick had a workhouse for sixteen inmates.

Sandbach had two small, adjacent poorhouses on The Hill, later the site of almshouses (SJ762606). There were also poorhouses in operation at Betchton Heath.[31]

Congleton Poor Law Union was formed on 13 January 1837, with thirty-one member parishes. The guardians initially considered enlarging the existing Congleton workhouse at High Town to accommodate 300 inmates. However, Congleton's location was felt by some not to be central enough. In June 1837, as an interim measure, the union began leasing the High Town workhouse for £80 a year. The existing matron was retained, a new governor appointed, and some small alterations made to the building. The premises at Sandbach and Betchton Heath also remained in use, but the Biddulph workhouse was closed.[32]

Eventually, in January 1844, a site for a new workhouse was acquired at Newcastle Road, Arclid Heath, next to the Rose and Crown Inn (SJ788624). The building was designed by Henry Bowman and intended to accommodate 370 inmates. It comprised three main sections: an entrance block containing the porter's lodge and boardroom, a long main block of two and three storeys, and a two-storey infirmary to the rear. Females were housed at the north of the site and males at the south. The central ground-floor section of the main block contained a dining hall at the front with the kitchen and laundry to its rear. To each side of the dining hall were schoolrooms at the front of the building and dayrooms for able-bodied adults at the rear. Dayrooms for the elderly were placed at the far end of each side.[33]

In 1847, increasing concern at the lack of accommodation for fever cases led to the creation of a separate fever ward. This was achieved by the modest expenditure of £85 on roofing over two washhouses in the girls' yard.

In 1872, the union increased its provision for vagrants. At Arclid, new tramp wards were erected at the south-west corner of the site. A separate casual ward, now a rare survivor of its type, was also erected at 86 Park Street, Congleton.[34]

The original workhouse infirmary block had twenty-six beds, thirteen for men and thirteen for women. It was extended in 1860 and again in 1873 to

The former Congleton Union workhouse (right) and 1900 infirmary (left), after becoming Arclid Hospital. Behind the infirmary are temporary ward blocks erected in 1940 for the Emergency Medical Service.

increase its capacity to fifty-eight beds. However, this still proved insufficient to meet the growing demands and in 1899–1900 a new infirmary was erected at the north of the workhouse. Designed by Alfred Price, it had ninety-six beds. The three-storey central section contained staff accommodation, with two-storey male and female wings to either side.[35]

In 1918, forty beds in the infirmary were allocated for military casualties. In addition, twenty pauper inmates were taken in from the Wirral Union workhouse, which was also being used as a military hospital. In September 1918, the Congleton casual ward, which had been closed the previous year, received ten German prisoners of war who were employed in agricultural work in the area.

In 1930, the workhouse was taken over by Cheshire Council and became a PAI. In 1934, it provided a night's accommodation for 260 men marching from Scotland to London to protest about high rates of unemployment. The site joined the NHS as Arclid Hospital, finally closing in 1993. The buildings were demolished to make way for housing.

GREAT BOUGHTON (TARVIN)

Great Boughton Poor Law Union formally came into being on 17 May 1837, with 101 member parishes and townships – the largest number in any union in England and Wales. The union encircled Chester, which had retained its Local Act status and thus thwarted the PLC's plans for dividing up the area.

Over the next twenty years, the Great Boughton guardians resisted the building of a union workhouse, much to the growing irritation of the PLB. The board's opinion of the guardians also suffered after the publicity given in 1852 to the union's treatment of a blind pauper named John Ince, whom one of the Great Boughton relieving officers, William Prince, had illegally tried to remove to Chester.[36] In 1853, the PLB decreed that the Great Boughton union covered too great an area and separated fifteen parishes in its western part to form the new Hawarden Union, and with the threat of further annexations to come.

The Great Boughton guardians then fell into line and in 1857 erected a workhouse on a 4-acre site on the east side of Heath Lane, Boughton Heath, Great Boughton (SJ424659). Designed by J. Harrison, it was intended to accommodate 100 inmates and its construction cost around £2,500 plus a further £500 for the land. The two-storey main building had a simple T-shaped layout, with the master and matron's quarters at the centre, male and female

An aerial view of the Tarvin Union workhouse showing its extensive area of vegetable cultivation. (Courtesy of Steve Martin)

accommodation to either side, and dining hall and kitchen to the rear in the stem of the 'T'. A separate two-storey infirmary lay at the rear of the site.

In May 1857, the guardians advertised for a master and matron for the workhouse. Applicants had to be man and wife, of good health, unquestionable character, and active energetic habits. Preference was given to those without encumbrance and with previous experience as Poor Law Officers. The joint salary was £70, with apartments and the usual rations.[37] James and Elizabeth Postlethwaite, previously at the Fylde Union workhouse, were the successful candidates.

In March 1871, after losing a further forty-four of its constituent parishes to the newly constituted Chester Union, Great Boughton was renamed the Tarvin Union.

In 1930, the site was taken over by Cheshire Council and became a PAI, with the infirmary operating separately as Tarvin Hospital. In 1948, the whole site joined the NHS as Heath Lane Hospital, providing care for the chronic sick. The hospital closed in 1967 and the housing of Heather Court now occupies the site.

MACCLESFIELD

Macclesfield had a workhouse from 1698, probably near the Market Place. In about 1748, it was re-established in a converted stable at Town's Yard, on the corner of Buxton Road and Commercial Road (SJ919740), now the Arighi Bianchi store car park.[38] In 1776, the establishment could house 160 inmates. In 1819, charges were brought against the workhouse master, Charles Salt. It was alleged that he was blasphemous, had stolen from an old woman, kept ducks that he fed on the inmates' bread, and was regularly inebriated. He was, however, acquitted.[39] In 1832, there were over 100 inmates and their annual earnings were about £200. Several of them went out of the house to work, and these received an additional meal.[40]

In 1776, workhouses were also in operation at Adlington (for up to forty-two inmates), Bollington (eighteen), Chorley (eighty), Pott Shrigley (twenty), Sutton Lane Ends (twenty), Gawsworth (twenty-eight), North Rode (six), and Rainow (thirty).

In 1782, Sutton, Rainow and Macclesfield agreed to co-ordinate their workhouse facilities. Sutton mainly housed children, Rainow focused on the elderly, and Macclesfield took adults, including transients.[41]

In 1785, Sutton opened a new workhouse on Walker Lane, Sutton Lane Ends (SJ924709). In 1832, its inmates comprised: five males, aged from 6 to 83 years, and twelve females, aged from 8 months to 86 years. Their former occupations were mostly in the silk and cotton trades. The three-storey building is now known as The Old Poor House.

The Rainow workhouse consisted of two cottages on Tower Hill, Rainow (SJ949757). The building is now a private residence.

Gawsworth's workhouse stood on Penningtons Lane (SJ900720). A row of cottages known as Moss Terrace now occupies the site.[42]

Macclesfield Poor Law Union began operation on 26 September 1836, with forty-one member parishes. The guardians soon commissioned plans for a workhouse to hold 580 inmates. However, there was intense local opposition to the scheme, particularly from workers in the town's declining silk-weaving industry. A local builder tendered for the work but was subjected to such abuse and intimidation that the plan was shelved.[43] Instead, the union continued to use the Town's Yard workhouse for able-bodied paupers, Sutton for children, and Rainow for old men and women.[44]

In 1842, the Chairman of the Guardians, Mr Thomas Itchenor Watts, again proposed that a new workhouse be built, and listed the faults with the old Macclesfield premises:

There is no classification; old and young, vicious and virtuous, mingle together, and there is scarcely such a separation of the sexes as to prevent intercourse with each other, even in the day time ... Much of the clothing and other property of the guardians is stolen and destroyed by the paupers. Not a week since, a pauper was admitted in a filthy state; there was no bathroom or probationary ward, and he was consequently turned amongst inmates only half cleansed.[45]

By the end of 1842, the workhouse was so overcrowded that scenes of violence were not uncommon. The official capacity was 220 inmates, but often reached 100 more than that. There were also problems with the accommodation at Sutton and Rainow.

In January 1843, the guardians agreed to build a new workhouse at a site they had acquired on Prestbury Road, Macclesfield (SJ909739). Architects Scott and Moffatt provided plans for the scheme, which was their only workhouse in Cheshire. Construction of the Tudor-style building was completed in 1845. At the east of the site was a small porter's lodge, behind which stood an L-shaped receiving block containing the porter's quarters, male and female vagrants' wards, boardroom, clerk's room and a stable. The main building, which faced east, had a three-storey central block set between a pair of cruciform two-storey wings. To the rear of the main block a supervisory hub connected to the dining hall, which was also used as a chapel.[46] By 1888, the hall's interior was decorated with frescoes containing the Ten Commandments, the Apostles' Creed, and the Lord's Prayer, the work of a pauper. There were also framed woodcuts and oleographs from illustrated newspapers.[47] Immediately to the south-west of the dining hall stood workshops used for oakum picking. To the rear of the workhouse was a three-storey hospital block, the north of which housed females, and the south males.

Later additions included a sixty-bed fever hospital to the south-west of the workhouse, built in 1853–54 at a cost of around £1,200, and a new seventy-bed hospital block to the south of the workhouse in 1879–81 costing about £6,000.[48]

In 1888, the 346 inmates included seventy-nine old women and ninety old men. Among the able-bodied females were twenty-one occupied as washers, twenty-two sewers and knitters, twelve scrubbers, twelve assisting women, four in the kitchen, four in the nursery, and four stocking darners. On the men's side were two joiners, one slater, one upholsterer, one blacksmith, three assisting the porter with the tramps, six men attending the boilers, three attending the stone-shed men, four whitewashers, four attending the pigs, two looking after sanitary matters, one regulating the coal supply, eighteen potato peelers, one messenger, twenty-six ward men, and two doorkeepers. There were twelve boys at work in the tailor's shop.[49]

The main building of the Macclesfield Union Workhouse, now converted to apartments.

By the 1890s, the workhouse had separate 'privilege wards' for the respectable aged poor. These wards were brightly decorated and had comfortable furniture. The inmates could wear their own clothes, retain a few of their own possessions, keep small pets, and had first pick of books and newspapers that came into the workhouse. Their meals were served to them in their own wards, and the food was of better quality than that for the paupers in the other wards. They were served tea from three o'clock to four o'clock every afternoon, except Sunday, and could hold an 'at home' for visitors. They could go in and out of the workhouse by their own door, and part of the grounds was reserved for them to walk in.[50]

After 1930, the site became a PAI run by Cheshire Council. From 1933, the medical facilities operated as West Park Hospital and were used for military casualties during the Second World War. The whole site joined the NHS as the West Park branch of Macclesfield Hospital. Medical use of the old buildings ended in 2008. The main surviving portions are the boardroom block (now a nursery), the main black (now residential use) and the 1881 hospital block (now a care home).

NANTWICH

A workhouse of sorts was established in Nantwich in 1677 at the end of Beam Street. However, its function was to provide work for the able-bodied poor who lived in their own homes and received relief there. It was combined with the town's House of Correction.[51] By 1748, there was a residential establishment for the poor in three cottages in Queen Street, off Pillory Street, opposite Love Lane.[52] In 1776, it could house thirty inmates.

A new, purpose-built workhouse was opened in June 1780 on Barony Road, Nantwich (SJ654533). Originally two storeys high, it had a U-shaped layout and a separate single-storey entrance block. In 1788, prison reformer John Howard reported that:

> It was clean, and great attention seems to be paid to the inhabitants. The rooms are too low, and the upper parts of the windows too far from the ceilings. Five shillings a month is allowed for tobacco and snuff, yet the use of tea, though purchased with their own money, is ordered to be punished by confinement in the dungeon. Aug. 1st, 1788, there were eleven men, sixteen women, ten boys, seven girls.[53]

The workhouse had several acres of land attached, which was worked by any inmates who were capable.[54] Animals were kept and there was a dairy. The workhouse children were educated, with spelling and copy books and easy readers being purchased for them.[55]

In 1731, a parish meeting in Tarporley authorised the churchwardens to 'take a house for a workhouse'. In 1773, there was an agreement to erect a poorhouse or workhouse at Portal Green (now Portal Lodge, SJ559633) to serve Tarporley, Eaton and Utkinton.[56] In 1776, however, there were still separate workhouses in use at Tarporley (for up to forty inmates), Eaton (twelve) and Utkinton (twelve), as well as at Baddiley (nine), Faddiley (four), Poole (eighteen) and Weston (twelve). Of these, only Weston was still active in 1803.

Audlem opened a workhouse in 1740. In 1776, the establishment could house ten paupers. It was inactive in 1803 and 1818. In 1832, however, its nine inmates comprised a man of 97, four men about 70, a woman of 75, two women aged 28, and a girl of 9. An 1842 tithe map indicates a 'poor house' just inside the parish of Audlem at what is now 1–4 Lodmore Lane, Burleydam (SJ613423).[57] An 1881 map identifies the site as 'Workhouse'.[58]

A workhouse was established in 1818 at Wrinehill. In 1819, there were ten inmates, the men being required to wear blue flannel and the women red. Breaking workhouse rules could result in nine hours' confinement in the 'dungeon'.[59]

A property in the parish of Newhall is identified as the Old Workhouse in the 1861 census.[60]

Nantwich Poor Law Union was formed on 18 February 1837, with eighty-six member parishes and townships. The union took over the Barony Road building, which in 1850 could house 250 inmates. In January 1853, the union lost eight of its members to the new Whitchurch Union.

In 1879–80, a home and school building for sixty children was erected at the west of the workhouse site to designs by John Aldersey Davenport of Nantwich. The ground floor, with separate boys' and girls' entrances, contained schoolrooms, dayrooms, mistress's apartments, dining hall and kitchen. The upper floor was occupied by dormitories.

In 1890–91, a seventy-bed infirmary, designed by Charles E. Davenport, was added at the east of the workhouse. In 1894, a new tramp ward, mortuary and other buildings were erected, followed in 1895 by a steam laundry and in 1903–05 by a nurses' home and additional female infirmary ward block.[61]

In January 1900, the workhouse master, Mr Pritchard, disappeared shortly before an audit of his accounts. After £150 was found to be missing, including around £12 for brandy, Pritchard, in his absence, was dismissed. He died in

An aerial view of the Nantwich workhouse site, later Barony Hospital. The U-shaped building (upper centre) is the original 1780 workhouse.

Canada in 1902. Mrs Pritchard retained her post as matron, but in December 1904 she and her 7-year-old daughter were found unconscious in bed after taking a large dose of laudanum. Only the daughter survived.[62]

In the early 1900s, the union set up a children's cottage home at The Mount on Crewe Road, Nantwich (SJ660523).

In 1930, the workhouse site was taken over by Cheshire Council and became Barony County Institution and Hospital. It joined the NHS as Barony Hospital, finally closing in 1994. The original workhouse building, now known as Bevan House, and several other blocks survive, converted to office or residential use.

NORTHWICH

In 1776, local workhouses were in operation in: Goostrey-cum-Barnshaw (for up to fifteen inmates), Newton (fifty), Over (thirty) and Weaver (thirty). Of these, only Over was still employing a workhouse in 1803. At that date, Bostock, Marston, Middlewich, Northwich, Wincham and Witton-cum-Twambrook were also maintaining paupers in workhouses. Northwich had no workhouse in 1832.

Middlewich's workhouse was in operation by 1786, when it was receiving able-bodied paupers from Wrinehill.[63] In 1832, the establishment had thirty inmates: fourteen male and seven female adults, one boy and eight girls. It was also then receiving paupers from the parish of Bostock.[64]

Northwich Poor Law Union was formed on 20 October 1836 and comprised sixty-one parishes and townships. In June 1837, the guardians invited tenders for construction of a workhouse 'on land adjoining the Bowling Green Tavern, in Leftwich' (SJ658731).[65] The location, on the London Road, some distance from the centre of Northwich, was said to have been chosen so that the sight of the inmates would not 'discommode or prove offensive to the citizens'.[66]

The new workhouse was designed by George Latham and broadly followed the PLC's model '200-pauper' plan (see page 26). Females were housed at the north of the site and males at the south. The yards at the west of the main block were for adults and those at the east for children.[67]

In 1850, an isolation block, with its own laundry, was added at the west end of the male side-wing. In 1853, a separate chapel was constructed above the single-storey dining hall.[68] A casual ward was erected at the north-east of the workhouse in 1859 and rebuilt on a larger scale in 1875.[69] In 1872, a separate fever hospital was built at the west of the site. In 1892, an extension at the south of the entrance range included a new boardroom and master's house, and allowed the workhouse capacity to be increased by eighty places.[70]

In 1930, the site was taken over by Cheshire Council and redesignated as a PAI, later becoming Weaver Hall old people's home, which closed in 1974. Only the front part of the buildings survives, now occupied by the Weaver Hall Museum.

In 1923, the union opened a children's home at The Lymes, 271 London Road, Leftwich.

RUNCORN

A workhouse existed at Grappenhall from around 1745.[71] It is said to have been located on Broad Lane. In 1803, Grappenhall's workhouse was being used by eighteen other townships, including Hatton and Hull-and-Appleton.[72]

By the 1820s, townships making use of the workhouse at Church Street, Warrington, included Grappenhall, Halton, Hatton, Moore, Norton and Thelwall.[73]

Runcorn Poor Law Union formally came into being on 26 August 1836, with forty constituent parishes and townships. In 1839, Runcorn was one of the small group of unions that were identified by the PLC 'which for the present decline to concur in providing an adequate Workhouse'.[74] The union's resistance in the matter continued until 1854 when, under the threat of the PLB's dissolving the union, the guardians agreed to proceed with the erection of a workhouse.[75]

A site for the building was acquired at the east of the village of Dutton, around 4 miles to the south-east of Runcorn (SJ581778). The choice of location aroused some opposition, particularly from ratepayers in Frodsham, who felt that it was more central to the union area and preferable in other respects.[76] Undeterred, the guardians pressed ahead and in February 1855 invited tenders for the erection of the building using plans by William Culshaw of Liverpool.[77] Culshaw's design was an unusual variation on the popular 'square' plan (see page 26). The building, accommodating 200 inmates, was a plain structure constructed in red brick. The Elizabethan-style frontage, which included the boardroom and porter's room, was surmounted by a turret with a clock. At the rear, it was linked to an axial range whose central corridor had rooms on either side. In contrast, the rear transverse range was only one room deep and wider than was usual. An infirmary was placed at the rear of the site.

The entrance block of the former Northwich Union workhouse, now home to the Weaver Hall Museum.

In October 1857, with construction approaching completion, the guardians advertised for a master and matron for the establishment. Applicants, who were required to be man and wife, were offered a joint salary of £80 plus rations.[78]

The medical provision was enlarged in 1881–82 by the addition of two small ward blocks linked to the rear of the existing infirmary by quadrant-shaped covered ways.

On the night of 17 August 1896, a fire occurred in the central tower of the workhouse, which was in the hands of painters at the time. The blaze spread rapidly but was brought under control within two hours. There were no casualties but considerable damage occurred.[79]

After 1930, the establishment became a PAI under the management of Cheshire Council. It joined the NHS in 1948 as Dutton Hospital, providing seventy-four beds for the chronic sick. The hospital was closed in about 1966. All the old buildings have been demolished and housing now occupies the site.

In April 1913, the union established a home for up to sixty children at Dutton Lodge, a large old house on Lodge Lane, Dutton (SJ581778). The girls received instruction in dressmaking, cookery, housewifery and laundry work, while the boys were taught joinery, gardening and shoemaking.[80]

An early 1900s view of the Runcorn Union Workhouse at Dutton.

The solid main block of the former Stockport Union workhouse, later Shaw Heath Hospital, photographed in 2001.

STOCKPORT

In 1730, Stockport erected a workhouse with an adjoining charity school.[81] In 1776, the workhouse could house sixty paupers. A new building, accommodating 170 inmates, was erected in 1812 on Daw Bank (now the approximate location of the Whitfield Centre, Viaduct Street, SJ891900). Its construction was funded by the enclosure and sale of some of Stockport's common lands. In 1834, the workhouse had 140 inmates, including thirty children under 10 years of age, all orphans. Almost all the adults were of unsound mind or very infirm health. About twenty inmates found occasional employment at the cotton mills, and their earnings nearly covered the cost of their maintenance.[82]

In 1776, the workhouse at Marple could accommodate nine inmates, but it was no longer in use by 1803.

Heaton Norris had a workhouse on Short Street (SJ891911). Four paupers were maintained there in 1803 and fifteen in 1813.

Stockport Poor Law Union was formed on 3 February 1837, its sixteen member parishes drawn from Cheshire and Lancashire. Like a number of other northern manufacturing towns, Stockport was the scene of some resistance to the 1834 Poor Law Amendment Act. On 23 January 1837, a meeting of local ratepayers was held in the town to nominate people for the forthcoming board of guardian elections. Several of those present criticised the Act as 'unchristian and unconstitutional' and urged that no guardians be nominated. Nonetheless, the election proceeded without incident.[83]

The union initially made use of the old workhouses at Daw Bank and Heaton Norris. The latter was initially used to house and educate children. It closed in 1838, but ten years later was converted for use as a fever hospital.[84] A new workhouse was erected in 1841–42 at Shaw Heath (SJ895895). Designed by Henry Bowman, the new workhouse was intended to accommodate 690 inmates. Its two-storey entrance block faced the main road at the south-west. The main accommodation block was a substantial red-brick building, largely four storeys high, with males accommodated at the north side and females at the south. Children's quarters and schoolrooms were placed in cross wings at each end of the main block, with the area to the front forming boys' and girls' exercise yards. To the rear, the men's and women's sides were separated by the kitchens, dining hall and bakery. A washhouse and a drying ground for laundering linen and clothes were placed on the women's side, and a smithy and pigsties on the men's side.[85]

Soon after the workhouse opened, a widespread manufacturing slump led to demonstrations and riots in many northern areas. On 11 August 1842, Stockport's workhouse was attacked by a mob of unemployed workers, who forced an entrance and helped themselves to bread and money. It was reckoned that 672 seven-pound loaves were taken away, and about £7 in copper. Constables, yeomanry, and infantry were drafted in and captured about forty of the rioters.[86]

In 1870, a hospital block for infectious and contagious cases was erected at the north of the workhouse.

In 1894, a *BMJ* report found that due to a trade depression, inmates in the Stockport workhouse were 'packed like sardines in a tin'. The management of the hospital appeared to be 'completely without plan or method' and the female wards were 'comfortless and barnlike'. Many wards were so crowded as to present a serious danger in the case of fire. Former schoolrooms had been pressed into service as wards for the old and infirm. There were no dayrooms and the men smoked in the wards, often being confined there for days on end during the winter. The workhouse staff, though, were praised for their energy and for doing their utmost for the patients under most discouraging circumstances. The report recommended the building of a new infirmary – a course of action also urged by the LGB, but to which there was local opposition.[87]

In 1901, after continuing pressure from the LGB, construction of a new infirmary began on a site at Stepping Hill, to the south-east of Stockport (SJ912875). It was formally opened in December 1905 by G.N. Andrew, Chairman of the Stockport Guardians. The buildings, designed by W.H. Ward, could accommodate 340 patients, plus thirty-six nurses and twenty-four other staff. The layout was a typical pavilion-plan design with a central administration block flanked by pairs of three-storey Nightingale ward blocks, all linked on each floor by an open-air walkway. Other blocks housed maternity and lying-in wards, nurses' home, laundry and mortuary. A porter's lodge stood at the site entrance on Poplar Grove.[88]

In 1930, the Shaw Heath site was taken over by Stockport Council and became a PAI. In 1948, it joined the NHS as Shaw Heath Hospital, known from 1954 as St Thomas' Hospital. After the hospital closed in 2004, the site was acquired by Stockport College, with plans to refurbish the main workhouse block. Some of the original buildings at Stepping Hill survive as part of a much-enlarged hospital.

WIRRAL

In 1832, a workhouse at Great Sutton had six inmates and one at Little Sutton had eight.

The Wirral Poor Law Union was formed on 16 May 1836, with fifty-six constituent parishes. At the guardians' first meeting, a week later, it was decided to build a new workhouse at Clatterbridge, at the centre of the union area, although some distance from the main population and commercial centre around Birkenhead. A 2-acre site was purchased on the road from Birkenhead to Chester (SJ320821) and William Cole was appointed architect.[89] There was disagreement between the guardians and the PLC as to the required capacity of the building. For economy, the guardians proposed limiting it to 130 places, while the Commissioners, with an eye to future population increase, recommended 200 places. As a compromise, the provision for inmates' accommodation was set at 130, while the staff and administrative facilities were designed to deal with 200. Part of the cost of the building was financed by a loan of £2,500 at minimal interest from one of the guardians, the Rev. R.M. Feilden.[90] Construction work was completed in August 1837.

The building comprised a long, narrow entrance block facing north-east, with the main accommodation block to its rear, the two connected by a short central link block. There were early problems with the workhouse roof when gales caused damage because of the lack of coping on the gable ends. The original water supply to the building may have been from the nearby brook, but in 1839 an order was issued to sink a 4-foot brick-lined well to provide water. There were originally no baths in the workhouse, such things being thought likely to be quite foreign to paupers at the time. In 1840, however, the master and matron were instructed to take the children to bathe at Bromborough.[91]

The workhouse was economically furnished. The new boardroom contained only an oilcloth-covered deal table, 12 feet by 4 feet, and twelve strong rush-bottomed chairs. The guardians enquired of the PLC as to whether double beds could be used in the inmates' dormitories. A month later, having received no reply on the matter, many double beds were purchased, some later being occupied by three children.[92]

In 1847, during a typhus and cholera outbreak in Birkenhead, the guardians opened a temporary fever hospital in the town, made permanent in 1851. The workhouse's own infirmary, originally having just four beds, was enlarged to twenty-five beds in 1857.

In 1861, the growing inadequacy of the accommodation and facilities at Clatterbridge led to nine parishes at the north of the Wirral being separated to form the new Birkenhead Union.

In 1894, a two-storey infirmary, designed by Alfred Culshaw, was opened at the north-east of the workhouse, with a chapel by C.O. Francis erected nearby in 1898. In 1906, a second infirmary was added, connected to the first and designed by John H. Davies. In 1927, a new 112-bed women's hospital designed by F.W. Finchett and costing £30,000 was opened.[93]

In 1930, the site was taken over by Cheshire Council and became known as Clatterbridge (County) General Hospital, shortened to Clatterbridge Hospital on joining the NHS. The original workhouse building had been demolished by 1939, with other older blocks following in 1997 as part of the hospital's modernisation.

By the 1920s, the union operated several children's scattered homes, with a receiving home for new admissions at 'Brynmore', 32 North Parade, Hoylake.

A post-1930s view of the former Wirral Union workhouse site. The workhouse main block has gone but the chapel and the 1894 and 1906 infirmaries can be seen right of centre.

GLOUCESTERSHIRE

BRISTOL INCORPORATION

In 1696, to enable a city-wide system of poor relief, Bristol's eighteen parishes obtained a Local Act, which created the Bristol Corporation of the Poor.[1] The Corporation, managed by a board of guardians, was empowered to set up workhouses and appoint paid officers.

The City Council lent the Corporation a building adjoining the Bridewell prison for use as a workhouse (ST588732). The New Workhouse, as it was known, housed 100 pauper girls, who were taught to read and to spin. On arrival, the new inmates were stripped and washed by the matron and given a set of new clothes. Their diet included 'Beef, Pease, Potatoes, Broath, Pease-porridge, Milk-porridge, Bread and Cheese, good Bear [Beer], Cabage, Turnips etc.' Prayers were said twice a day, with a church service on Sunday. Sickness among the inmates was common and included conditions such as measles and smallpox. The girls worked at their spinning for ten and a half hours a day in summer, a little less in winter. After their initial training, they were hired out to local manufacturers. However, the coarseness of the yarn they produced resulted in complaints and low payment rates.[2]

In 1698, the Corporation purchased a former sugar merchant's house at the south of St Peter's Church (ST591731). Previously occupied by the Treasury as a mint, the building became known as the Mint Workhouse and was used to house the elderly, boys and young children. In August 1699, 100 boys were moved in and were occupied in 'spinning Cotten Wool, and weaving Fustians', for which they generated the creditable income of £6 per week. They were also taught to read and, unlike the girls, to write. Next, elderly inmates were admitted. They were clothed and given 'such Employments as were fit for their Ages and Strengths'. Finally, young children were taken in and put in the care of nurses.[3] In 1709, the girls at the New Workhouse were moved to the Mint Workhouse, which later became known as St Peter's Hospital.

The Bristol scheme was not without its critics. In 1711, an anonymous pamphlet claimed that the workhouse was 'crowded with idle, lazy and lewd people'. The economics of the scheme were also questioned as the workhouse's running costs consumed almost half the annual poor rate, for the benefit of just 170 inmates.[4]

In 1797, there were 350 inmates, of whom sixty-three were in the workhouse's 'pest house' – a form of isolation hospital. The only work was oakum picking. The building was infested with vermin, particularly bugs, due, it was said, to the number of old and diseased persons there. The inmates ate their meals in their lodging rooms.[5]

In 1832, the master reported that the usual number of inmates was about 560 but had fallen to 320, with 94 having died from cholera and the others discharged at their own request. He also related that the establishment was mostly inhabited by 'lunatics, idiots, sick and old worn-out persons, and children'.[6]

In 1834, St Peter's was said to be a strictly run establishment. It was:

The Bristol Incorporation's St Peter's workhouse, destroyed during the 'Bristol Blitz' in 1940.

extremely well regulated; the sexes are kept separate, and the house steward is empowered to confine offenders, in case of flagrant misconduct. Vagrants are kept separate from regular inmates. Prostitutes wear a yellow dress, and single pregnant women wear a red dress; they are kept separate from the rest and not allowed to associate with the children. The children are taught to read, to knit, and to sew and when of sufficient age are sent to service. They are well clad, decent in appearance and respectful.[7]

Able-bodied men were employed in breaking stones at the Clifton Hot Wells, while infirm men made laces and plaited straw. Women were occupied in knitting and winding worsted.

During the 1832 cholera outbreak at St Peter's, the Corporation rented and subsequently purchased the old prison on Manor Road, Stapleton (ST627762). The building was erected by the Admiralty in about 1779 to hold prisoners from the wars with the American colonies and, after 1793, with France.

The Corporation's Local Act status largely exempted it from the 1834 Poor Law Act and it continued in operation, employing the St Peter's and Stapleton workhouses.

In 1867, a report by the *BMJ* praised the facilities at Stapleton. In the imbecile department of the main building, the male part consisted of a dining room, two dayrooms, and five sleeping wards, containing over fifty people, who were attended to by three paid nurses, assisted by the most competent of the patients. The dayrooms were light and cheerful, and were furnished with, among other things, a bagatelle table. The beds occupied by patients subject to epilepsy had well-padded sides to them, and those used by patients who were in the habit of passing their urine under them were covered with macintosh, and each had an opening in the centre for the water to run through into a vessel placed below. There were excellent bathrooms and lavatories, with a plentiful supply of hot and cold water. The workhouse laundry facilities were noted as being particularly good.[8]

New male and female infirmary pavilions were opened at Stapleton in 1868, each containing thirty-two beds, with 1,800 cubic feet of space per bed. There was a major redevelopment of the main building in about 1890, together with the erection of a single-storey entrance block on Manor Road and a chapel.[9]

In 1898, after its boundaries were extended to cover all of urban Bristol, the city was administered as a Poor Law Union. The new union absorbed many of the parishes previously included in the adjacent Barton Regis Union and took over the Barton Regis workhouse at Eastville. The much-reduced Barton

The frontage of the Bristol Incorporation workhouse at Blackberry Hill, Stapleton.

Bristol's former Quaker workhouse, photographed in 2013.

Regis Union then built a new workhouse at Southmead (see page 194). This arrangement lasted until 1904, when the Barton Regis Union was wound up and many of its parishes were added to a further enlarged Bristol Union. The St Peter's workhouse ceased receiving inmates in 1898 but continued to serve as the Bristol Union's offices.

In 1902–04, the guardians erected children's cottage homes at Frenchay Road, Downend (ST644768). The scheme, designed by La Trobe and Weston, housed 168 children in a crescent of seven pairs of semi-detached houses. There was also a school/communal building and a convalescent home.[10] The buildings were demolished in 1983 and housing now covers the site. By 1908, a further 192 children were housed in sixteen scattered homes, with a headquarters home at 11–19 Snowdon Road (ST628759).

During the First World War, the Southmead workhouse became a military hospital. From 1921, it operated under its own administration, acting solely as an infirmary for the union's acute medical cases. In 1924, a large pavilion-plan hospital known as Southmead Infirmary was built at the south-east of the workhouse.

In 1930, the union's responsibilities were taken over by Bristol City Council. Southmead immediately became a municipal general hospital. Much expanded, Southmead Hospital is now a major hospital, with some of the original buildings still standing. The Eastville and Stapleton workhouses became PAIs, with Eastville housing the aged and chronic sick. Eastville was demolished in 1972 and modern housing occupies the site. By the Second World War, Stapleton was mainly used for the care of mental cases and the aged and infirm. It subsequently became Manor Park Hospital, later Blackberry Hill Hospital, which closed in 2008 and has now been converted to residential use. The St Peter's building was destroyed by bombing in 1940.

BRISTOL QUAKERS

In 1680, the Society of Friends (Quakers) set up a scheme in London in which stocks of flax were purchased for supplying the Quaker poor to spin at home or in prison. This project's treasurer, John Bellers, later developed plans for a 'College of Industry' – a co-operative, self-sufficient, humanitarian community where up to 200 labourers and 100 of the impotent poor would live and work together. Although Bellers's utopian plans were never implemented, their influence can be seen in two subsequent workhouse developments in Bristol and London.[11]

The Bristol scheme, which began in 1696, was originally intended to provide employment for seven poor Quaker weavers and the instruction of children. It proved so successful that in 1700 a new building was erected in New Street, St Jude's (ST596733), at a cost of £1,300, 'for willing Friends to work in and the aged and feeble to live in'. The premises incorporated an orphanage, a school, and an almshouse, all together housing forty-five inmates, including twenty-four paupers and ten apprentices. The inmates were mainly employed in the manufacture of worsted cloths known as cantaloons. Workhouse residents dined according to a schedule of diet that repeated every two weeks. Old people in the workhouse received pocket money of 2s per week plus a tobacco allowance.[12]

A survey of Bristol in 1861 recorded that the site was still 'used as an asylum for poor Friends'. In 1867, the building was extended at the south-east and the courtyard was roofed over to create a hall. Part of the site was also used as an infants' and boys' school and part housed the New Street Mission.[13] Quaker ownership of the site ended in 1929 when it was sold to the Bristol Churches Tenements Association for conversion to workmen's flats. The building was taken over by Bristol City Council in 1961 and became known as New Street Flats. In 2013, the building was sold to a property company for refurbishment as modern apartments. A new Quaker meeting house was erected on the site of the adjacent burial ground in 1958.

CHELTENHAM

In about 1730, the Royal Oak Inn, at the south side of Cheltenham High Street, was converted for use as a workhouse. In 1776, the establishment could accommodate thirty-six inmates. After it burned down in 1778, premises were leased in Day Lane (now Grove Street). A new workhouse, with a large workshop on its ground floor and accommodation above, was erected in 1789 on a leased site. From 1797, the inmates were employed in the pin-making trade. In 1808, a new purpose-built workhouse opened in the town on what is now Knapp Lane (SO943225). The following year, to celebrate the golden jubilee of George III, over 100 inmates dined on beef, pudding and strong beer.[14] Accommodation for the insane was added in 1810.[15] In 1811, Cheltenham adopted Gilbert's Act.[16]

From around 1808, Coberley's workhouse was located to the west of the village at Booker's Cottages, now a private residence (SO956161).[17]

In 1824, Prestbury opened a workhouse on what is now Queenwood Grove (SO979243). Yarn and spinning wheels were provided to employ the women and children.[18]

In 1827, at a cost of £466, Charlton Kings erected a workhouse on Church Street, opposite the end of New Street, where a nursery now stands (SO964504).[19] An inventory of the premises in 1835 included a tailor's bench, a shoemaker's stall and a maniac's chain.[20]

Cheltenham Poor Law Union was formed on 16 November 1835 and had thirteen member parishes. Initially, the new union continued to use the existing workhouses on Knapp Lane and at Charlton Kings, the latter used to house children. A site for a new workhouse was provided by Admiral Sir Tristram Ricketts in part of the grounds of his house, The Elms, at the junction of Swindon Road and Carlton Place, Cheltenham (SO945231). Designed by Edward Cope, its design appears to have been slow to finalise. The guardians first invited tenders for construction of the building in October 1838, but after revising the plans, final requests for tenders appeared in March 1840.[21] Further tenders were invited in November 1844 for the erection of an additional four rooms to be used as hospital wards.[22] Following the opening of the new workhouse in 1842, the children were transferred to Knapp Lane and the Charlton Kings premises closed. The establishment initially held 250 inmates, but further

A 1978 view from the north of the hub and splayed wings of the former Cheltenham Union workhouse. (Photo by Steven Blake, reproduced with permission)

additions and alterations to the buildings in 1849–50 raised its capacity to 581 places. The old Knapp Lane workhouse was then closed and sold, with National and Infant Schools being built on the site in 1856.

A mid-1850s map featuring the new workhouse indicates that males were housed at the west of the site and females at the east. An entrance block at the south contained the guardians' boardroom and offices. To its rear, a long narrow range, with schoolrooms on its ground floor, was linked to a central hub from which transverse ranges radiated at each side, with dayrooms on their ground floor and dormitories above. The north side of the hub contained a chapel, perhaps originally also used as a dining hall. Its north side connected to two further ranges, running to the north-east and north-west. The one on the men's side housed the kitchen and a dayroom, and that on the women's side contained a bakehouse and dayrooms. At the end of these two ranges were cross-wings housing fever rooms. At the north of the site, a laundry was placed on the women's side, and a stone yard on the men's side. A vagrants' ward had an access gate from St Paul's Road. The space between the various wings was divided into exercise yards for the various categories of inmate, one identified as the 'Lewd Women's Yard'.[23]

In November 1874, an official inquiry was held at the workhouse into numerous charges against the master and matron, Mr and Mrs Welch, namely that they had: inflicted punishment without reporting it to the guardians; been absent from house after hours; not visited the men's wards at night; not reported the property of deceased paupers; misappropriated property of the guardians; scalded the milk and kept a number of fowls; fed visitors from the workhouse supplies; disposed of lard, and not accounted for money received from the sale of rags and bones; improperly cut up the pigs and kept the best joints preserved; given lumps of fat, cow's udder, lights and pipes to the paupers; used burnt sugar to colour the beef tea; failed to report complaints; bullied the inmates; and allowed drunkenness in the house.[24] The LGB accepted that many of the charges had been proved and the immediate resignations of the master and matron were demanded.

In 1882, the guardians acquired the rest of The Elms site. The old house was used as a home for up to 100 pauper children, while its garden provided space for new buildings. The following year, a new casual ward was erected at the north of the garden.

A major building programme, designed by J.T. Darby, was undertaken in 1886–87. It included parallel male and female infirmary blocks at the centre of the garden area, a chapel to the south, a new laundry and master's house, and additions to the entrance block and to Elm House.[25]

After 1904, for birth registration purposes, the workhouse was identified as The Elms, Swindon Road.[26]

From 1930, the site was run by Gloucestershire Council and became a PAI, then joined the NHS as St Paul's Hospital. After its closure in the 1990s, the buildings were demolished except for the chapel. The site is now occupied by St Paul's Medical Centre plus some modern housing.

CHIPPING SODBURY

In 1776, parish workhouses were in operation in Chipping Sodbury (for up to forty inmates), Westerleigh (twenty-two) and Yate (forty). Of these, only Chipping Sodbury's was still active in 1803, when ten inmates were maintained there, and in 1813, when the number was just four.

A row of cottages known as the Old Workhouse was built in 1798 on Frith Lane (formerly Workhouse Lane), to the south of Wickwar (ST723872).[27]

Frampton Cotterell had a workhouse at the south side of Church Road (ST660820), dating from 1824.[28]

A workhouse was erected at Hawkesbury Upton in 1825.[29] Another existed at Iron Acton by 1826.[30] A poorhouse in Yate stood at the south side of St Mary's Church, later the site of a National School (ST714827).

Chipping Sodbury Poor Law Union was formed on 30 March 1836, with twenty-three member parishes. The new board of guardians had their first meeting at Chipping Sodbury Town Hall on 31 March 1836. A review of existing workhouses within the union revealed that the Wickwar workhouse could accommodate forty adults or thirty adults and twenty children. However, the board decided to use the nearer and larger workhouse at Hawkesbury Upton for adults, while children were placed at Iron Acton, where there was a pin manufactory.

In September 1836, the guardians advertised for a new mistress for the Iron Acton establishment. She was to be a middle-aged female who understood the cutting out and making of clothing for the females, was accustomed to superintending pin-heading, and would teach the children needlework.[31]

It was subsequently decided that the existing premises had insufficient capacity and that a new workhouse should be built, with capacity for 160 inmates. A suitable site was eventually found on what is now Station Road, Yate (ST718824), and construction was completed in May 1840. The architects were Scott and Moffatt and the building was typical of their designs (see page 27). Males were housed at the east of the site and females at the west.

The arched entrance gateway had the guardians' boardroom to its left and a schoolroom to its right, with boys' and girls' yards to the rear. The main accommodation block was three storeys high at the centre, where the master and matron had their quarters, with two-storey wings at either side. At its rear, the dining hall separated the men's and women's yards. A block running across the south of the site had the infirmary at its centre and tramps' accommodation at its eastern end. A now-demolished single-storey section containing the washhouse and laundry were placed at the rear of the women's yard.

In 1905–06, a new boardroom was erected at north-east of the site, facing onto the road. In 1921, rotary handwashing machines were installed in the laundry, which by then also had piped water and gas. In 1922, the men's labour yard was closed, a piano was bought for the dayroom, and occasional lantern slide shows were put on. In 1926, the first car park was provided. In 1927, the vagrants' wards were closed and new nurses' quarters were erected in their place. The following year, a fire in the roof of the master's quarters destroyed the clock, dome and finial that surmounted the building.[32]

In 1930, the workhouse was taken over by Gloucestershire Council and became a PAI. During the Second World War, some of the buildings were used as an emergency hospital. After 1948, the rear part of buildings became the Ridgewood old people's home. The site is now used by local businesses and community groups.

The former Chipping Sodbury Union workhouse at Yate – a well-preserved example of a classic Scott and Moffatt design.

CIRENCESTER

In 1724, the Cirencester vestry agreed to convert Chesterton House, a large old property at the edge of the town, for use as a Workhouse.[33] The building stood at the south side of what is now Watermoor Road (SP024014). The inmates were employed in woollen and yarn manufacture. In 1776, the workhouse could house 120 inmates. and the same number were maintained there in 1803. In 1810, the parish adopted Gilbert's Act, which excluded the able-bodied from indoor relief.[34] Inmates were still expected to work, however. In 1812, their employment included working on the roads and pin-making. A year later, pin manufacture was dropped as being uneconomic, but a new wool-carding machine was acquired. Income was also derived from selling garden produce and fattened pigs.[35] In 1828, of the fifty-one inmates, twenty-seven were 'infirm', six were 'idiots', four were 'unwell', one blind, one deaf, one 'infirm and cripple', two were unspecified, and three women were pregnant.[36] In 1829, a proper access road (Workhouse Lane, now Quern's Road) was constructed, linking the workhouse to Quern's Hill.

In 1797, Fairford adopted Gilbert's Act and opened a workhouse in a converted barn at the south of the Crofts, later the site of the cottage hospital (SP154010). Its female inmates spun flax and worsted.[37] Twenty-three paupers were maintained there in 1803, and thirty-nine in 1813.

In 1803, the parish of South Cerney relieved nine of its paupers in a workhouse. From 1831, there was a poorhouse at Caudle Green, Brimpsfield (SO943106), as identified on an 1837 tithe map.[38]

A property in the parish of Coates is identified as the Old Workhouse in the 1841 census.[39]

Cirencester Poor Law Union was formed on 21 January 1836. The guardians decided to demolish the old town workhouse and erect a new building on the same site. They advertised for plans for a workhouse for 300 inmates, and in March accepted those from John Plowman of Oxford. Building commenced that summer and was completed the following year.

Plowman's design was a variation on the PLC's model 'square' plan (see page 26), with males housed at the east of the site and females at the west. The front block originally had entrance doors either side of the centre. The one to the left led to the boardroom and office, the one at the right to the porter's lodge and workhouse interior. A schoolroom was placed further to the left, and receiving wards to the right. The centre rear of the entrance block linked to a central hub whose ground floor contained the dining hall, with the master and matron's quarters above. On the women's side were the kitchen, scullery, able-bodied dayroom and laundry, with dormitories on the upper floor. On the male side were the old and able-bodied men's dayrooms, with dormitories above. The rear block contained the infirmary and wards for imbeciles and epileptics. The town's old lock-up, originally on Gloucester Street, was relocated to the west side of the workhouse in 1837.

In 1872, the guardians invited tenders for the erection of four tramp cells at the workhouse.[40] Works in 1896 included a new committee room, new lavatories and WCs, and extensions to the girls' day and night wards.[41]

A visitor in 1890 noted that inmates were allowed visitors on Mondays and Fridays, from 1 p.m. to 4 p.m. The ward for the chronic sick was described as a bright scene, with yellow quilts, gay pictures, books and flowers. In contrast, the children's quarters were clean but very bare, with no pictures, games or other entertainment. Almost all the children were illegitimate. The orphans were boarded out in nearby villages. Able-bodied inmates were occupied in stone breaking, oakum picking and gardening. The food was judged as very good, varied and well cooked. Two days each week it comprised boiled bacon and two vegetables, two days meat and two vegetables, two days pea soup, and the other day beef and potatoes.[42]

After 1904, for birth registration purposes, the workhouse was identified as 24 Quern's Hill.[43]

In 1930, the site became a 200-bed PAI run by Gloucestershire Council. In 1948, it joined the NHS as Watermoor Hospital, then was converted to council offices in about 1980. Most of the original workhouse buildings survive.

CLIFTON (BARTON REGIS)

In the early 1770s, a workhouse existed on Chalk Lane (now Chalks Road) in the parish of St Philip & St Jacob.[44] In 1776, up to 100 inmates could be housed there. A workhouse later operated on the west side of Pennywell Road, later the site of Brecknell, Dolman & Rogers' engineering works (ST599736). It was described by Eden in 1797, at which date it was shared with the parish of St George and had eighty-five inmates:

> It is pleasantly situated and appears to be clean and comfortable. There are 2 or 3 beds of flocks and feathers in each room. Bill of fare in the Workhouse: Breakfast–every day, milk pottage. Dinner–Sunday, Thursday, bread and cheese; Monday, rice milk; Tuesday, Friday, pease soup; Wednesday and Saturday, pickled beef and vegetables. Supper–every day, bread and cheese or

The front block of the former Cirencester Union workhouse, now Cotswold District Council offices.

butter. 3 pints of beer are allowed to each person on meat days, and a quart on other days. One lb. of bread is given out daily and 9oz. of cheese every week. Once a month 12lbs. of butter are distributed, and at particular seasons better fare is provided, more especially for the sick.[45]

St George subsequently had its own workhouse, on what is now Hudds Vale Road (ST623739). The site was later the home of the Crown Pottery.

In 1776, Stapleton's workhouse could house 100 inmates. In 1795, the inmates comprised five men, seven women and eight children. The children were employed in spinning flax and hemp, but their earnings were 'very inconsiderable'.[46] It had ceased operation by 1803.

At the end of the eighteenth century, Westbury-on-Trym had two workhouses in use. One occupied former almshouses at the north of the parish church, the other was a building known as Long Entry. In 1801, with both premises in a poor state of repair, the parish adopted Gilbert's Act and erected a new workhouse, next to the church, which opened in 1804. The building, designed by Henry Wood, measured 81 by 36 feet and was 35 feet high. Its total cost of £3,587 included fifty-two iron bedsteads. The men worked at gardening or picked oakum, while the women did the domestic work, mended stockings or picked oakum. The children knitted stockings for use by the house or for sale.[47] In 1832, the inmates comprised six men, aged from

45 to 90; twelve women, from 20 to 86; and four children under 10. In more recent times, it has been suggested that the good food and care received by the inmates were such that 'even today it would be unlikely for an old person in a geriatric ward to receive such good treatment'.[48]

In 1810, Winterbourne resolved to adopt Gilbert's Act and establish a work-house.[49] In the years 1813–15, however, it had no long-term inmates.

Clifton's poorhouse or workhouse was located at the east side of Church Lane, Clifton Wood, on the hillside above Mardyke (ST575725). In 1859, the building was converted for use as a boys' industrial school.

In 1835, Assistant Poor Law Commissioner Charles Mott reported on his visit to the Pennywell Road workhouse, which was 'filthy in the extreme, the appearance of the inmates dirty and wretched'. In one miserable-looking room, he discovered a 'poor distressed lunatic … his clothing was extremely ragged; his flesh literally as dirty as the floor; his head and face were much bruised, apparently from repeated falls.' It transpired that the man had been in that state for years. In a room elsewhere in the building, another such indi-vidual, 17 years of age, had been confined for four years. He was almost naked, wearing only a coarse shirt. The explanation from the parish officers for this was, 'because he tears his clothes'.[50]

Clifton Poor Law Union was formed on 9 April 1836, with twelve member parishes. Initially, the union continued to use three former parish workhouses. Children were housed at Hudds Vale Road, able-bodied adults at Pennywell Road, and the aged and sick at Clifton Wood. Eventually, the guardians decided to build a large, general workhouse at Eastville.

The new workhouse, for 1,180 inmates, was erected in 1845–46 at 100 Fishponds Road, Eastville (ST613748), to designs by Samuel T. Welch. Its entrance block was at the south-west. To the rear, a central spine containing the dining hall and chapel divided the male and female sides, with several ranges at each side, parallel to the entrance block. The buildings to the north-east of the complex probably included both medical wards and accommodation for the mentally ill ('lunatics') and the intellectually impaired ('imbeciles' and 'idiots'). Children also had their own accommodation. At the Fishponds Road entrance there were stone-breaking yards and a casual ward for the overnight accommodation of vagrants. The stone yards were also used by able-bodied non-inmates who, at certain periods, attended each day to perform labour in return for out-relief.

In October 1867, inspectors from the *BMJ* found much to criticise. In the male infirmary, each ward was allowed the use of one washbasin and one towel a week; in the female department, similar arrangements existed, except that

An early 1900s view of the workhouse at 100 Fishponds Road, erected in 1847 by the Clifton Union.

there was only one basin for the use of the patients in both lying-in wards. In one of the sick wards, the only basin was reserved for making poultices in, while a bucket served not only for washing the wards, and the patients' hands and faces, but also any bad legs, or wounds, requiring such treatment, and lastly, the plates and cups. In another ward, if the patients wanted to bathe any sores, they had to do so in their chamber pots. All the towels were in an extremely dirty condition.[51]

In 1877, the Clifton Union was renamed Barton Regis (an old name for that part of Gloucestershire). This was at the request of the residents of Clifton, who felt that the name of the parish was increasingly being tarnished when events such as outbreaks of smallpox in other, more urban, parts of the Clifton Union received publicity.

Eastville had its own burial ground at the south of the workhouse, which was in use until 1895. Around 4,000 workhouse inmates were interred there in unmarked graves, including unbaptised infants who were buried in an area referred to as 'under the wall'.[52]

In 1894, another *BMJ* report praised several aspects of the workhouse. The sick wards were furnished with bright curtains, pictures and flowers, and in the dayroom for infirm women, the inmates could sit and sew, look at periodicals, tend growing plants, and brew their own tea. However, staffing levels for the care of the sick were said to be inadequate. No night nurses were provided for the sick and infirm wards, whose inmates numbered 586, and the old and infirm men were tended only by untrained male nurses.[53]

In 1898, the newly constituted Bristol Poor Law Union absorbed several parishes from the Barton Regis Union and took over the Eastville workhouse.

In 1900–02, Barton Regis built a new workhouse at Southmead, intended to house 110 inmates plus twenty-four casuals. It was designed by A.P.L. Cotterell and W.H. Thorpe in the English Renaissance style. The main buildings had a pavilion-plan layout, with walkways linking the separate blocks. The central block contained the master's quarters, with dining hall, kitchens and boiler house to the rear. Accommodation blocks lay to each side, males to the north and females to the south. A small block for married couples lay to the north of the male block. To the rear of the main building were a laundry on the female side, and a carpenter's shop on the male side. A twenty-eight-bed hospital block for females and children lay at the south of the site. The site entrance, on Southmead Road, had the boardroom offices at its north side and receiving and casual wards at the south. Stables, a carriage shed and mortuary block stood at the western corner of the site.[54]

In 1904, the Barton Regis Union was wound up and its member parishes distributed between the Bristol and Chipping Sodbury Unions.

A car stands outside the entrance of Dursley Union workhouse in this view from the 1920s. (Courtesy of Andrew Barton)

DURSLEY

By 1763, Wotton-under-Edge had a workhouse at the south side of Potters Pond (ST759932).[55] It could accommodate fifty inmates in 1776, and seventy-five paupers were maintained there in 1802–03. In 1834, the establishment had a resident matron but was very much a poorhouse, no work being done in it. Its inmates, comprising twenty-six old people and children, were well fed, with meat dinners on four days a week, and bread and cheese on other days. The elderly were allowed 2oz of tea and 4oz of sugar a week.[56] The building was later used as an infants' school and then as a mortuary.

North Nibley had a workhouse by 1764. It occupied Chantry House, on Church Lane (ST735961).[57] In 1803, there were nineteen permanent inmates, but none in 1813.

In 1779, Dursley established a workhouse in the Church House, on Silver Street, Dursley (ST756980). It stood where steps now lead up to St James' Church.[58] It was used to relieve seventy-eight paupers in 1803 and thirty-four in 1813.

In April 1780, the inhabitants of Uley met to consider the provision of a workhouse.[59] Its subsequent premises are said to have faced down from the top of Fop Street, on the opposite side of the road to the chapel (ST784981).[60] Twenty-nine paupers were maintained there in 1803, and sixty in 1813. By 1834, it was 'an unwelcome place for all who can keep out of it', with stone-breaking the sole form of labour for its thirty-eight inmates.[61]

Church House, at Churchend (SO739035), was the Slimbridge parish workhouse in 1781.[62] It was used to relieve eighteen individuals in 1803 and ten in 1813.

A building at what is now 41–45 Hopton Road in Cam (ST758993) served as a workhouse in the nineteenth century.[63] In 1813, the parish maintained twenty-nine paupers there. The property was later known as Workhouse Cottages.

In 1813, Coaley maintained seven paupers in its workhouse. In 1830, it occupied part of a cottage opposite the parish church on Coaley's main street (SO770107).[64]

In 1830, the parish of Kingswood, placed in Wiltshire until 1844, raised money to build a workhouse at Kethroe's Green, later referred to as Horsecroft.[65]

Dursley Poor Law Union was formed on 4 April 1836, with eleven constituent parishes. Initially, the existing workhouses at Kingswood and Uley were retained by the union. In May 1836, the guardians advertised for a governor and matron to superintend both establishments.[66] A new workhouse for 300 inmates was erected in 1837–39 on what became known as Union Street, at the south-west of Dursley (ST755979). Designed by Thomas Fulljames, it was a variation on the PLC's model 'square' plan (see page 26). Stone for constructing the workhouse was taken from a quarry in Hermitage Wood. The building came into use in September 1839.

In 1892, a lack of able-bodied female inmates led to the employment of a resident cook. The post was advertised at 7s per week, working from 4.30 a.m. until 8.30 p.m.[67]

In 1930, the site was taken over by Gloucestershire Council and became a PAI. It was closed at the start of the Second World War but subsequently housed evacuees. After the war, the building was demolished and replaced by an infants' school. The site is now covered by the housing of Harrold Close.

GLOUCESTER

A Local Act of 1702 enabled Gloucester to form an incorporation to administer poor relief across the city. A workhouse was in operation in 1703–04, but by 1707 the incorporation had virtually ceased functioning and individual parishes resumed their poor-relief responsibilities. The incorporation was active again from 1727 to 1740 and established a workhouse in the former New Bear Inn, at the corner of Castle Lane and Quay Street (SO828186). It closed in 1757 through financial difficulties, but reopened following a further Local Act in 1764.[68] In 1775, the establishment could house 200 inmates, who were employed 'principally in pin-making; but the aged and infirm pick oakum. The women in washing, brewing, and other household work.' A master was employed at £15 a year, a matron at £10, a schoolmaster at ten guineas, and an apothecary at £20. Several paupers were also employed: a schoolmistress at threepence a week, a porter at threepence a week, and a nurse at a shilling a week.[69] In March 1830, a lengthy investigation into the management of the workhouse led to the instant dismissal of the master, who had held the position for fourteen years.[70]

Norton had a workhouse by 1787. It was replaced in 1794 by a leased house at Cold Elm (SO856239), which was run by a contractor until 1800, then given up.[71]

Gloucester Poor Law Union was formed on 30 April 1835, with thirty-five member parishes. In 1837–39, the union erected a workhouse for 300 inmates at the south side of what is now Great Western Road, then named Workhouse

Members of the City Council's welfare committee in front of the old Gloucester workhouse, prior to its demolition in 1961.

Lane (SO838186). The architects were Scott and Moffatt and the building was typical of their designs (see page 27).[72] The single-storey reception block had a central entrance archway and included a porter's lodge, boardroom and chapel. To the rear was a three-storey accommodation block with a central supervisory hub containing a kitchen on the ground floor, and the master and matron's quarters above. The original infirmary, at the rear of the site, was demolished in 1850 to make way for the South Wales Railway. In 1852, a new infirmary, designed by Jacques and Son, was opened at the west of the work-house. In 1873, a vagrants' ward, designed by William Jacques, was erected at the western edge of the site.[73]

From 1899, boys were housed at Tuffley Court, Tuffley (SO830148) and girls at 73–75 Bristol Road (now the Linden Tree pub), Gloucester. In 1902, Ladybellegate Lodge, on Ladybellegate Street (SO829184), was purchased for use as a children's receiving home but subsequently housed aged women. From 1908, aged men were housed at Somerset Lawn, on Spa Road, Gloucester (SO828178).

A visitor in to the workhouse 1890 noted that there were 230 inmates and thirty children. The staff included a tailor and shoemaker who taught the boys their trades, many of whom subsequently emigrated to the Colonies. The girls learned needlework, knitting, cookery and other household skills to equip them for employment in domestic service. Twice a week, the children had a treat of 'bread cake' – ordinary bread with currants and a little sugar. Wardswomen (inmate nurses) and washers were allowed half a pint of beer a day, and men over 60 an ounce of tobacco a week.[74]

In 1908, the guardians bought the 7 acres of Budding's Field, immediately opposite the workhouse. In 1911, a casual ward, designed by Walter B. Wood, was erected at the south-east corner of the field. Later known as the Wayfarers' House, it had two association wards for fifteen inmates each, and ten single sleeping cells. The inmates slept in canvas hammocks slung 3 feet from the floor. There were also twenty stone-breaking cells.[75]

In 1914, construction began of a new infirmary on Budding's Field, also designed by W.B. Wood. It had a central administration block and nurses' home, with male and female ward pavilions to either side. In 1914, before it was completed, one of the pavilions was taken over as a Red Cross hospital for the war-wounded. Building recommenced in 1919.[76]

In 1930, the union's responsibilities passed to Gloucester Council. The workhouse site became Great Western House PAI. The buildings were demolished in 1961 and the site is now a car park. In 1936, the infirmary site became the City General Hospital, now Gloucestershire Royal. The old administration block still survives.

NEWENT

In 1751, Bromesberrow opened a poorhouse at Woodend Street (SO753348). By 1826, the establishment was run as a workhouse under a governor. From 1829, many of its inmates worked on local farms. Following a fire, the property was rebuilt in 1848.[77]

From 1768, Newent had a workhouse in a large house at Crown Hill (now Ross Street, SO719262), at the north of the town. The master, employed at £10 a year, supervised the labour of the adults, who mostly worked at spinning and knitting, and taught their children to read and write, and the girls to sew and knit. Children were also employed in heading pins. In 1776, the establishment could accommodate 150 inmates. The parish had adopted Gilbert's Act by 1803.[78] Sixty-nine paupers were maintained in the workhouse in 1813.

Dymock opened a workhouse in 1769 in a church house at the south-east corner of St Mary's churchyard (SO700312). In 1776, it could house thirty paupers. Management of the workhouse was mostly contracted out until 1796 when the vestry employed a resident master, who also acted as assistant Overseer.[79] For over thirty years, parishioner John Hill occupied the post. In March 1805, the death occurred of 85-year-old workhouse inmate James Drew, who at one time had possessed a considerable estate in the parish.[80]

Staunton had a workhouse by 1794.[81] A new workhouse was established in the parish in about 1822.[82]

In 1803, Redmarley D'Abitot maintained twenty-nine paupers in a workhouse on the Causeway (SO751312). Known as Church House, it was later used as the village bakehouse and then as a post office.[83] It was restored in the 1970s for use as a private residence.

Hartpury established a workhouse in 1788. The parish maintained nine paupers there in 1803. In 1823, the workhouse was at Sloper's Farm, Corsend (SO795252).[84]

In 1818, a workhouse was erected on Moat Lane, Taynton (SO731214), next door to a cottage already used as a poorhouse. The workhouse was initially shared with Tibberton and later also admitted paupers from Huntley. The three-storey building, which had very few road-facing windows, is now known as Hill View House.[85]

Newent Poor Law Union was formed on 23 September 1835. Its eighteen member parishes were drawn from Gloucestershire, Herefordshire and Worcestershire. The union took over the existing Newent workhouse, and in February 1836 the guardians invited tenders for its 'enlargement, repairs, and alterations'.[86] It could then house 160 inmates.

The workhouse occupied two adjacent buildings, linked together on the first floor with a passageway through to the rear of the site. An additional range was added at the west of the workhouse in 1867–68. In 1883, eight vagrant cells 'with hopper grid and tunnel' were built and alterations made to the existing vagrant wards, for which C.N. Tripp was architect.[87] In July 1904, the reconstruction of the workhouse hearse was carried out at a cost of £5 3s 6d.[88]

The workhouse was closed in 1918 due to a lack of inmates and the site was put up for sale. In 1922, it was acquired for the sum of £1 by Gloucestershire Council and became Newent Grammar School, removing the need for local children to travel by train to attend schools in Gloucester.[89] After the school relocated in 1965, the premises became a venue for youth groups. The south-west section of the buildings survives and in recent years has been used by various local community organisations.

Unusually, the Newent Union workhouse adjoined a pub, the King's Arms (left), opened in around 1820 and still in operation.

The Northleach Union workhouse in the early 1900s, when a greenhouse had been erected. The chapel stands at the left of the picture.

NORTHLEACH

Northleach established a workhouse in about 1724 but it had closed by the 1750s, after the parish had reverted to giving only out-relief. A new workhouse was opened in 1795 at Millend, where the inmates were initially employed in spinning. During a surge in pauper numbers in 1800–01, some inmates were hired out for stone quarrying, road making and harvest work. In the early nineteenth century, the usual number of inmates was around twenty.[90]

In 1803, Aldsworth housed thirteen paupers in a workhouse, although this may have been located in a neighbouring parish.[91]

Northleach Poor Law Union was formed on 18 January 1836, with thirty member parishes. Later that year, the union erected a workhouse at East End, Northleach (SP118144). Its design, by George Wilkinson, was based on the PLC's model 'square' plan (see page 26). It had a central octagonal hub from which radiated four wings, each having a cross-wing at the end. Most of the building was two storeys high, although the east and west cross-wings had three floors. The north wing was originally single-storey but later heightened. By 1867, a separate chapel had been erected at the south-west of the site.

The workhouse was the subject of an 1867 report by the *BMJ*, which found much to criticise. The old men's dayroom was described as a 'bare and stony cell', the only furniture being a table and two forms without backs. The floor consisted of large stone slabs, broken and uneven, and the windows had no blinds. The young men's day room contained only three very old men, of whom two were picking oakum, and one feebly darning a pair of braces. This room, like the previous one, was whitewashed, its lower half coloured a dirty pink, giving the whole a dull and tawdry look. There were windows on both sides, over 6 feet from the ground, precluding sight out. Both these rooms were 'dirty, ill kept, and desolate'. There was no workhouse library. The able-bodied women's ward contained seven women, four of whom were single mothers, while the other 'able-bodied' women were described as senile imbeciles. The girls' accommodation was good, however, with the thirteen inmates engaged in sewing. The only two boys in residence were taught with the girls. The vagrants' ward, at the west end of the frontage, received the greatest condemnation. It comprised a one-stalled stable, with no bath or drainage. The bedding consisted of old straw on the floor and three old, tattered counterpanes. The only convenience was a large open tub in the corner. Vagrants were given no supper and only a scanty breakfast before being required to break a bushel of gravel or pick a pound of oakum. The high spot of the inspectors' visit was the workhouse kitchen, where 'the bread, cheese, milk, and beer, were so good that we did more than taste them'.[92]

In 1868, the town police station, located in the old Northleach House of Correction (SP108149), took over the provision of nightly accommodation for passing vagrants, who were housed in some of the building's old cells.[93]

In 1930, the workhouse site was taken over by Gloucestershire Council and became a PAI. It joined the NHS in 1948 as Northleach Hospital, finally closing in 1987. The building is now a care home for the elderly.

STOW-ON-THE-WOLD

A workhouse was in operation in Bourton-on-the-Water by 1783, in a property rented by the parish. Its running was contracted out from 1787, but it had ceased use by 1803. In 1834, the vestry decided to refurbish the building, by then being used as a poorhouse, and reopen it as a workhouse.[94]

There was also a small workhouse at Bledington, where seven paupers were maintained in 1803.[95]

Stow-on-the-Wold Poor Law Union was formed on 25 January 1836, with twenty-eight member parishes. That June, construction began of a workhouse for 200 inmates at the north-east of the town, on what became known as

A distant view of the Stow-on-the-Wold Union workhouse from the tower of St Edward's Church.

Union Street (SP195257). It was designed by George Wilkinson and based on the PLC's model 'square' plan (see page 26).

Even before building work had begun, the guardians were advertising for a master and matron for the workhouse. In a rather unusual arrangement, the master was also expected to act as clerk to the union and the matron as workhouse schoolmistress. A joint salary of £70 was offered at the outset, rising to £120 when the workhouse came into operation, which was expected to be in the following November.[96]

A report in 1861 recorded that fifteen of the inmates had been continuously resident for five years or more. Jane Waring had been in the workhouse since it had opened because of her 'weak intellect, and having illegitimate children'. Joseph Haynes had been an inmate for eight years due to 'old age, and a great dislike to work'.[97]

In 1872, the guardians invited tenders for the erection of new tramp wards and the conversion of the porter's lodge into receiving wards.[98]

In March 1907, an elderly inmate of the workhouse named John Mason, a fiddle player for Morris dancing, was visited by folk-song collector Cecil Sharp. Over a two-day period, Sharp transcribed several traditional dance tunes that Mason played for him.[99]

In 1930, the workhouse was taken over by Gloucestershire Council and became the East View PAI, then joining the NHS as East View Hospital. The building was demolished in the 1970s and housing now occupies the site.

STROUD

A workhouse was erected in 1724–25 at the north side of Parliament Street, Stroud (SO855051). It was a long building, two storeys high plus attics, with sixteen bays of windows.[100] In 1776, it could house 100 paupers. The inmates were usually occupied in some branch of the cloth-making industry. In 1803, however, the total earnings of the sixty-five inmates was only £87, less than a fifth of the £450 it cost to run the workhouse.[101] By 1824, the establishment had become a poorhouse, with no labour required from its then thirty-nine inmates, who were mostly elderly. In 1834, the building was said to be old, inconvenient, and with no arrangement for separating the sexes. It was, however, very clean.[102]

Horsley had a workhouse by 1726, near Horsley Cross. In 1728, it was said to be so crowded that it was more like a playhouse than a workhouse. In about 1769, the parish erected a new workhouse for 100 paupers at Shortwood Green. Its inmates were employed in spinning.[103] Fifty-four paupers were maintained there in 1813.

In 1726, Bisley established a workhouse in a property on Joiners Lane (SO903054), where sixty paupers could be housed. In 1728–29, the income generated by the inmates was just a quarter of the workhouse's running costs of £115.[104] In 1776, the workhouse could house fifty inmates. In 1813, fifty-one paupers were maintained there.

Minchinhampton erected a workhouse in 1727 at the south end of Workhouse Lane, now Chapel Lane (ST873999). In 1776, it could house 100 inmates. In 1803, seventy paupers were maintained there, with their labour generating the substantial income of £242.[105]

King's Stanley also built a workhouse in 1727, adjoining an existing alms-house. A female keeper, appointed in 1729, received a payment for each inmate, plus part of the income from their spinning work. In 1732, a surgeon from Leonard Stanley undertook to treat the inmates instead of paying poor rates.[106] In 1776, the establishment could hold seventy inmates. When the workhouse was auctioned off in 1836, it was described as a substantial building with five large ground-floor rooms, six bedchambers, five garrets, and a large court and garden. The site had 150 feet of frontage and a well.[107]

A workhouse occupied part of Painswick's old town hall, at the south side of Victoria Square (SO866096). From 1796, inmates were occupied in pin-heading.[108] Fourteen paupers were maintained there in 1803, and thirteen in 1813. In 1817, the parish adopted Gilbert's Act.[109]

A workhouse was built in Rodborough in about 1738. Its use had lapsed by 1767 when the church house, to the south-west of the churchyard and previously used as a poorhouse, was converted into a workhouse. In 1782, three tenements at the west of the church were converted for the purpose. In 1786, the vestry decided to use one part of the church house as a penitentiary for prostitutes and another to house the idle poor.[110] Thirty paupers were maintained in the workhouse in 1803, and twenty-one in 1813.

Avening probably had a workhouse from 1744. In 1776, it could house twenty inmates. It closed in 1783 but had reopened by 1813, when eighteen paupers were maintained there.[111]

Miserden had a workhouse or poorhouse at a location variously referred to as The Down, Downhill (Down Hill), and 'near the Dillay'.[112]

In 1782, Randwick built a workhouse at the west of the church, replacing the old church house on the site. By 1811, the inmates were occupied in pin-making. In 1829, most of the female inmates did spinning, while the men worked on the roads. The inmates numbered fifteen in 1831.[113] The building was demolished in 1884 to make way for the glebe house.

By 1812, Leonard Stanley had erected a parish workhouse on Marsh Road (SO804033).[114] Fifteen paupers were maintained there in 1813.

By the 1820s, Stonehouse had a poorhouse in a row of cottages on Woodcock Lane.[115] The 1901 census referred to the location as the Old Workhouse.[116]

Stroud Poor Law Union was formed on 2 April 1835, with fifteen member parishes. It initially employed the existing workhouses at Minchinhampton and Horsley. In 1837–39, a workhouse for 500 inmates was erected at the north side of Bisley Road (SO863049). In April 1837, Samuel Mynett, who was working on construction of a new well for the workhouse, was killed when a box of stones fell 70 feet onto him.[117]

William Mason was originally appointed as architect but Charles Baker subsequently took over the role. The building employed the relatively uncommon double-cruciform layout. The entrance block at the south had a central archway. At the centre of the site, a three-storey block contained a chapel and administrative facilities. To each side were cruciform, three-storey accommodation blocks, one for men and one for women, each having an octagonal hub.

In September 1849, a young 'idiot' inmate named Charles Ireland literally boiled to death after the steam heating the bath in which he had been placed was carelessly left on by the boilerman, William Chew. The attending nurse, Eliza White, had also failed to test the temperature of the water. After an inquiry, Chew resigned and White was reprimanded.[118]

On 1 September 1856, the Bishop of Gloucester consecrated a 3-acre cemetery on Bisley Road, opposite the workhouse. Three days later, inmate William Lewis was the first to be interred there.

In 1899, improvements to the building included a new mortuary and vagrants' block at the east of the workhouse, and a rebuilding of the entrance block and master's quarters.

After 1904, for birth registration purposes, the workhouse was identified as 1 Bisley Road, Stroud.[119]

In 1930, the site was taken over by Gloucestershire Council and became a PAI. By 1939, the buildings were in a poor condition, and it was decided to close the establishment. During the Second World War, the premises were used to house military personnel but then stood empty for many years. The site was converted to residential use in the mid-1990s, with most of the original buildings retained.

Part of the Stroud Union's massive three-storey double-cruciform workhouse, now converted to housing.

A view of the Tetbury Union workhouse not long after it was rebuilt in 1905–06.

TETBURY

A workhouse existed in Tetbury by 1741. In 1776, it could house sixty inmates. A new building was erected in 1790 at the east side of what is now Gumstool Hill (ST 892931). Spinning was among the inmates' tasks, and the workhouse contractor in 1814 and 1822 was a local worsted manufacturer.[120]

In March 1837, a property previously used as Shipton Moyne's parish workhouse was put up for sale by auction.[121]

Tetbury Poor Law Union was formed on 31 March 1836, with thirteen member parishes. The guardians took over the existing Tetbury parish workhouse and made alterations with advice from Sampson Kempthorne, the author of the PLC's model workhouse plans. It had a large, square main building facing north-west, with several smaller blocks at each side.

By 1902, the workhouse was in urgent need of improvement and enlargement, and the LGB pressed the guardians to erect a new building on a different site or else face the union being dissolved. A site was found at the north of the town, near Wisteria Cottage, and plans were prepared by V.A. Lawson. However, the estimated £11,000 cost of land and construction was beyond what the guardians would be able to borrow. The situation was eventually resolved after some land adjoining the existing site became available to lease. This allowed the necessary additions and improvements, again designed by Lawson, to be made for just £3,850. The main building now had a T-shape layout, with an administrative section at the front centre, and male and female accommodation to each side. The stem of the 'T' at the rear housed the dining hall and kitchen. A separate laundry stood at the south-east. A date stone from the 1790 workhouse was incorporated into the rear of the main block. Sick wards and nurses' accommodation were placed in a block on the new land at the north-east of the site.[122]

In 1918–19, the building was used as a hospital by the Australian Flying Corps, the pauper inmates being boarded out at neighbouring institutions. In 1930, the establishment was taken over by Gloucestershire Council and redesignated as a PAI. After it closed in 1936, the premises became the Cotswold Maternity Home and Children's Hospital, later the Cotswold Hospital, which operated until the mid-1960s. In the 1980s, the Gloucestershire Constabulary used the building for training sniffer dogs. Since 1996, it has been used as a nursing home for the elderly.

TEWKESBURY

In 1724, Tewkesbury's vestry resolved to establish a workhouse, but it is unclear whether this took place. A similar resolution in 1756 led to house in Mill Bank (SO889325) being fitted up for the purpose.[123] In 1776, workhouse could house thirty-six inmates. After the parish obtained a Local Act in 1792, a board of Guardians of the Poor was appointed and a House of Industry was erected on the Gloucester Road (SO889321). The architect may have been the gaol designer George Byfield. The building had a main block of three storeys, increasing to four at the rear where the ground sloped away. There were originally wings at each side, probably single-storey out-buildings, and small separate roadside block.[124] In 1903, eighty-three paupers were maintained in the workhouse. They worked for local manufacturers, who sent materials into the workhouse. In 1832, the inmates comprised thirty-eight males and thirty-nine females, their ages ranging from under 5 years to over 80.

In 1771, the parish of Deerhurst began boarding its paupers at Winchcombe. By 1789, Deerhurst had its own small workhouse, which was still in use in 1813.[125]

In 1776, Overbury's workhouse could accommodate eleven inmates.

By 1790, Twyning had a workhouse on Hill End Common.[126] In 1803, fourteen paupers were maintained there.

The former workhouse originally erected by the Tewkesbury Incorporation in 1792.

In 1793, Forthampton replaced an existing poorhouse with a workhouse near the parish church. The contractor running it received £80 a year plus any income from the paupers' labour. In 1793, the inmates comprised one man, five women and eight children. The workhouse operated until at least 1803, when it comprised a cottage for the master and another housing just two men and two women. The women's quarters were provided with spinning wheels for flax and wool.[127]

Tewkesbury Poor Law Union was formed on 16 November 1835 and comprised twenty-three parishes from Gloucestershire and Worcestershire. The union purchased the existing House of Industry.

In April–May 1839, there were four attempts to set the building on fire. On the final occasion, an inmate named Ann Ella, about 15 years of age, was suspected of placing a burning coal, wrapped in a piece of rag, beneath one of the beds. On being taken into custody, she confessed to the crimes and was placed in the town gaol to await a court appearance. In each case, the chief damage was the destruction of some articles of clothing, and minor injury to the furniture and floors of the building.[128]

After 1904, for birth registration purposes, the workhouse was identified as 'The Infirmary, Gloucester Road'.[129]

In 1930, the site was taken over by Gloucestershire Council and became Holmwood House PAI. In 1948, it joined the NHS as Holm Hospital, providing geriatric care until its closure in 1969. After a period of dereliction, the building was renovated in the early 1990s to become Shepherd Mead retirement homes.

Some early residents of the homes claimed that a ghost inhabited the buildings. In the adjacent retirement bungalows, built on the site of the former workhouse graveyard, the sounds of crying children have also been reported.[130]

THORNBURY

A property deed of 1728 refers to a workhouse at the west end of Tytherington.[131]

Thornbury established a workhouse in 1739 in two adjacent properties at the east side of St Mary's Street, near the present-day entrance to the Aldi supermarket site (ST637900).[132] In 1776, the establishment could house eighty inmates. In 1832, the inmates comprised nine women and seven men, who were mostly aged, and fourteen boys and fifteen girls.

In 1776, workhouses were also in operation at Aust, for up to eight inmates, and at Elberton and Littleton-upon-Severn, each housing twenty. All had ceased use by 1803.

Alkington, a tithing in the parish of Berkeley, had a workhouse from 1791. It stood about a mile to the east of Berkeley village, adjacent to Coldelm Farm (ST686985).[133] In 1803, fifteen paupers were maintained there. In August 1804, 58-year-old inmate William Smart hanged himself from a beam in his lodging room. An inquest returned a verdict of lunacy.[134]

Berkeley's Ham tithing and Stone chapelry had a joint workhouse where thirty-one paupers were maintained in 1803. It was situated just to the south of Ham Green (ST679981).[135] Its 'manufactory' ceased operation in 1811.[136]

The Berkeley tithings of Hinton, Breadstone and Hamfallow relieved seventeen paupers in a workhouse in 1803, and the same number in 1813. In the latter year, the parish of Rangeworthy gave indoor relief to eight paupers.

In 1803, Redwick with Northwick, a tithing and chapelry in the parish of Henbury, relieved five paupers via a workhouse.

In Olveston, Down House on Foxholes Lane (ST611873) was used as the parish workhouse from about 1814.[137]

Almondsbury had a workhouse on The Scop (ST604841). It is now divided into residential properties and known as Belgrave Buildings.

Thornbury Poor Law Union was formed on 5 April 1836, with twenty-one member parishes. Initially, the union retained the workhouses at Almondsbury, Alkington and Thornbury, while the premises at Olveston, Ham and Hinton were also available if needed.[138] In May 1838, after lengthy and sometimes disputatious deliberations, a site for a new workhouse was acquired on Gloucester Road, Thornbury (ST641905). Designed by Sampson Kempthorne, it combined elements of his '200-pauper' and 'square' plans (see page 26). Additions during construction include adding an extra storey over the chapel for use as fever and idiot wards, and converting the bakehouse into a boys' schoolroom. The building came into use in May 1839.

In April 1848, the guardians invited tenders for altering and enlarging the workhouse.[139] In 1881, a new vagrants' ward, designed by J.Y. Sturge, was erected at the west of the workhouse.[140] A new porter's lodge was added at the site entrance in 1888.[141] In 1899, the guardians sought tenders for a new infirmary, designed by G.H. Oatley.[142] The long building, placed at the southeast of the workhouse, had a two-storey central portion and single-storey male and female ward wings to either side.

In 1930, the site was taken over by Gloucestershire Council and became a PAI. After 1948, it was known as Thornbury Hospital and continued in use until the 1990s. In 2000, the buildings were converted to residential use.

Now converted to residential use, the former Thornbury Union workhouse still bears a reminder (inset) of its previous identity.

WESTBURY-ON-SEVERN

Longhope had a parish workhouse from the 1770s but it had closed by 1803. Another establishment, opened after 1816, was still in operation in 1835.[143]

In 1789–90, Westbury-on-Severn erected a parish workhouse on the west side of the High Street (SO715141). In 1795, a pin-making company in Gloucester contracted to employ the inmates for seven years.[144] In 1803, the labour of the ten inmates generated an income of almost £25. Thirty-three paupers were maintained in the workhouse in 1813.

In 1791, Newnham erected a workhouse on the site of an existing establishment.[145] The new building may be that which survived until 1875 at the north-west corner of the churchyard. In 1809, the workhouse had up to twenty paupers, whose work included spinning, weaving and tanning.[146] The parish adopted Gilbert's Act in 1815.

In 1790, Mitcheldean opened a workhouse in a rented house, initially with fifteen inmates who were occupied in spinning hemp or in heading pins for Gloucester manufacturers. From around 1810, the establishment was used primarily as a poorhouse.[147] The parish adopted Gilbert's Act in about 1822.[148]

In 1791, Awre proposed erecting a workhouse, but its absence in 1803 suggests that this may not have taken place. The parish adopted Gilbert's Act in

1822 and took over an existing building as a workhouse.[149] In 1851, a property in Blakeney, the parish's largest settlement, was said to have been the parish workhouse for many years.[150]

In 1820, the Littledean vestry agreed to build a workhouse to replace its old poorhouse, whose inmates were moved to the new premises in 1822. The governor was Richard Elsmore, formerly in charge of Stonehouse workhouse. In 1823, the parishes of Abenhall and Flaxley also began using the workhouse.[151] Although the three parishes adopted Gilbert's Act, they did not formally establish a Gilbert Union.[152]

Westbury-on-Severn Poor Law Union was formed on 28 September 1835, with thirteen member parishes. Initially, the union took over the existing Westbury parish workhouse at a rent of £60 per annum. In 1836, the PLC authorised an expenditure of £500 on its enlargement, for which Thomas Fulljames was architect.

In 1869, the workhouse was substantially altered and extended. The architect for the scheme was Alfred W. Maberley. Following the rebuilding work, the building consisted of three main sections. Fronting onto the road at the east were the boardroom, porter's lodge, vagrants' wards and stables. To the rear, separated by inmates' airing yards and the master's garden, was a long, brick-built, three-storey block, which incorporated the old parish building.

An aerial view of the Westbury-on-Severn Union workhouse. (Courtesy of Jerry Green)

This block contained the master's quarters, dayrooms, kitchens and an infectious ward. A large new two-storey block at the west contained a dining hall with a chapel above, schoolrooms, dayrooms and dormitories.[153]

At the end of September 1882, the board of guardians appointed Mr W.B. Waterer as new master of the workhouse. At their next meeting, however, they decided to revoke their decision. It had come to light that, six months earlier, Waterer, then master of the Holbeach workhouse, had been found guilty of the manslaughter of one of the inmates there.[154]

In 1898, the guardians invited tenders for the erection of new vagrants' wards, receiving wards, porter's lodge, committee room, laundry, kitchen and stores.[155] The architect was W. Fitzgerald Jones. In 1901, the workhouse's earth closets were replaced with water closets.

After 1904, for birth registration purposes, the workhouse was identified as 1 High Street, Westbury on Severn.[156]

In 1930, the site was taken over by Gloucestershire Council and became a PAI, later a county council welfare home known as Westbury Hall, which was closed in 1969. The housing of Colchester Close now covers the site.

WHEATENHURST

Eastington erected a parish workhouse in 1785 at Chippenham (now Chipman's) Platt (SO782063). In 1803, twenty-five paupers were maintained there, but only four in 1815. A keeper of the workhouse was appointed in 1819, and two looms were bought in 1827.[157]

Frampton-on-Severn opened a workhouse in 1786. It had six beds, though in 1792 had nine inmates. In 1796, a Gloucester pin-maker was contracted to run the workhouse and to teach the inmates how to head pins. The vestry had resumed running the workhouse by 1803, but the inmates continued to work at pin-heading, generating an income of £37 in that year. The workhouse then fell out of use until 1820, when it was refurbished and its operation again contracted out. In 1833, the inmates were still occupied in pin-heading, although the establishment was by then described as a poorhouse rather than a workhouse.[158]

Arlingham may have adopted Gilbert's Act by the 1820s and had a workhouse on Church Road.[159]

Wheatenhurst Poor Law Union was formed on 21 September 1835, with fourteen member parishes. The union took over the existing Chippenham Platt site and invited tenders for 'altering and enlarging' the workhouse, with

Thomas Fulljames as architect.[160] Following the work, the workhouse was a substantial, triple-pile, three-storey building and featured a canted central bay-window at its rear to facilitate supervision of the exercise yards.

Eastington was close to main Gloucester to Bristol Road, a popular route for travelling vagrants. In September 1866, the guardians issued a handbill announcing that the sergeant at Whitminster police station, about 2 miles from the workhouse, had been appointed as Assistant Relieving Officer for the relief of vagrants, and was empowered to issue tickets for admission to the work-house's casual ward. The public were warned that they should on no account give money to tramps and vagrants, and only give relief in kind to those who could produce a ticket from a 'distant' union.[161]

In 1930, the workhouse site was taken over by Gloucestershire Council and redesignated as a PAI. After 1948, it became The Willows Hostel for Aged Persons. The building now houses the Camphill Communities' William Morris College for people with learning disabilities and other special needs.

The Wheatenhurst Union workhouse, viewed from its grounds in about 1910.

WINCHCOMB

In 1746, the Overseers at Winchcomb (now Winchcombe) established a work-house in the old Abbey House (also known as Water Abbey), at the north side of what is now Abbey Terrace, Winchcombe (SP023283).[162] In 1776, the premises could house seventy inmates. The contractor in 1789 was Richard Warner, who received £490 for the year. He was required to return to departing inmates all the goods and furniture they had brought with them on entering the workhouse.[163] In 1813, forty paupers were maintained in the establishment. Abbey House was demolished two years later.[164]

In 1783, the Bishop's Cleeve Overseers began making use of the Winchcombe workhouse, for which privilege they paid 30s per year plus 3s per week for each pauper placed there. In 1801, Bishop's Cleeve and Woodmancote established a joint workhouse at what is now 40 Station Road, Bishop's Cleeve (SO961277). John Philips was initially paid £180 a year to farm the parishes' poor, though this decreased when the number of paupers declined. Woodmancote opened its own poorhouse in 1808 on Gambles Lane.[165]

Winchcomb Poor Law Union was formed on 16 January 1836. In March of that year, the guardians invited tenders for the construction of a new work-house. The building was erected at the west of the town, on the north side of Gloucester Street (SP019281). It was designed by the Sampson Kempthorne and based on his model '200-pauper' layout, although its eventual capacity was only 118 places.[166]

In 1847, alterations and enlargement work increased the capacity of the workhouse to 140 places. A fever hospital was erected at the west of the workhouse site in 1878. The building was enlarged in 1913 to create a general-purpose infirmary capable of housing the workhouse's sick and bed-ridden inmates. As well as providing separate male and female wards, each with their own dayroom, the improvements included the installation of hot and cold running water, hot-water heating and gas lighting.[167]

In 1915, the death was reported of inmate Elizabeth Hall, who had entered the workhouse on 5 May 1836, almost eighty years earlier. Said to be of weak intellect, she had never left the institution.[168]

In 1930, the premises were taken over by Gloucestershire Council and became a PAI. After it was closed in 1934, a boys' home was established at the site. The premises were requisitioned during the Second World War, then afterwards disposed of by the council. Modern housing now covers the site.

HEREFORDSHIRE

BROMYARD

Bromyard had a workhouse by 1754. A contractor was running the establishment in 1774 and 1781.[1]

In 1774, the township of Winslow began using privately operated workhouses 15 miles away in Hereford, variously run by Mrs Symson, Sarah Morris, Thomas Morris and Edward Morris. In 1781, the township of Linton also contracted with Thomas Morris, who was paid £24 a year, plus £1 for each adult and 8s for each child he received. Each inmate in his workhouse was to receive:

> Meat, drink, washing, apparel, lodging and all other necessaries, phicisions, surgeons, apothacaries etc. Theire breakfast every morning will be milk porridge, onion broth, they shall have a hot beef, mutton, pork … with vegetables on every Sunday, Tuesday and Thursday of every week. The other four days their dinner shall be hasty pudding with flower and milk and toast, cyder or beer etc. and whatever the season of the year shall produce. Their supper shall be bread and cheese etc.[2]

From 1737, the parish of Cradley made use of the Ledbury workhouse. By 1780, it had its own premises.[3] The 1891 census suggests it was located near Storridge.[4]

Later references to the property's sale indicate the existence of a parish workhouse in Stanford Bishop.[5]

Bromyard Poor Law Union was formed on 30 May 1836, with thirty-three member parishes. A new workhouse for 120 inmates was built at Bromyard Downs, Linton (SO670541). The architect was George Wilkinson, whose design was based on the PLC's model 'square' plan (see page 26).

In 1893, there was a widespread outbreak of smallpox, with tramps often implicated in spreading the disease when travelling between casual wards. A man named Thomas Taylor, who had worked in disinfecting the workhouse, died after becoming infected. On 20 July, the union clerk was instructed to obtain tenders for installing concrete and wood-block flooring in the female tramp ward and other wards that had been used for housing smallpox patients.[6]

In July 1909, the workhouse was in a state of disarray for several months following a breakdown in relations between the master, Richard Byard, and the porter, Thomas Lodge. Lodge's complaints against the master included that he did not properly pay for the accommodation of members of his family and for the food consumed by them and their visitors. Lodge also claimed that a pet lamb kept by the master's children was fed on milk intended for the inmates. In his turn, the master accused the porter of insubordination and a failure to record the names of every visitor to the workhouse. Eventually, the master and matron, the assistant matron, the porter and his wife, who was the workhouse nurse, were all forced to resign.

In 1930, the workhouse became a PAI run by Herefordshire Council. The site joined the NHS as Bromyard Hospital, finally closing in 1993. The surviving buildings are now in private residential use.

DORE

Madley appears to have had a workhouse by 1730.[7] In 1803, the parish maintained nine paupers in a workhouse. In 1813, the number was nineteen.

In 1815, the parish of Abbey Dore made an agreement for use of Vowchurch workhouse.[8] The 1881 census indicates that it was near St Bartholomew's Church.[9] A parish workhouse also existed at Kentchurch.[10]

The Dore (or Abbey Dore) Poor Law Union was formed on 27 March 1837, with twenty-nine member parishes, two of which lay in Monmouthshire. Two weeks later, the union's new board of guardians met for the first time at the Red Lion Inn, Abbey Dore (now the site of Abbey Dore Court).

Neither of the old Madley and Kentchurch workhouses was deemed suitable for use by the union. Consequently, a new workhouse for 80–100

The former Bromyard Union workhouse, with its date of construction recorded above the entrance (inset).

A distant view of the former Dore Union workhouse.

inmates was built in 1837–38 on a piece of land called 'Upper Drew' to the north of Abbey Dore (SO384326), for which a loan of £2,000 was taken out from the Exchequer. The land was bought from one of the original guardians, William Hamp, who then resigned from the board. The architect for the building was John Plowman, who was also responsible for the workhouses at Hereford and Ross. When approving the plans, the PLC noted that they lacked any special workrooms, a mill room, bakehouse, washing places and a dead house.[11]

The main workhouse building was built around two yards, one for males to the north, and one for females at the south, each being divided diagonally to separate adults from children. The male and female yards were separated by the dining hall and kitchen. An entrance block at the west contained the guardians' boardroom, dayrooms and a receiving ward. To the rear lay the original infirmary block. A porter's lodge and casuals' ward were in a separate block to the north, with a stable block to its east. A turret clock for the main building was donated by William Hamp.[12] A stone stable with stalls for twelve horses was erected in 1838.

The first master and matron were James and Ann Hughes, who had previously had charge of the workhouse at Ledbury.

The workhouse suffered outbreaks of typhus fever in 1847 and 1852. As a result, the height of the infirmary was increased to provide two new rooms over the existing ones. In the 1890s, a separate isolation block was added at the south-east of the workhouse.[13]

Between 1930 and 1935, the workhouse was a PAI run by Herefordshire Council. During the Second World War, part of the premises was used by the firm of Chalmers as a tractor factory. After the war, the buildings were bought by a Mr Woodhouse, who converted them into cottages now known as 'Riverdale'.

HEREFORD

In 1697, following the example of Bristol the previous year, Hereford obtained a Local Act for the 'erection of hospitals and workhouses for better employing and maintaining the poor'.[14] Whether any workhouse was actually erected under this Act is unclear.[15]

In 1766, Hereford's St Nicholas parish made an agreement with Judith Haswell, described as 'Mistress of the Workhouse', for the maintenance of its poor.[16] By 1776, five of the city's parishes were operating their own small workhouses: All Saints (for up to eighteen inmates), St John Baptist (twenty), St Martin (seven), St Nicholas (ten) and St Peter (fifteen, in two workhouses).

In 1783, all six Hereford parishes set up a joint workhouse in the old General Infirmary premises, at what is now 162 Eign Street (SO504401).[17] In November 1795, there were fifty-six inmates, mainly old people and children. They were employed in spinning mop yarn and carding wool for saddles, while a few worked out of the house. Their diet comprised: breakfast – Sunday: water gruel and bread; rest of the week: broth and bread; dinner – Sunday, Tuesday, Thursday: beef and vegetables; other days, bread and cheese; supper, every day: bread, cheese and beer. The joint arrangement ended in 1796 and each parish then made its own arrangements.[18] At its sale in 1807, the Eign Street building had 'two parlours forward, two parlours backward, and on the principal floor four lodging-rooms, with attics over, a spacious garden and cellars, with offices behind'.[19]

By the 1830s, Hereford had three workhouses in operation, one in All Saints parish, one in St John the Baptist, and one in St Nicholas, on Quaker's Lane (now Friars Street).[20]

Allensmore had a workhouse by 1780, when a contract was made for its management.[21] In 1814–15, the parish provided workhouse relief to one person.

In 1783, the Overseers at Burghill contracted to pay John Monington the annual sum of £105 for the following three years to receive and maintain all the parish's poor in sufficient 'meat, drink, washing and clothing', and all other necessities other than medical fees. However, he was not to admit any children over the age of 8 years, if healthy and well.[22]

In 1798, advertisements were placed for a 'person in trade' to run the workhouse at Lugwardine, jointly rented by the parishes of Lugwardine, Burghill, Holmer and Brinsop.[23]

Hereford Poor Law Union was formed on 28 April 1836, with forty-five member parishes. Initially, the union took over the All Saints workhouse (for able-bodied males), the Quaker's Lane workhouse (vagrants), and the St John's workhouse (all other classes).[24] A new workhouse for 250 inmates was built in 1836–37 at the south side of Commercial Road, Hereford (SO515402). The architect was John Plowman, whose design followed the PLC's model 'square' plan (see page 26). Females were housed at the east side of the workhouse and males at the west. The front block had two entrances, one leading to the boardroom and offices, the other into the main workhouse. At the end of 1849, the main block was enlarged at each side, increasing the workhouse's capacity to 300 places.

Work performed by the inmates included oakum picking, stone breaking, pounding bones and cleaning hair. The workhouse had extensive vegeta-

The entrance block of the former Hereford Union workhouse, photographed in 2001.

ble gardens and a dairy, whose produce was sometimes sold, and pigs were purchased for fattening. In 1850, extra land was bought, new piggeries and cowsheds erected, and a farm manager appointed.[25] Boys in the workhouse received agricultural training, and at the end of 1850 a new girls' school was opened on the new land, where the girls were taught dairy work.[26]

In the mid-1870s, new male and female infirmary blocks were erected along the north-east side of the workhouse. A chapel, designed by Capel N. Tripp and funded by voluntary donations, was added to the west of the workhouse in 1879.[27]

In March 1903, after inspectors had condemned the workhouse as obsolete and insanitary, the guardians debated at length whether to erect a new building on a different site or remodel the existing building. The latter course was eventually followed. In October 1903, some space was freed up in the workhouse when the union opened a home for up to thirty-two children at Ivy House, on Ledbury Road, Tupsley (SO526402).[28]

After 1904, for birth registration purposes, the workhouse was identified as Union Buildings.[29]

In 1907, the master and matron of the workhouse were a Mr and Mrs Harding. Their son, Gilbert, who was born in that year, became a well-known radio and TV personality in the 1950s on shows such as *Twenty Questions* and *What's My Line?*

In around 1920, the workhouse adopted the name Longfield Buildings. In 1930, the site became a PAI run by Herefordshire Council. In 1937, the large new Hereford County Council Hospital was erected on the St Guthlac's Priory site at the north-west of the Institution. An Emergency Medical Service hospital was erected in 1940 and the pauper inmates transferred to other institutions in the county. In 1948, the whole complex joined the NHS as Hereford County Hospital. The front portion of the workhouse building and the chapel survive.

KINGTON

Kington had a workhouse by 1734, when paupers in the parish of Almeley were threatened with curtailment of their relief unless they went to the establishment.[30] In 1776, the workhouse could house forty paupers. In 1813, Kington maintained thirty-one inmates there. By 1832, the parish had closed the workhouse, deciding that giving paupers a weekly allowance was a cheaper option.[31]

A workhouse at Pembridge was in operation by 1763, when Thomas King was its keeper.[32] In 1776, the establishment could house thirty inmates. In 1812, the parish contracted with John Caldwell to run its workhouse for a period of three years.

Kington Poor Law Union was formed on 25 August 1836. Although the majority of its twenty-six member parishes lay in Radnorshire, the greater part of its population was in Herefordshire, where it was placed for Poor Law

The frontage of the former Ledbury Union workhouse.

administrative purposes. The new board of guardians met the following day and appointed a Building Committee to locate a site and obtain it for a workhouse. Advertisements were placed for plans for a building to house 150–250 persons. It was eventually decided to adopt the plans submitted by H.J. Whitling, which were based on the PLC's model 'square' plan (see page 26). In order to reduce costs, the design underwent a number of amendments, and the revised version, for 170 inmates, was approved by the PLC in December 1836, with tenders for the construction work invited soon afterwards.[33] The following year, the workhouse was erected at the east side of Kingswood Road, to the south of Kington (SO298558).

In 1900–01, a detached infirmary was erected at the south of the workhouse. During the early part of the First World War it was used as a Red Cross hospital. In December 1917, the workhouse received inmates from the Knighton Union, which had been also taken over by the Red Cross.[34]

In 1906, a new water supply was connected to the site at a cost of £1,600. In 1920, electric lighting was installed, and a radio provided by voluntary subscription.[35]

In 1930, the site was taken over by Herefordshire Council and became a PAI. After 1948, it became Kingswood Hall old people's home and was rebuilt in about 1962, retaining only the old infirmary. Modern housing now covers the site.

LEDBURY

Ledbury had a workhouse from 1733.[36] In 1776, it could house up to 100 inmates, and in 1813, the parish maintained forty-five paupers there. It stood between Back Lane (now Church Street) and Church Lane (SO711377), and part was later used as a boys' school.[37] Inmates were sent out each day to work for farmers or other local employers. Some worked at Mr Watts' pin factory, which was attached to the workhouse. In the years 1815–18, the workhouse was increasingly afflicted by problems caused by the financial impropriety or incompetence of its managers and their lax supervision of the inmates, many of whom were viewed as malingerers. The soaring cost of running the workhouse eventually led to its closure in November 1818.[38]

A property known as Perrins Cottage (SO645414), on the A417 at the south of Ashperton, is said to have once housed the parish's workhouse.[39]

The 1881 census identifies a property at Colwall Stone, Colwall, as the Old Workhouse.[40]

Ledbury Poor Law Union was formed on 2 June 1836, with twenty-two member parishes. A new union workhouse for 150 inmates was built in 1836–37 to the north-west of the town on what is now Orchard Lane (SO707381). The architect was George Wilkinson, whose design followed the PLC's model 'square' plan (see page 26). In January 1837, with building work nearing completion, James Hughes and his wife Ann were appointed as master and matron. Each of the union's parishes was requested to bring its paupers to the workhouse, 'properly clean', on specified mornings in the last week of February.[41]

Mr and Mrs Hughes were soon succeeded by William and Sarah Dyer, the first of numerous staff changes that took place over the next decade. This was perhaps a reflection of the Ledbury guardians' particularly zealous scrutiny of the workhouse's operation and management. The guardians were also unusual in their attitude towards illegitimate children, in that they preferred to flout official policy and take the cheaper option of giving their mothers out-relief rather than requiring them to enter the workhouse. In 1838, the board also decided that when such children reached the age of 7, out-relief payments would end but their mothers could let their children be received into the workhouse.[42]

Staff problems reached a low point in 1849 when the master and matron, William and Mary Benwell, were forced to resign after just three months in the post, along with the schoolmistress, Amelia Hickman. All three had become regular companions in beer drinking, both inside the workhouse and outside, including sessions before breakfast. Hickman had also been seen leaving the Benwells' private quarters, sometimes straightening her apron as she left.[43]

After 1904, for birth registration purposes, the workhouse was identified as 1 Belle Orchard, Ledbury.[44]

In 1930, the site was taken over by Herefordshire Council and renamed Belle Orchard House PAI. After 1948, it became Belle Orchard House old people's home, replaced in 1977 by a new building on an adjacent site. The workhouse's central hub and inner cross-ranges have been demolished and the surviving sections are now in private residential use.

LEOMINSTER

A workhouse existed in Leominster from about 1729.[45] From 1759, it occupied the infirmary section of the ancient priory, to the north-east of the town centre (SO499593). In 1832, the inmates comprised thirteen males and ten females, aged from below 1 year to over 60.

In 1761, John Preece received £12 a year for operating a workhouse in Monkland. By 1795, James East's payment for the undertaking had risen to £30. In 1821, after deciding to close the workhouse, the vestry agreed to hire a house 'to lodge poor people'.[46]

In 1776, Shobdon had a workhouse housing up to twenty inmates. Nine paupers were maintained there in 1803.

In the parish of Kimbolton, a pair of cottages at Lower Stockton is named the Old Workhouse (SO521608).

Kingsland had a workhouse by 1784, when Edward Stevens was contracted to 'take unto him the poor of the parish'.[47] A half-timbered building still known as The Poorhouse, was located on Longford (SO444615).

Hope-under-Dinmore's workhouse was active in 1797, indicated by the survival of the establishment's rules from that date.[48]

At Ivington, in the parish of Leominster Out, there was a workhouse in what is now Bury Cottages, just north-east of the church (SO475566).[49]

Leominster Poor Law Union was formed on 15 June 1836, with twenty-five constituent parishes. A union workhouse was constructed in 1836–38 based around the existing priory establishment. The architect was George Wilkinson, who incorporated the old building into a design that broadly followed the PLC's model 'square' plan (see page 26). A single-storey entrance block at the west of the workhouse contained the boardroom and clerk's office to the south, a waiting hall at the centre, and porter's room and receiving room to the north. Males were placed at the west of the site and females at the east. Children were housed

The former Leominster Union workhouse, now partly used as a youth hostel.

at the south of the site and the adults in the old priory building at the north. To the rear of the entrance block, the men's and boys' yards were separated by the boys' accommodation range. Running parallel to the entrance block were the chapel-cum-dining hall and boys' and girls' rooms. Girls' accommodation lay at the rear, separating the women's and girls' yards.[50]

In July 1846, inmate John Besley wrote to the PLC with numerous complaints against the long-serving master and matron, Thomas and Elizabeth Woolley. His accusations included that they had frequently treated inmates cruelly, served short rations at mealtimes, supplied their own sons with basket-loads of provisions and vegetables from the workhouse, and brewed beer on the premises. An inquiry by an Assistant Commissioner led to mild rebukes for the Woolleys and a suggestion that Besley might usefully be given out-relief.[51]

A Royal Commission report in 1909 described the workhouse as 'old and unsatisfactory' and the guardians as 'slack and uninterested and unintelligent'. One guardian, a publican, was said to have brought twenty-six drunken voters to the most recent election. At a board meeting, the one female guardian described her visit to the house of a dead pauper and found the body had been attacked by rats. A discussion about the board providing a mortuary ended after another guardian (the landlord of the house in question) intervened and said that the harm had been trifling. A tour of the workhouse revealed a large rat-hole in the boys' ground-floor dormitory. The bedclothes were not clean, and there were no pillowcases. The girls slept in double beds, their bath was dirty, and there were cockroaches in the basins, the latter dismissed by the matron who said there were always cockroaches in workhouses. Although the floors were well scrubbed and externals looked fairly clean, some of the cupboards were very dirty and the bedding in the babies' cots concealed stores of dirty food. In the sick wards, the nursing appeared insufficient – one mentally deficient patient was constantly disturbing the other patients and seemed in great discomfort, but was not removed on the grounds of economy. The accommodation for casuals was unsatisfactory: there was no bath in the women's ward, and they were locked in at night with no means of communication with outside. The matron maintained that there was a bell to the porter's lodge but it was shown to be broken. The master, newly appointed, seemed apathetic, with no real interest in his work. By 11.30 a.m. he had already had some beer, although the board was sitting.[52]

In 1930, the site became a PAI run by Herefordshire Council. It joined the NHS as the Old Priory Hospital, then from the 1980s was used as Herefordshire Council offices. In 2000, part of the building was taken over for use as a youth hostel.

In 1920, the union opened a children's home at 46 Etnam Street, Leominster, later known as Norfolk House Children's Home.[53] The property is now part of a retirement scheme.

ROSS

In 1728, the parish of Ross was bequeathed land on Dean Hill, with access to Corpse Cross Street (now Copse Cross Street, SO600239).[54] A workhouse was subsequently erected on the site and in 1776 could accommodate 100 inmates. In 1832, the workhouse – said to be only for the reception of the aged and infirm poor – was home to ten men, aged from 47 to 49; eight women, aged 30 to 78; two boys; and three girls. Those who were capable were employed in the domestic work of the house.[55]

In 1790 and 1799, the Bridstow vestry recorded agreements for the erection of a workhouse but it is unclear if it was ever built.[56] In 1804, the parish maintained four paupers in a workhouse.

Ruardean had a workhouse by 1803, when seven paupers were maintained there. In 1816, a married couple managed the establishment.[57]

In July 1811, 'a large dwelling-house, now used as a work-house, with a garden adjoining', at Hoarwithy, in the parish of Hentland, was put up for sale by auction.[58]

Overseers' accounts at Weston-under-Penyard indicate the operation of a workhouse there from 1814 onwards.[59] What is now The Hostelrie Hotel, at Goodrich (SO574194), served as the parish's workhouse from 1819.[60]

In 1803, Upton Bishop relieved eight paupers in a workhouse. A property in the parish, at Upton Crews (SO645271), is now a private residence known as the Old Workhouse.[61] The 1881 census identifies another Old Workhouse near the east end of Church Road, Howle Hill, Walford.[62] In 1838, the former workhouse at Peterstow was put up for sale.[63] A tithe map of 1842 locates a workhouse at Llangarron.[64]

Ross Poor Law Union was formed on 12 April 1836, with twenty-nine member parishes. In 1836–37, a new workhouse was erected on the Copse Cross Street site and extended onto adjacent land, with its entrance on Alton Street. Designed by John Plowman, it could accommodate 160 inmates. Due to various delays, the building did not come into use until January 1838. In the interim, the union made use of the Weston-under-Penyard and Upton Bishop workhouses. Teething problems with the new building's 'warming apparatus' led to the contractor suggesting that springs be fitted on the doors, as the

The only surviving part of the former Ross Union workhouse.

inmates habitually left them open.[65] The workhouse by then had a bakery, which supplied both the inmates and the union's outdoor poor.

By the 1860s, the workhouse was becoming overcrowded. In 1866, its accommodation for the sick was criticised as 'barely sufficient', with 'itch' (scabies) cases being housed in one of the receiving wards if there were also fever cases in the house.[66] A move to a new location was briefly considered but rebuilding on the existing site was eventually decided upon.

The new buildings, erected in 1872–73, were designed by Messrs Haddon Brothers of Hereford. The three-storey main block faced east and was based on the then popular corridor plan. The master and matron's quarters were at its centre, with men's and boys' accommodation at the north, and women's and girls' at the south. To the west of the main block stood the inmates' dining hall, the kitchens and the laundry. A children's playground and single-storey school-room also stood to the west of the main block. The Alton Street entrance was flanked at the west by administrative offices and receiving wards, and at the east by an infirmary and fever wards. The administrative block contained the guardians' boardroom, clerk's office and waiting room for relief applicants. The two-storey infirmary had a central section containing nurses' rooms and stairs, with a wing for males to the west and females to the east. A separate fever block stood at the east of the infirmary.[67] A casual ward was erected at the north of the site, with its own entrance from Dean Hill. It included both sleeping cells and labour cells, with six hammocks for 'one half of the male wards and the female wards to be supplied with bedsteads'.[68]

After 1904, for birth registration purposes, the workhouse was identified as 3 Alton Street, Ross-on-Wye.[69]

By 1914, the older inmates had mixed dayrooms and individual cubicles in their dormitories, and fixed mealtimes had been abandoned. Inmates even had trips to the local cinema every Saturday.[70]

In 1930, the establishment became a PAI under the control of Herefordshire Council. After 1948, as part of the NHS, it was known as Alton Street Hospital, later Dean Hill Hospital, providing care for people with learning disabilities. Most of the buildings were demolished in 1992, with only the administrative block on Alton Street retained as part of the new Ross Community Hospital.

WEOBLEY

Eardisland had a workhouse from 1761, when Thomas Owen received £6 6s a year, plus disbursements, to operate it. In 1776, when the establishment could hold fifteen inmates, John Miles was paid the princely sum of £60 to do the job. At one time, the paupers in the workhouse were occupied in spinning and weaving. In 1822, inmates were forbidden to keep a dog or fowls.[71] The workhouse building, said to be near an old house called Ruscote at the south-west of the village, survived until 1917, when it burned down.

In 1776, a workhouse for up to twenty inmates was in use at Dilwyn. A workhouse also existed at Woonton, in the parish of Almeley, where a garage now stands (SO351522).[72]

Weobley Poor Law Union was formed on 9 April 1836, with twenty-one member parishes. A new workhouse for eighty inmates was built in 1836–37, on what is now the B4230, to the north-west of Weobley (SO393521). George Wilkinson was appointed architect[73] and his design followed the PLC's model 'square' plan (see page 26). In October 1836, the guardians advertised for the supply of fifteen single and fifteen double wrought-iron bedsteads, for delivery at the workhouse in the second half of January 1837.[74] The following month, they invited plans and proposals for heating the building with warm water.[75]

On 21 August 1837, the new master of the workhouse, William Heathcote, with his wife Jane Frances Heathcote as matron, took up their posts and lived in the workhouse with ten of their twelve children. The following year, at the age of 45, William died at the workhouse after a short illness. His wife

Jane may have stayed on for some time as her two youngest children, Jesse and Emma, also died at the workhouse, one in January and the other in early February 1839.[76]

In 1867, the guardians invited tenders for the building of a fever ward at the workhouse.[77] In 1874, the guardians were authorised to spend £900 on the erection of sick wards at the south-east of the site.[78]

In 1908, the guardians agreed to receive children from the Bromyard Union into the workhouse in return for a weekly payment. However, the arrangement was soon halted by the LGB, who viewed the separation of women and children at Weobley as inadequate.[79]

After 1930, the site was taken over by Herefordshire Council and redesignated as a PAI. The site later became known as Whitehill House and housed offices for Weobley Rural District Council. The buildings are now in residential use.

The well-preserved structure of the former Weobley Union workhouse, now a listed building.

17

SHROPSHIRE
(SALOP)

ATCHAM (& SHREWSBURY)

Pontesbury established a workhouse in 1732, on what is now Brookside, at the foot of what became known as Workhouse Bank (SJ399059).[1] In 1776 it could house twenty inmates, and in 1813 the parish maintained twenty-two paupers there. They wove linen cloth, which was used as clothing for the outdoor poor. Despite a purge of its inmates in 1817, the workhouse's running costs were said to be ruinous end excessively expensive. The building was later converted to four cottages, now replaced by modern houses known as Birch Row.

Condover had a workhouse by 1741, when the closure of an existing establishment was noted. A new one was erected in 1769, probably in the grounds of Condover Hall. The parish maintained fourteen inmates there in 1802, and seventeen in 1813. It relocated in 1820 to a house on the Great Ryton Road (SJ490057).[2]

In 1750, Berrington contracted to board out its poor at the Wellington workhouse, but the experiment was not repeated.[3]

Cound had a workhouse from 1758 until 1795, its inmates being employed in cloth manufacture.[4]

In 1761, Westbury erected a workhouse on the Shrewsbury Road, to the east of the village (SJ360094), where the inmates were employed in spinning and weaving. In 1769, the parish began placing paupers at the Pontesbury workhouse. Westbury's workhouse was reopened from 1791 to 1801 and produced textiles such as linsey, stockings, table linen and bedcovers.[5]

Alberbury parish registers indicate that Alberbury township had a work-house by 1766.[6] In 1780, it stood at the north of the churchyard (SJ358149).[7] In 1813, the township maintained two paupers in a workhouse, and the par-ish's Wollaston Quarter maintained nine.

From around 1782, Cardeston leased a workhouse from the lord of the manor. Although its inmates spun and wove flax in 1786 and 1794, it was generally more like a poorhouse.[8]

In 1776, Leighton had a workhouse accommodating twenty inmates. In 1792, it joined the Montgomery and Pool Incorporation.

Ruckley had a poorhouse at the west of the village, now known as Duffy's Cottage (SJ532000).[9]

Bausley erected a workhouse in about 1779, funded by a loan of £165 from Alberbury's parish funds. At various times, workhouses were also in operation at Astley and Upton Magna.[10]

In 1792, Atcham and nine other parishes[11] were incorporated under a Local Act, gaining powers, among other things, to operate a common workhouse. The existing workhouse of one member parish, Cound, was briefly consid-ered for incorporation use, but was rejected as being unsuitable.[12] Instead, a new workhouse was erected at Cross Houses, in the parish of Berrington (SJ539076). The H-shaped building, designed by John Hiram Haycock, was three storeys high and constructed in red brick. The ground floor included the boardroom, dayrooms and school, while the upper floors contained dor-mitories and the master and matron's quarters. Females were housed at the south of the building and males at the north. The first inmates were received in November 1794.

Atcham Poor Law Union was formed on 18 November 1836, with forty-five member parishes, four of which lay in Montgomeryshire. The union took over and adapted the existing Cross Houses workhouse. In 1842, growing pressure on the inmates' accommodation led to use of the boardroom, school-master's room and nurses' room to increase the capacity of the workhouse to 240 places.[13]

A new infirmary was erected in 1850–51 to a design by Edward Haycock, son of the workhouse's original architect. It was erected at the rear of the main block and echoed its appearance, being an H-shaped red-brick build-ing, though only two storeys high at its east side. One other difference was in its arch-shaped windows, whose frames were made from an important local product, cast iron.[14]

In 1871, the union absorbed the parishes belonging to the recently dissolved Shrewsbury Incorporation and was renamed the Atcham and Shrewsbury

The Atcham Union (formerly Incorporation) workhouse and chapel in about 1916.

Union. The Cross Houses workhouse was then considerably enlarged, taking its capacity to 550 inmates. Three-storey wings were added to each side of the main block. The original section was then used to house the aged inmates, while the side-wings contained schoolrooms, playrooms and dormitories for the boys and girls. The 1850 infirmary was adapted to accommodate the able-bodied inmates, with an infants' room and cook's stores on the women's side, and a workshop and coal store on the men's. A dining hall and kitchens were constructed linking the former infirmary to the main block – the plans included a 'tramway' running from the dining hall serving area through to the infirmary. In about 1872, a new infirmary was erected at the north of the orig-inal buildings. Fever wards were erected at the west of the new infirmary, and a block containing a porter's lodge and casual wards at the site entrance. A chapel was built in front of the main block, slightly skewed from the normal east–west orientation so that its entrance door faced the workhouse. In 1896, new receiving wards and vagrant cells were added at the west of the site entrance. In 1903, a nurses' home was erected at the west of the site, and a matron's house at the north-east of the 1872 infirmary.[15]

At an inspection in 1909, the inmates included seventy-five children, of whom twenty-two were illegitimate, and 100 cases in the infirmary. The site was noted as being in open country and included many acres of garden and fields. The infants were all happily playing in a hay field and in hot weather had their meals outdoors. The large kitchen garden provided healthy occupation to the old men, who were able to work a little. The infirm and convalescent sick were seated in wide courtyards outdoors, enjoying the sun and the air. The atmosphere of dreary desolation, common in town workhouses, was remarkably absent. There were only nine men on the workhouse's able-bodied diet, and of those only one was fit for stone breaking. The master suggested that this was due to the introduction of sawing wood as a labour task, which had practically emptied the house of able-bodied men. The inspector's one criticism was that the cells in the casual ward, which were only about 4 feet by 8 feet, were each used to accommodate two tramps in wooden bunks placed close together.[16]

During the First World War, the workhouse was home to Berrington War Hospital. After reverting to civilian use, it became the Poor Law Hospital for Shropshire, renamed Cross Houses Hospital in 1948. It was later used as offices by the Shropshire Health Authority. In 2004, the site was redeveloped with only the original main building, the 1850 infirmary and the chapel surviving.

In 1908, the union began using scattered homes in Shrewsbury. They included 'Leedale' on Underdale Road, 'Grasmere' on London Road, 'Besford House' and 'Belle Vue House' on Trinity Street, and 'Pen-y-Bont' on Betton Street. There was a receiving home at 143 Abbey Foregate.

BRIDGNORTH

Worfield had a workhouse from 1729, when it was said to 'frighten some of the idle into industry'.[17] In 1776, the establishment could house twelve inmates. At one time it occupied part of what are now cottages and a post office on the village main street (SO758956). In 1832, it was home to fifteen women, one man, seven children and 'an idiot, aged 30'. At that date, the workhouse was said to be so comfortable that the poor of the adjoining parish tried to gain settlement there, and one former inmate later chose to pay to lodge there.[18]

In 1776, Claverley's workhouse could house twenty inmates. A new workhouse was erected in 1818.[19] An L-shaped building at the south side of the Bull Ring was formerly the workhouse (SO792933).[20]

In 1789, the Bridgnorth parish of St Mary Magdalene erected a workhouse on Bernard's (or Barnet) Hill, Lower Town (SO721928). In 1832, the inmates comprised five females, three of whom were children, and six males, all of whom were former labourers or servants. The building still exists, now converted to private residential use.

Bridgnorth's other parish, St Leonard's, had a workhouse at the west side of the North Gate (SO715933) and linked to the parish's House of Correction.[21] In 1740, John Jolley of Nantwich was contracted to manage the parish's poor there. In 1832, the inmates were fourteen adults and three children.

In 1813, the parish of Chetton maintained eleven paupers in a workhouse.[22]

Morville's workhouse was at Morville Heath (SO682936). Built in Elizabethan times and once used as almshouses, the building is now derelict.

Bridgnorth Poor Law Union was formed on 31 May 1836, with twenty-nine member parishes. Initially, the union retained four existing workhouses: two at Bridgnorth, one at Quatt, and the other at Chetton, which was closed after a few months. The able-bodied were placed in St Leonard's, where a former sergeant major was appointed as master, and the elderly and infirm were housed at St Mary Magdalene.[23] The children were accommodated at Quatt, the establishment subsequently developing as a farm school and then as a District School (see page 265).

In 1848–49, the union erected a new workhouse on Innage Lane, at the north of the Bridgnorth (SO714934). The PLC authorised an expenditure of up to £4,000 on the building, which was to accommodate up to 200 inmates. The architects may have been the local firm of Griffiths and Penzer, who did other work for the union at that period.[24] Unlike the plain appearance of many earlier union workhouses, the Bridgnorth guardians chose an elegant, Tudor-style frontage, resulting in the final cost being about £5,300. The main building, at the south of the site, had an E-shaped layout, with offices and guardians' boardroom at the centre, and male and female inmates' accommodation to each side. A dining hall and kitchen were located at the rear of the centre. Later additions to the buildings included an infectious block in 1875, an infirmary, and a casual ward at the east of the site.

In 1930, the site became a PAI run by Salop Council. It subsequently became a residential home for the elderly known as Innage House. In 1994, the surviving buildings, renamed Andrew Evans House, reopened after being converted to flats.

CHURCH STRETTON

Church Stretton had a workhouse from about 1710. It stood on the west side of the High Street, where the Silvester Horne Institute now stands (SO452936).[25] In 1776, it could house sixty-six inmates, but in 1832 had none, though was said to sometimes have a few.

The unusually stylish façade of the former Bridgnorth Union workhouse.

A view from the south-east of the former Church Stretton workhouse main block during its demolition in 1959. (Courtesy of Shropshire Archives, ref. PH/C/19/5/142)

Cardington erected a poorhouse in the 1790s, thought to be at the south-west of the village. In 1803, the inmates totalled five, of whom three were aged over 60 and disabled.[26]

A former farmhouse at Hatton, in the parish of Eaton-under-Heywood, once served as a workhouse (SO467902). Later becoming the Blue Bell Inn, the property is a now known as Hatton Cottage.[27] The parish also used a property at Soudley as a workhouse.[28]

A workhouse existed in the parish of Wistanstow.[29]

Church Stretton Poor Law Union was created on 20 July 1836, with fourteen member parishes. The union initially retained existing workhouses in Church Stretton, Wistanstow and Soudley. Plans were commissioned from Edward Blakeway Smith for rebuilding the Church Stretton workhouse on the existing site. In 1837, however, following local pressure for the establishment to be moved out of the town, the guardians purchased a long, narrow site at Little Ashbrook, on the Shrewsbury Road to the north of the town (SO455942). Advertisements were placed for new plans for a workhouse to hold between 100 and 120 inmates. The chosen design was by one of the guardians, Thomas D. Duppa, although Edward Blakeway Smith appears to have made a significant contribution to its being put into practice.[30] The building was completed early in 1839. The following year, the old High Street building was sold and converted into two cottages.

The new building's design was a variation on Sampson Kempthorne's model 'square' plan (see page 26) although the entrance block, central cruciform section and rear infirmary were all separated. Males were housed at the north of the site and females at the south.

In 1867, it was reported that other than mothers of illegitimate children, there were rarely any able-bodied inmates. At the same time, the aged and infirm and children were very well cared for.[31]

New tramp wards were erected in 1884 at the east of the workhouse. In 1891–92, a new infirmary designed by A.B. Deakin was added at the north of the tramp wards.

In 1930, the site became a forty-bed PAI run by Salop Council. Part of the building was used as a children's home and for a period also housed 'mental defectives'. The institution closed in 1939 and the buildings were demolished in about 1959. St Lawrence Primary School now occupies the site, with only the 1891 infirmary surviving as swimming pool changing rooms.

CLEOBURY MORTIMER

Cleobury Mortimer opened a workhouse in about 1737 at an isolated location to the north-west of the town (SO670763). In 1776, the L-shaped, two-storey building could hold sixty inmates. In 1796, inmate Mary Morriss died after fifty years in residence.[32]

Workhouses were in operation at Neen Savage by 1784[33] and at Milson by 1790.[34]

Kinlet had a workhouse by 1803.[35] It was located at Buttonbridge.[36] In 1832, its twelve inmates comprised 'the Assistant Overseer and his Wife, an old married pair, 3 sickly women, and 1 idle young labourer with his wife and 3 children'.

Farlow's parish workhouse was at the west side of Oreton Common (SO639800). The property is still known as The Workhouse. The parish of Rock also operated a workhouse, which the 1851 census suggests was in the vicinity of Far Forest Village Hall (SO729745).[37]

Cleobury Mortimer Poor Law Union was formed on 15 July 1836, its seventeen member parishes drawn from Shropshire, Herefordshire and Worcestershire. The union adopted the existing Cleobury Mortimer workhouse, and in 1837 the PLC authorised the relatively modest expenditure of £450 on its enlargement. The additions involved extending the existing side wing at the north of the building and erecting a matching side wing at the south, creating a U-shaped building. Internal work included the construction of additional staircases and divisions to allow segregation of the different classes of inmates. The rear yard was also divided into male and female parts, each with a three-seater privy. Males were housed at the north side of the building and females at the south.

In 1839, the front range, which contained a schoolroom, was extended to the south to provide a boardroom on its ground floor.[38] In 1849, a separate block was erected at the west of the workhouse. It contained a brewhouse, cleansing house, vagrants' wards, receiving wards, refractory wards and a mortuary.[39] The area between the two buildings was divided into separate airing yards for the different classes of inmate.

The site was taken over in 1930 by Salop Council and put up for sale. From August 1932 until September 1936, the buildings were used as a youth hostel known as Styper House. At the start of the Second World War, the premises served as a camp for refugees from Europe.

The former workhouse buildings have all been demolished and a caravan park now occupies the site.

CLUN

Bishop's Castle had a workhouse by 1776, when it could accommodate twenty-five inmates. In 1797, the establishment, on Church Street, was run by a contractor and had fourteen inmates, who were chiefly 'old, infirm and insane'.[40]

Lydham also had a workhouse by 1776, when it could hold twelve inmates.

Clun had a workhouse that occupied a former malthouse on the north side of the river (SO301808). It was accessed by a path to the left of what is now 23 High Street.

Lydbury North's workhouse was a large, part half-timbered building at the west of the village, now two houses known as Tudor Cottage and Gravenor House (SO 350860).[41] In 1832, the establishment had fifteen inmates: eight females, aged from 5 to 60 years, and seven males, aged from 4 to 66 years.

Clun Poor Law Union came into being on 18 July 1836, with nineteen member parishes. Initially, the union took over the existing workhouses at Clun and Bishop's Castle, the latter used to house children. At the time of the 1841 census, the Clun workhouse was being run by Joseph and Mary Brown. The thirty-five inmates ranged in age from 6 months to 65 years. The Bishop's Castle workhouse was in the charge of a relieving officer, William Robertson, with twenty boys and thirteen girls among its thirty-five inmates.[42]

At first there was some reluctance on the part of the guardians to build a new workhouse. Eventually, in 1841, the guardians acquired a site for a new building at what was then known as Potter's Close, Bishop's Castle (SO322888). This was despite opposition from the parish of Clun, which wished to be the administrative centre of the union that carried its name.

The design for the new workhouse for 150 inmates was by H.J. Whitling, but the scheme was beset by problems. There were delays in getting the plans approved by the PLC; the guardians' vice-chairman was found to have 'borrowed' money advanced to pay the builder; and Whitling made unauthorised changes to the design, eventually leaving the country in embarrassment.[43] Another architect, Edward Haycock, completed the project and the workhouse was finally opened towards the end of 1844. Its layout was based on the PLC's model 'square' plan (see page 26), with its entrance on what is now Union Road. Females were housed at the south of the site and males at the north. No separate sick wards were included in the design.

In January 1846, brother and sister Francis and Mary Anne Williams were appointed as workhouse master and matron. Within a few months, the master's conduct and competence were raising concerns – his transgressions included being absent without leave and turning the men's yard into a poultry yard, with

An early 1900s view of Cleobury Mortimer Union workhouse and its extensive vegetable gardens.

The east front of Stone House, the former Clun Union workhouse at Bishop's Castle in 1964. (Courtesy of Shropshire Archives, ref. PH/B/16/12/11)

birds and bread and water everywhere. Williams resigned soon afterwards but two weeks later was found in bed in the workhouse, having cut his own throat.[44]

After 1904, for birth registration purposes, the workhouse was identified as Stone House, Clun.

In 1930, the site was taken over by Salop Council and became Stone House PAI, later a geriatric hospital, which closed in 1964. The old buildings were demolished soon afterwards. A hospital and care home now occupy the site.

DRAYTON

A workhouse was operating in Market Drayton (formerly known as Drayton in Hales) by 1735.[45] In 1739, a trust was set up under the will of the former vicar, Richard Price, to fund the instruction of poor children and other benevolent activities. By 1757, a workhouse financed by Price's legacy existed at the south side of Shropshire Street, Little Drayton, at its junction with what is now The Old Armoury (SJ672339).[46] In 1776, it could house seventy-five inmates. The building was enlarged in 1788. The inmates were engaged in farm work, spinning and oakum picking. In 1829, they numbered thirty-five, at which date the establishment had only fifteen beds.[47]

At Child's Ercall (Ercall Parva), plans were being made for a workhouse in 1732.[48] In 1735, however, the parish was sharing the Market Drayton workhouse, and in 1803 it was sharing a workhouse with Spoonley, a hamlet in Adderley parish.

In 1776, Hodnet had a workhouse for up to twenty paupers, which was used by twenty-six in 1803. It stood on the west side of what is now Webster's Lane (SJ620280).

Mucklestone had a parish workhouse at Ireland's Cross, near Dorrington. The plain brick structure adjoined four tenements known as The Almshouses.[49] It was unused in 1803, but the parish maintained two workhouse inmates in 1813.

Stoke-upon-Tern had a workhouse on a site of 2 or 3 acres, where nine paupers were maintained in 1803, and nineteen in 1813.[50]

Drayton Poor Law Union was formed on 3 October 1836, with twelve member parishes. Initially, the union took over the Shropshire Street workhouse, which was enlarged to house 100 inmates. Use was also briefly made of the old workhouses at Spoonley and Hodnet, and an old workhouse at Cheswardine was rented for a few months but never used.

In 1838, to allow for further expansion at Shropshire Street, the guardians purchased a neighbouring block of cottages at the west of the workhouse.

Plans for additions and alterations were then prepared by Samuel Pountney Smith to provide for the accommodation of a total of 207 inmates. Pountney Smith, who was also a building contractor, carried out the construction work, which cost £1,120. Further development of the original building was hindered by the guardians' inability to obtain freehold ownership of the site, which was vested in Richard Price's charitable trust. Eventually, in 1849, plans began to be formulated for a completely new workhouse.[51]

In 1851, a 5-acre site was purchased at Little Drayton Common, on the south side of Buntingsdale Road (SJ661334). A competition for plans was won by Thomas Denville Barry, but the construction cost of his original design proved beyond the guardians' budget. A much-pruned version, accommodating just 128 inmates, was eventually adopted.

The workhouse was based on the model 'square' design (see page 26) but lacked the usual entrance block, so that the building's octagonal hub and side-wings became its frontage. The hub, which had axial corridors running

A 1965 view of the frontage of Quarry House, the former Drayton Union workhouse. (Courtesy of Shropshire Archives, ref. PH/M/6/19/10)

through it, contained receiving wards to the front and master's quarters to the rear. The west wing contained a boy's day school and able-bodied men's dayrooms, with dormitories above. The east wing included similar accommodation for women and girls. The north wing housed the kitchens. Blocks for aged paupers and isolation wards were at the rear.[52]

New vagrant wards designed by George A. Craig were erected in 1898. The following year, a new infirmary, also by Craig, was added at the north-east of the workhouse. It had a two-storey central portion and single-storey wings at each side.[53]

A report in 1909 described the workhouse as: 'a very comfortable one, well ventilated and very clean'. There was a farm connected with the workhouse, managed by the master and worked by the inmates, which supplied the house with milk and vegetables. The staff then comprised the master and matron (married), labour master and mistress (married), one trained nurse, cook and laundress.[54]

After 1930, the workhouse was taken over by Salop Council and became the Quarry House PAI, later Welfare Home, which closed in around 1990. A housing estate now occupies the site. The Shropshire Street building, later used as a drill hall, survived until 1967.

ELLESMERE

Ellesmere had a parish workhouse by about 1733, where the inmates were occupied in spinning and weaving. From 1781, the parish's poor were farmed by a contractor who could profit from any productive work by the inmates.[55]

By 1776, Baschurch had a workhouse that could accommodate six inmates.

In 1791, following the path taken by Shrewsbury seven years earlier, the parishes of Ellesmere, Baschurch, Myddle and Hordley, plus the chapelry of Hadnall, were incorporated under a Local Act and erected a House of Industry at Swan Hill, Ellesmere (SJ404355), which opened in January 1795. Like Shrewsbury's establishment, it had a three-storey, H-shaped main building constructed in red brick, though only 150 feet in length compared to Shrewsbury's 180 feet. Males were accommodated in the west wing and females in the east wing, which also contained a chapel.[56] A block at the north of the workhouse was probably an infirmary. A graveyard lay at the north-west of the site.

In November 1795, the inmates comprised fifty women, thirty-four men and 114 children. All their clothing was manufactured in the house. Flannels were also made for sale, and a hop-bag manufacture had been started. Special apartments were provided for persons of good character judged to have unde-servedly fallen into reduced circumstances. All the inmates dined together, however. According to Eden, 'notwithstanding the promised advantages, it is said that the incorporated parishes are in general now heartily sorry they ever engaged in the erection of a House of Industry'.[57]

The parishes' sorrow was presumably due to the failure of the establishment to produce the expected financial savings. Apart from the initial cost of the site, building, furnishing and legal expenses, which totalled £7,000, the pro-jected annual expenses amounted to £3,500 – over twice as much as under the previous system.[58] In 1795, perhaps reflecting this situation, it appears that Baschurch made an agreement to erect a workhouse on Nobold.[59]

In 1832, the House of Industry's inmates comprised eighty-two males and eighty-one females, their ages ranging from 1 week to 89 years. The able-bodied males were employed either in cultivating the institution's land or in manufacturing clothing for the use of inmates. The less capable were occupied in picking oakum. The boys were taught weaving, shoemaking or tailoring. The women were employed in washing, ironing, sewing, baking, cleaning the house, cooking, and attending to the sick, while the girls were taught to sew and knit stockings for the inmates' use.[60]

In 1803, the Flintshire parish of Overton maintained twenty-three pau-

The entrance to the Ellesmere Union workhouse in about 1920.

pers in a workhouse. In 1832, the establishment, located at Lightwood Green (SJ385406), was described as a 'very small and incommodious' brick cottage. Despite this, places there were also rented by Bangor (Flintshire), Worthenbury, Halghton and Penley. The house was said to be little used, but its threat was effective in deterring relief claimants. The paupers were farmed out at 2*s* a week to a contractor, who was also provided with the house and a few acres of land rent free. He also benefited from all the labour he could extract from the inmates, who were mostly children and the aged. The contractor was a brickmaker and any paupers who were capable assisted him in the manufacture. Otherwise, there was virtually no regulation of the inmates in the establishment.[61] The building is now a private residence.

On 14 November 1836, the incorporation was replaced by the Ellesmere Poor Law Union. Its nine member parishes and townships included five previously in the incorporation. In March 1837, a further eight Flintshire parishes were added. The union took over the incorporation workhouse, which then housed 350 inmates.

After inspecting the workhouse in June 1869, the PLB found it 'highly objectionable' that most of the adult males slept two to a bed. The guardians were requested to provide an adequate number of single beds.[62] In the same year, new tramp wards were erected.

Unlike most other workhouses in the county, Ellesmere did not become a PAI in 1930 but was closed and demolished soon afterwards.

LUDLOW

In the 1670s, a property known as Lane's House (later Lane's Asylum), at Old Street, Ludlow (SO513744), was converted into a workhouse for employing the town's poor in making serges and woollen cloths.[63] In 1776, it could hold forty inmates. In 1788, the establishment was 'a dismal, neglected house, in which … the poor of that parish and ten others were farmed'.[64] In 1828, the inmates were being with provided with flax and hemp, wool for spinning and knitting stockings, and leather for making shoes.[65] The premises comprised a central half-timbered house and a building at each side, that to the north not now surviving.

In 1835, the Ludlow Overseers advertised for plans for a plain, two-storey workhouse to accommodate 100 paupers.[66] Although the scheme appears not to have progressed, an 1835 directory locates a workhouse on Gaolford (now Upper/Lower Galdeford), with Samuel Oliver as its master.[67]

A house on Roman Road, at the southern end of Leintwardine (SO404737), served as the parish's poorhouse, later converted to a workhouse.[68]

Corfton, in the parish of Diddlebury, had a workhouse by 1787 that was still in use in 1836.[69]

Ludlow Poor Law Union came into being on 15 July 1836, a quarter of its thirty-two member parishes lying in Herefordshire. The Ludlow guardians inherited the existing workhouses in Ludlow, Leintwardine and Corfton, with the latter then being closed. A plan was briefly considered for converting the Leintwardine premises into the union's workhouse. However, it was soon decided that a completely new building was required. Land was acquired at the junction of New Road and Gravel Hill in Ludlow (SO514753) and advertisements placed for plans for an establishment to hold 250 inmates. The chosen submission, by local architect Matthew Stead, was based on the PLC's model 'square' plan (see page 26), though with an unusually substantial entrance block, a two-storey infirmary linked to the main building, separate accommodation for lunatics and for elderly married couples, and the provision of central heating. The yards between the building's four wings were each to be divided diagonally, creating eight in total. Stead's initially assessment of the construction cost was just over £2,000. Two months later, however, he amended his estimate to be nearer £4,500. The guardians instructed him to revise his design to reduce the cost, with stone being used instead of the originally proposed brick construction. John Collins of Leominster was awarded the building contract at £3,070.[70] It soon became apparent that Collins lacked the skill or experience for such a big job and the work began to overrun. Changes to the plans, such as installing open fires instead of the central heating, and reinstating a cupola over the central hub, led to further costs and delays. When the first inmates moved in, in May 1839, the total cost had risen to £6,750.[71]

The Ludlow guardians, mostly farmers and Anglican clergymen, were notably penny-pinching and strict in their outlook. Inmates performing demanding duties such as nursing the sick were denied the ration of beer or extra food that was customarily provided in other workhouses. On more than one occasion, the board voted to reduce the salaries of its officers, only to be overruled by the central authority.[72]

Despite regular outbreaks of infectious diseases such as measles, diphtheria and 'the itch' (scabies), the guardians were reluctant to provide separate accommodation for such cases. Eventually, in 1874, a new sixteen-bed 'infectious hospital' was erected at the south-west of the workhouse. In 1883, the infirmary was extended and a new mortuary and piggeries erected.[73] In 1904, the

The entrance to the former Ludlow Union workhouse, now the local
community hospital.

guardians sought tenders for the construction of vagrants' cells, in 1906 for a
further extension of the infirmary, and in 1907 for a new receiving ward and
nurses' rooms.

After 1930, the workhouse was taken over by Salop Council and became a
PAI. In 1948, it joined the NHS as East Hamlet Hospital. The surviving part of
the building now forms part of Ludlow Community Hospital.

MADELEY

Much Wenlock had a workhouse by 1731. It was a rented stone building on
the north side of Downs Lane, just beyond Farley Brook (SJ625001), and in
1776 could hold thirty paupers. From 1788, an apothecary was retained to
attend workhouse inmates. In 1793, all twenty-seven inmates were women
or children. The older pauper children were usually apprenticed to Lancashire
cotton mills.[74] In 1832, there were six men, six women and eight children in
residence, the men being employed in road mending.

By 1734, Broseley had a workhouse at the south side of Harris's Green
(SJ672018). In 1776, it could house forty inmates. In 1813, seventy-five of the
parish's poor were workhouse residents.

Little Wenlock had a poorhouse by 1750. It also began farming its poor with Thomas Hazlehurst, a contractor with his own premises in Wellington. By 1814, the parish had its own workhouse at the south side of Coalmoor Road at Little Worth (SJ652069). Sixteen paupers were maintained there in 1814–15.

From around 1766, the poor of Madeley were farmed by a contractor who operated a workhouse at Madeley Wood. In the 1780s, the parish took over direct responsibility for its indoor poor. A new workhouse costing £1,000 was erected in 1796–97 at the Brockholes, now Belmont Road, to the east of Ironbridge (SJ677035). It was referred to as a House of Industry, indicating that the inmates were expected to engage in productive labour. An advertisement for its first manager specified that he should have some knowledge of manufacturing coarse linens and woollens.[75] In 1803, forty-four paupers were maintained in the establishment. In 1832, the inmates comprised seven men, thirteen women and twenty children.

In 1776, a parish workhouse for twelve inmates was in operation at Buildwas. It occupied a timber-framed cottage at what is now 2 Leighton Road (SJ629049).

In the early 1800s, Benthall established a House of Industry at Mine Spout, on the present-day Spout Lane (SJ668028). In 1813, eighteen paupers were maintained there. The property is now known as The Croft.

The entrance (left of centre) and boardroom (centre-right) of the influential Madeley Union workhouse.

From about 1784, Dawley had a workhouse in a rented property. In 1813, the parish purchased premises for its own House of Industry on the west side of Dawley Green Lane, now Bank Road (SJ686080, later occupied by the Rising Sun Inn).[76] In the same year, thirty-six of its paupers received workhouse relief.

Madeley Poor Law Union was formed on 6 June 1836 and comprised twelve member parishes. The union initially retained the workhouses at the Brockholes and at Broseley, the latter being used to house the elderly. Broseley was closed in 1838 but reopened in 1842 during a surge in unemployment in the area. Thereafter, it was chiefly used as an out-relief station.

In 1849, children in the workhouse were being taught in the boardroom and the schoolmaster was described as an 'infirm cripple'.[77] In the same year, the union joined the new South East Shropshire School District and began making use of its school at Quatt (see page 265).

Despite regular complaints by the PLB about defects in the accommodation at the Brockholes, the guardians did little more than make minor alterations and piecemeal repairs. In 1863, one of the union's own medical officers, F.H. Hartshorne, reported that the workhouse was poor and dilapidated. The only toilet facilities were four wretched privies in the yards and the only means of washing was out of galvanised buckets in the dayroom.[78] Another report in 1867 concluded that the premises were 'in all essential respects unsuitable for occupation as a workhouse'.[79] Eventually, in 1868, the PLB ordered the closure of the Brockholes workhouse and so forced the guardians' hand.

A new workhouse was erected in 1871–75 at a site on Beech Road, just to the north of Ironbridge (SJ674039). It was designed by G.C. Haddon and was the first entire workhouse to adopt the pavilion-block principle. It was constructed in pink-brown brick decorated with yellow, red and blue brickwork. A long front block had an entrance archway at its centre. To the rear, a central pavilion contained a kitchen at its north end and a chapel at the south. The central block was flanked by the inmates' pavilions, with males housed at the east and females at the west. An infirmary was placed at the north-east of the site.[80]

In July 1898, it was reported that the workhouse inmates had to eat their meals in silence, the master stating that this was the custom in all such institutions.[81] There was, in fact, no official rule requiring silence at mealtimes, only that 'decorum' be maintained.

After 1904, for birth registration purposes, the workhouse was identified as 'The Beeches'.[82]

After 1930, the workhouse became Ironbridge PAI, accommodating the chronic sick and cases of epilepsy. After 1948, it joined the NHS as Beeches Hospital, then became the Lincoln Grange care home for the elderly. In 2018, after a decade of standing empty, the buildings were converted to residential use.

The surviving part the old Brockholes building is now a private residence.

NEWPORT

In 1748, Newport was using a workhouse in Wellington run by the contractor Thomas Hazlehurst.[83] The parish had its own workhouse from 1755 in a leased property in Norbroom.[84] In 1776, the workhouse could accommodate eight-een inmates. It subsequently occupied premises at the south side of Workhouse Lane, now 34–40 Vineyard Road (SJ747194). In 1832, the inmates comprised nine females, aged from 9 to 80 years, and five males, aged from infancy to 74 years. The males included two former tradesmen and one 'idiot'. The build-ing, now three cottages, had unusually high ceilings, perhaps providing for the use of looms.[85]

By 1776, Edgmond had a workhouse for up to sixteen paupers.[86] In 1825, a local magistrate, Thomas Leeke, inspected the establishment and found it in a very bad state, with a leaky roof letting rain into the bedrooms, windows with-out glass, and missing floorboards. The twenty inmates, nine of whom were children with their parents, were filthy, badly clothed, starved and idle. There were insufficient beds and bedding – a young woman who had been sickly for some months slept on the floor with just sheet and blanket and straw beneath her. There was no resident superintendent.[87] In 1832, the inmates comprised twelve females aged from 1 to 8 years, and nine males from 6 to 72 years. The 1841 census identifies the 'Old Workhouse' as located on the Shrewsbury Road, between the New Inn and Lamb Inn.[88] In 1778, a workhouse was referred to in the Edgmond township of Pickstock.[89]

In 1776, Forton's workhouse could hold ten inmates. It had ceased use by 1803.

The High Offley workhouse accommodated up to thirty paupers in 1776, but was unused in 1803 and 1813.

Gnosall's first workhouse, in 1733, was a converted barn. From 1738, its limited capacity resulted in some paupers being sent to the workhouse at Penkridge. In 1774, Gnosall erected a new workhouse at the bottom of the High Street, where it meets Stafford Road (SJ828206). In 1783, the parish purchased an additional property for the purpose at the south of the church, later the site of a school, now a day nursery (SJ829208). It had nine inmates in 1803 and thirty-five in 1813. The governor from 1823, Thomas Betteley, is buried at the north side of the church-yard. The 1774 building was replaced in 1832 by two almshouses.[90]

Tibberton had a workhouse by 1803, when it maintained four paupers there.[91]

There was a workhouse in Lilleshall village by 1804. In 1810, it relocated to premises owned by the Duke of Sutherland at the east side of what is now School Road, Donnington (SJ709140). It had forty-nine inmates in 1817 and was then enlarged.[92]

Chetwynd was employing a workhouse by 1813, when the parish relieved nine paupers there.

Newport Poor Law Union was formed on 5 October 1836, with six of its sixteen parishes lying in Staffordshire. The union decided to adopt the exist-ing workhouse in Newport for the able-bodied and young children, and that at Gnosall for the aged, infirm and older children. However, both buildings required considerable repair and improvement, and while that was being car-ried out, use was made of the old parish premises at Chetwynd and Lilleshall.

In December 1839, James Betteley, the governor at Gnosall and probably Thomas's son, was dismissed for financial irregularities. The Assistant Poor Law Commissioner for the area, William Day, subsequently visited Gnosall and found the workhouse to be dirty, the children louse-ridden, and their educa-tion very unsatisfactory – their teacher, 68-year-old Mary Sage, was said to be querulous and decrepit and was not teaching the children writing or arithme-tic as required by official regulations. Rather put out by Day's complaints, the guardians recorded that in their opinion, the children ought not to be taught writing and arithmetic.[93]

In 1854, under growing pressure from the PLB, the guardians agreed to build a new general workhouse in Newport to replace both the existing establishments. In the interim, the children were removed from the 'wretched' building at Gnosall to the Stafford workhouse.[94]

A 3-acre site was acquired on Long Marsh Lane, now Audley Avenue (SJ751187). The building was designed and constructed by John Cobb, a local architect and builder, although Edward Haycock was also credited as having certified its completion in May 1856. The two-storey red-brick front range had a central section containing the entrance, porter's lodge, committee room, and master and matron's quarters. Female inmates were accommodated to the left and males to the right. To the rear of the centre, a single-storey central spine housed the dining hall and kitchen. This connected to a single-storey range, running parallel to the road, which contained stores, together with laun-dry facilities on the women's side and a dayroom on the men's side.[95]

The Audley Avenue frontage of the former Newport Union workhouse.

Casual wards were added at the rear of the site in 1873. A twenty-nine-bed infirmary, designed by Fleeming & Son, was opened at the east of the workhouse in 1908 at a cost £3,100.

In 1930, the workhouse became a PAI run by Salop Council, later known as Audley House old people's home. It was sold off in 1986 and the buildings converted to residential use.

In 1898, the union opened a boys' home at Doley Common, Gnosall (SJ817215).[96] The girls were placed at Miss Roddam's certified home on Newport Road, Edgmond (SJ731196).[97]

OSWESTRY

Ruyton-in-the-Eleven-Towns had a workhouse by 1753, when the burial of inmate John Davies was recorded on 14 April.[98]

In 1756, Llansilin rented a building from the Chirk Castle estate for use as a workhouse.[99] The building was located on the Rhiwlas Road, at the north of the village (SJ209284). Its furniture comprised an old table, an iron pot, three fire grates, eight pipkins, frying pan, four bedsteads, eleven blankets, three rugs, seven sheets, one feather bed and two chaff beds.[100] In 1776, it could house forty inmates.

Kinnerley had a workhouse by 1774, when John Rattenbury was contracted to run the establishment. The arrangement ended the following year when Rattenbury was found to be deficient in his duties. In 1784, the parish began renting a property belonging to Robert Mansell of Edgerley, Junior, for use as a workhouse.[101]

In 1776, workhouses were in operation in Oswestry Parish (for thirty inmates), Oswestry Town (thirty) and Whittington (twenty). Although not mentioned in the 1776 survey, a workhouse at West Felton is said to have been in use at around that time.[102]

Selattyn's parish records indicate the existence of a workhouse in 1788.[103] The first steward and matron were Thomas Cooper and his wife, who held the post for nearly thirty years.

In 1791, the parishes in the Oswestry Hundred,[104] together with Chirk and Llansilin in Denbighshire, were incorporated under a Local Act 'for the better Relief and Employment of the Poor'.[105] In 1794, the incorporation opened a House of Industry at Morda Bank, Morda (SJ289279). Designed by John Hiram Haycock, the building was based on that adopted by the Shrewsbury Incorporation a decade earlier. The three-storey main block, constructed in red brick, was a shallow, inverted U-shape. The building's construction and furnishings cost around £7,700. Its capacity was put at 700 places.[106]

Paupers sent to the workhouse were required to have been provided with new clothing. For men, this included a coat, waistcoat, breeches, two shirts, two pairs of stockings, a pair of shoes and a hat. For women, it comprised two caps, two handkerchiefs, two shifts, two aprons, one bedgown, three petticoats, two pairs of stockings, a pair of shoes and a hat. Unmarried pregnant women were stigmatised through having to wear special clothing and eat at a separate table.

In 1811, single mothers were given a vegetable diet or meat soup with the meat removed. A woman named Mary Jones, also known as Red Moll, had a chain and log attached to her leg after she absconded from the workhouse and returned with child. After tipping a plate of broth over the master's head, Jones was fitted with the scold's bridle – a metal headpiece, part of which held her tongue in place to prevent her from speaking.[107]

In 1800, four cells were built for the solitary confinement of dissolute persons, together with a room for the apothecary to examine new admissions for infectious diseases. In 1810, a school based on Joseph Lancaster's system was set up for the children at the workhouse.[108]

In 1819, the inhabitants of Oswestry resolved to abolish the House of Industry, 'great frauds having been detected in its management'.[109] The deceptions were found to date back as far as 1801 and had been continued by the current master, Thomas Armston, after he was appointed in 1809. The institution survived, although changes were made in its administration, including the appointment of a permanent paid Overseer.

In 1823, small two-storey annexes were erected at each end of the main building, linked to it by single-storey corridors. At least one of these, the eastern one, was used to house lunatics.

The original intention of the House of Industry was to be self-financing, using income generated by the labour of the inmates, who were to keep one sixth of any earnings. Such hopes proved unfounded, and by 1836 the incorporation had accumulated debts of £10,700.

The incorporation's Local Act status made it largely immune from the 1834 Act, and its parishes refused to join a new Poor Law Union unless the existing debt could be spread among all of such a union's members. That option not being taken up, the incorporation remained in existence until 1930, continuing to use the workhouse at Morda.

A chapel, designed by Samuel Pountney Smith, and dedicated to St Anne, was erected at the north-east of the site in 1882–83. In 1891, a sixteen-bed isolation hospital was erected to the south-east of the workhouse. It later became the Oswestry and Chirk Isolation Hospital, and then Greenfields Hospital. A nurses' home was added at the east of the workhouse in 1904.

In 1907, it was reported that £8 a month was being spent on tobacco for the workhouse inmates, with about 100 smokers having to be supplied.[110]

In 1930, the workhouse became a PAI run by Salop Council, later known as Morda House Welfare Home. Most of the main building was destroyed in a fire in 1982. The only surviving part was the western annexe, now converted to a house. The chapel and nurses' home have been demolished but the former isolation hospital is now Morda's village hall.

SHIFNAL

Shifnal established a workhouse in the early 1730s. In 1773, a site for a workhouse was being sought on land at Lizard Common, to the north-east of the town.[111] In 1776, the workhouse could accommodate forty inmates. By 1788, it occupied premises on Park Lane (now Park Street) at the south of Shifnal, rented from the Jerningham estate (SJ748072). In 1816, the establishment was deemed to be 'very unfit and unwholesome from its situation and want of accommodation'.[112] Accordingly, the vestry made plans to buy the building plus an acre of adjacent land from Sir George Jerningham. Sir George subse-

An early 1900s view of the Oswestry Union workhouse at Morda.

quently donated the site, and a new building, designed by James Smith, was erected the following year. The two-storey building, constructed in red brick, had a long range running alongside the main road, with short forward wing at one end.[113]

In 1779, Albrighton erected a workhouse/poorhouse, originally known as the Parish House, which now forms 35–37 Station Road, Albrighton (SJ814043).[114]

Sheriffhales, placed in Staffordshire until 1895, had a workhouse comprising two small buildings at the north end of Church Street (SJ760122).[115]

Shifnal Poor Law Union came into being on 2 June 1836, with fifteen member parishes, four of which lay in Staffordshire. The union took over the existing Park Street building. The Sheriffhales workhouse, which would have usefully served as a union school, was owned by the Duke of Sutherland and deemed exempt from being made available to the union. Additional land at the rear of the Park Street site was, however, purchased from the Jerningham family to allow enlargement of the existing building. Construction work was carried out in 1840–41, with Francis Halley as architect and contractor. The main additions were a long rearward extension of the short forward wing and a single-storey range parallel to it at the rear of the south end of the building. A new porter's lodge, probation ward and refractory rooms were added in 1842.[116] The capacity of the workhouse was then 150 places.[117]

New casual wards and offices, designed by J. Farmer, were added in 1896. A new infirmary was erected at the south of the workhouse in 1901–02. It fea-

The frontage of the former Shifnal Union workhouse, photographed in 2001.

tured a two-storey central section with single-storey male and female wards at either side. A mains water supply was connected to the workhouse site in 1903.

In 1930, the workhouse became a PAI run by Salop Council. It joined the NHS as Park Street Hospital, later renamed Shifnal Hospital. For a period, the 1902 infirmary operated as Shifnal Cottage Hospital before becoming part of Shifnal Hospital. A section of the main workhouse building survives, now converted into the apartments of Park Court.

SHREWSBURY

In 1604, Shrewsbury town corporation ordered that money be raised for 'settinge the poor to work' and the castle repaired for the purpose.[118] In 1627, it was ordered that the 'Jersey house be made a work-house' with 'Jersey cloth' being manufactured there.[119] The establishment was at the bottom of Barker Street, later becoming the St Chad's parish workhouse.[120] By the 1750s, the other town parishes of St Alkmund, St Julian, St Mary, and Holy Cross were also operating workhouses.[121]

In 1784, five Shrewsbury parishes and Meole Brace were incorporated under a Local Act.[122] The incorporation opened a House of Industry in the former Shrewsbury branch of the London Foundling Hospital, on what is now Ashland Road (SJ486120). Its brick-built, long main block was three storeys high, plus attics, with short cross-wings at each end. Each cross-wing was linked to a small single-storey annexe, the western one also connected to a low L-shaped block further to the west. The interior already included features such as a boardroom, chapel, kitchen, classrooms and dormitories. Although not originally designed as a workhouse, the building was adopted as a model by the other incorporations subsequently formed in the region, such as Ellesmere, Oswestry and Atcham.

The workhouse was described at length in Eden's 1797 survey. On different days, the inmates' dinners featured butcher's meat and 'garden stuff', stewed meat with potatoes or other 'garden stuff', hasty pudding with butter and treacle sauce, bread and cheese, and yeast dumplings. Breakfast was either broth or milk porridge, and supper variously comprised broth, mashed potatoes or pease soup. Food portions were weighed out by the steward. The larder, kitchen and dining hall tables and seats were cleaned immediately after each meal, as were the dormitories, either before or after breakfast, their windows being opened and doors locked. To avoid infectious diseases, new inmates were carefully examined, washed, and clothed if necessary. The beds were provided with clean sheets at least once a month, and the inmates with clean linen once a week. The inmates, if capable, worked from 6 a.m. (or 7 a.m. in winter) to 6 p.m., with a half-hour break for breakfast and an hour for dinner. No work was required on Sundays, at Christmas, Easter or Whitsun, on Shrewsbury Show day, and on Saturdays after 3 p.m. The children were taught reading and other useful subjects, and had their hands and faces washed and their hair combed every morning. The adults were chiefly employed in a woollen manufactory, and instructed in scribbling, cording and spinning. Those who had been shoemakers, tailors, carpenters, etc., were set to work at their different occupations. Inmates could keep one sixth of their weekly earnings, except in cases of misconduct such as drunkenness, profanity, disobedience, pretending sickness, damaging material or implements, or lewd, immoral or disorderly behaviour. The 'decent and orderly' were separated from the 'profligate and debauched' and a proposal had been made to house prostitutes and other 'abandoned' females in a separate building. Adjoining the workhouse were two ranges of buildings, one of which dealt with new admissions, who were stripped and washed, with infectious cases being kept until cured. The other was the infirmary, where the sick and infirm were placed in male or female wards, under the care of proper nurses.[123]

Despite Eden's positive portrait, the institution failed to live up to the incorporation's initial hopes, largely due to inadequate supervision by its directors. Despite being provided with a wealth of machinery such as spinning jennies and looms, the income generated by the inmates' labour fell far short of expectations. In 1798, the steward of the establishment since 1784 was dismissed after being charged with 'extravagant and unexplained expenditure in beer, flour, etc.'. His successor, after eight years in the post, underwent a similar fate. The next steward, after governing for eleven years, was transported for embezzlement.[124]

The incorporation was dissolved in 1826 and re-formed under a new Local Act as the Shrewsbury Poor United District.[125] Each parish's financial contribution was now based on its use of the House of Industry. Admissions then declined, and St Chad's and St Alkmund's also established poorhouses of their own.

From around 1831, the eastern annexe of the building was used as a lunatic asylum. The western annexe, originally used to house weaving looms, was by then being used to hold a school.

The incorporation's Local Act status made it largely immune from the 1834 Poor Law Amendment Act, and it and its workhouse continued in operation, although typically less than a quarter of its 350 places were occupied. The incorporation was dissolved in 1870 and reconstituted as the Shrewsbury Poor Law Union. The following year, however, the PLB amalgamated Shrewsbury with the adjacent Atcham Union to form a new Atcham and Shrewsbury Poor Law Union (see page 232).

In 1878, the incorporation workhouse was sold to Shrewsbury School, who still occupy the building. The interior was refitted and the exterior enhanced by additions such as the clock tower.

WELLINGTON

Wellington had a workhouse by at least 1748, when the poor were farmed by a tailor named Thomas Hazlehurst, who received a quarterly payment for providing inmates with food, clothing, medical care and, if required, burial. He also obtained income from the inmates' labour. From 1748, the workhouse also received paupers from Newport, and in 1750–51 from Berrington.[126] In 1776, then self-managed by the parish, the workhouse could house fifty-six inmates. In 1797, it was relocated from Street Lane (now Holyhead Road) to the south side of Walker Street (SJ649114). Extra sleeping rooms were added to the building in 1805. In 1832, there were about forty inmates, who were 'either weak in intellect, or too old or too young to work'.[127]

In 1760, Wrockwardine's indoor poor were also being farmed by Thomas Hazlehurst for a payment of £50 a year. By 1782, contractors were no longer being employed and the parish rented a building to use as a workhouse. In about 1801, new premises were built about half a mile west of the village on land owned by the Tiddicross charity – the property is now known as Tiddie

The Shrewsbury Incorporation workhouse after being remodelled by
Shrewsbury School.

Cross (SJ612119). Two years later, John Hollis was contracted to run the workhouse for £50 year. The inmates received bread, cheese, beer, and beef or
mutton at least once a week. In 1814, the establishment included kitchens, five
bedrooms containing thirteen beds, a 'dead room' containing several spinning
wheels, a pantry and a brewhouse.[128]

Ercall Magna (High Ercall) had a workhouse by 1751.[129] A new building
was erected in 1814 at Waterside, on Sytch Lane, to the north of Waters Upton
(SJ629197). In 1832, the inmates comprised three males aged from 4 to 35
years, and nine females aged 25 to 70. The building survived until the 1960s.

Wellington Poor Law Union was formed on 4 June 1836, with eleven constituent parishes. Initially, the union inherited the Walker Street workhouse
and those at Ercall Magna and Wrockwardine. The guardians decided to use
Walker Street as the main workhouse and to house children at Waters Upton.
The Wrockwardine premises had intermittent use up until 1841.

In 1838, the guardians decided to expand the accommodation at Walker
Street and additional land was purchased at the rear of the existing building. Plans obtained from Thomas Baddeley involved the rebuilding of most
of the Walker Street frontage and the addition of a new three-storey wing
at its centre rear. Just over halfway along its length, the new wing incorporated indentations with angled corners, similar to the central hub of the PLC's
model 'square' plan (see page 26). This was perhaps allowing for the possibility

of the later addition of cross-wings along the same lines.[130] After enlargement, the capacity of the building was 156 places, with 90 places at Wrockwardine for the children.[131]

A slump in trade in 1843 led to many unemployed coal miners entering the workhouse, which, despite its enlargement, became dangerously overcrowded. In some cases, inmates were sleeping four to a bed, and the vagrant wards were converted to inmate use.

In 1874–75, a new union workhouse was erected on the north side of Street Lane, Wellington (SJ648109). Designed by Bidlake and Fleming, it accommodated up to 350 inmates. The T-shaped corridor-plan main building was of red brick and three storeys high. Ancillary blocks including an infirmary, fever hospital and school. The school, at the rear of the workhouse, was closed in 1884 when the children started to attend a local board school.[132]

After 1930, the Street Lane site became a PAI run by Salop Council. During the Second World War, patients from several Birmingham hospitals, including the Children's Hospital, were evacuated there to avoid German bombing. The establishment joined the NHS as the Wrekin Hospital. In 1993, the main building was converted into a nursing home.

The Walker Street site was later occupied by the Union Brewery, and some of the surviving workhouse building now forms part of Wellington Library.

In 1916, the union established a children's home at Brooklyn House, 135 Watling Street, Wellington. In 1928, the home moved to The Mount, Haygate Road, Wellington.[133]

WEM

A workhouse existed in Wem by 1740.[134] In 1776, it could accommodate thirty paupers. In 1832, when it occupied a three-storey building at the west end of the High Street, the inmates were reported as comprising eighteen men aged from 40 to 80, and eight females aged from 30 to 50.

In 1756, the parish of Prees contracted with John Bennett for the care and maintenance of paupers in the workhouse.[135] In 1776, it could hold sixty inmates. In 1803, twenty-seven paupers were maintained in the establishment, which was located at Prees Heath.

In 1819, the Ightfield churchwardens purchased a property in the parish for use as a workhouse.[136]

Wem Poor Law Union was formed on 16 November 1836, with twelve member parishes. Initially, the union took over the existing Wem and Prees

The surviving part of Wellington's Walker Street workhouse is now part of the town's library.

Opened in 1875, Wellington's former Holyhead Road workhouse still provides care for the elderly.

workhouses, with the intention of housing able-bodied inmates at Wem and the aged and infirm at Prees. However, legal complications with the ownership of both sites led the guardians to seek alternative accommodation. This materialised in the shape of a recently built two-storey house on a 5-acre site on what is now Love Lane, off the Whitchurch Road, to the north of Wem (SJ514297). Plans for the conversion and enlargement of the building were provided by Robert Graham and construction work began in February 1838. The PLC authorised an expenditure of £2,800 on its construction, which was intended to be for 200 inmates, although the final capacity was set at 150 places.[137]

In the final layout, the main building formed a U-shape, whose base – which included the original house – faced eastwards onto Love Lane. Exercise yards were created either side of the building's southern range. The new workhouse was fully operational in September 1838.

An official inspection in 1867 gave the establishment a generally positive report:

> The management of the house is very good; the wards are always clean and well ventilated. The drainage and water supply are both good, rendered so indeed at a very considerable outlay of money. In no union in my district do the Regulations of the Commissioners as to diet, clothing, &c., appear to be more carefully observed.

The workhouse also had a paid nurse. On the negative side, it was noted that: 'The internal arrangements are in many respects defective, and the very confined area and bad aspect of the airing courts, are in my opinion very objectionable.'[138]

After 1904, for birth registration purposes, the workhouse was identified as Love Lane, Wem.[139]

In 1930, the site was taken over by Salop Council and for several years was used as a PAI.[140] The building later had various uses, including housing a chicken farm. By the 1970s, it had been converted to Landona Cottages, then in about 1990 became Landona House care home.

WHITCHURCH

Malpas had a workhouse by 1738, when it was maintained by William Winstanley.[141]

In 1776, the Whitchurch parish workhouse, on Newtown Road (SO540415), could hold forty inmates.[142] In 1790, plans were made to enlarge

The entrance and east wing of the former Wem Union workhouse.

the building, but it was subsequently decided that a new building on an out-of-town site would be preferable. In 1792, declaring that its poor 'were very numerous, and ... supported and maintained ... at a great and burthensome expence', the parish followed the example set by Shrewsbury and obtained a Local Act 'for the better relief and employment of the poor'.[143] All local residents possessing land rated at £20 or more were incorporated as Guardians of the Poor and elected twelve of their number as Directors.

A 10-acre site for the new workhouse was found at the east side of Claypit Street (SJ545420). A competition to design the building was won by William Turner and construction began in September 1793. In July 1795, the existing inmates at Newtown Road were transferred to the new premises. The H-shaped main building faced to the south-west and was constructed in red brick. It was three storeys high, with two-storey additions later constructed at each side. The ground floor included a directors' boardroom, kitchen, dining hall for 100, laundry, bakehouse, punishment cells, male and female workrooms and a schoolroom, also used for daily prayers.[144] Women and children were housed at the east side of the building and men at the west.

In 1832, it was recorded that there were sixty-three inmates, thirty-six male and twenty-seven female, their ages ranging from 8 months to 89 years. Those capable of working were generally employed according to their former occupation, which in most cases was agricultural work. They

An early 1900s view of the Whitchurch Union workhouse and its Arts and Crafts-style chapel (left).

The South East Shropshire District School at Quatt.

received a gratuity every Saturday night, according to the work they had done during the week.

Whitchurch's Local Act status made it largely immune from the 1834 Poor Law Amendment Act and it determinedly continued in operation, resulting in the PLC having to create a union based at Wem. In 1852, however, the directors finally agreed to the incorporation's dissolution. The following January, the Whitchurch Poor Law Union was created, taking in twenty-five parishes and townships from Nantwich and other neighbouring unions in Shropshire, Cheshire and Flintshire.

Later additions to the Claypit Street workhouse included a separate infirmary at the north of the site and a casual ward block, complete with sleeping and work cells, at the west corner. In 1881, a 150-seat chapel was built to the south-west of the workhouse at a cost of £639. It was one of the first workhouse chapels to adopt the Arts and Crafts style, which was then in vogue.[145]

After 1930, the site became a PAI run by Salop Council. It joined the NHS as Deermoss Hospital, now Whitchurch Community Hospital. Most of the original buildings have gone but the chapel and south-west wing survive.

SOUTH EAST SHROPSHIRE DISTRICT SCHOOL

William Wolryche Whitmore, the first chairman of the Bridgnorth board of guardians, strongly believed that pauper children should be housed and educated away from what he viewed as the corrupting effects of the workhouse. To put this idea into practice, he offered the guardians a property on his own estate, a former dower house in the village of Quatt (SO756883), for use as a residential school, housing around fifty children.

In 1845, industrial training – in agricultural work for boys and domestic skills for girls – was introduced at the school and an additional 4 acres of farmland were acquired. In 1848, the school's master, Henry Garland, reported that the boys were employed in the cultivation of the land and the management of up to four cows, eight pigs and a pony. The girls were employed in the house, in dairy work, washing, ironing, baking, sewing, knitting, and making their own clothes. Some of the skimmed milk and potatoes produced on the farm was consumed by the school itself, while the rest, plus butter, pigs and calves, was sold at market prices in Bridgnorth. The children rose at 5.30 a.m. in summer and at 6.45 a.m. in winter. They then worked until 8, had school from 9 to 12, dined at 1, and resumed work from 2 until 5. Supper at 6 was followed by an hour or more of play, weather permitting. As the children sang in church, they also practised the psalms and chants for the following Sunday. The day closed with prayers.[146]

In 1849, Bridgnorth joined with the Cleobury Mortimer, Seisdon and Madeley Unions to form the South East Shropshire School District. The School District took over the Quatt site, acquired extra land, and enlarged the buildings to increase the school's capacity to 150 places. The additions included two schoolrooms, a dining room, dormitories, a washhouse, laundry, bath, coalhouse, stable, cart house, tool house, and various farm buildings.[147]

The school employed three male and one female industrial trainers but no domestic staff, all the domestic work being done by the inmates and the older children tending to the needs of the younger ones. The older boys and girls were taught in one schoolroom, and the younger children in another. There were separate playgrounds for the sexes, but the children all took their meals together. Some of the boys were apprenticed to trades, others became gentlemen's servants. All the girls went into service.[148]

The training model adopted at Quatt proved influential and was widely imitated. By the end of the century, however, District Schools (or 'barrack schools' as they were referred to by their critics) had fallen out of favour, with cottage homes, scattered homes and boarding out becoming increasingly adopted. Following the withdrawal of Seisdon and Madeley from the School District, the LGB decided that the Quatt School should close at Michaelmas 1904.

The building, now owned by the National Trust, was converted into apartments in 2012.

18

WORKHOUSE
RECORDS

LOCAL RECORDS

Prior to 1834, the administration of poor relief, including poorhouse and workhouse operation, was chiefly carried out by individual parishes. Their records include:

Overseers' poor rates account books
Settlement and removal records
Vestry minutes
Workhouse inventories, rules, admission books, etc.

Following the 1834 Poor Law Amendment Act, extensive records were kept by the unions in each area. These include:

Boards of guardians' minute books
Admission and discharge registers for workhouses, children's homes, etc.
Indoor pauper lists (six-monthly summaries)
Registers of births, baptisms, deaths and burials
Religious creed registers (1869 onwards, also include admission details)

The survival of local Poor Law records is very uneven and, for some unions, virtually zero. Those that do survive are mostly held in the relevant county and metropolitan offices. There are usually restrictions on access to records less than 100 years old containing personal information.

Record repositories often produce research guides relating to their poor relief records and have online catalogues of their archive holdings. The National Archives' online Discovery system (discovery.nationalarchives.gov.uk) also includes the catalogues for many local archives. The Workhouse website (workhouses.org.uk) includes a summary of the records surviving for each union and where they are held. It also lists the parishes encompassed by each union.

The main local archives holding Poor Law records in the area covered by this book are listed below, together with their websites and the names of the former counties and unions they cover, where this may not be obvious from the repository's name:

- Anglesey Archives (anglesey.gov.uk/archives)
- Bristol (bristolmuseums.org.uk/bristol-archives)
- Carmarthenshire (carmarthenshire.gov.wales/libraries)
- Ceredigion Archives (archifdy-ceredigion.org.uk) Cardiganshire
- Cheshire Archives (cheshirearchives.org.uk)
  Cheshire unions except Stockport, Wirral and Birkenhead Unions
- Conway Archives (conwy.gov.uk/archives)
- Glamorgan Archives (glamarchives.gov.uk)
  Bridgend, Cardiff, Merthyr and Pontypridd Unions
- West Glamorgan Archives (swansea.gov.uk/westglamorganarchives)
  Swansea and Neath Unions
- Gloucestershire (gloucestershire.gov.uk/archives)
- Gwent Archives (gwentarchives.gov.uk) Monmouthshire
- Gwynedd Archives (gwynedd.llyw.cymru/archives)
  Merionethshire and Caernarvonshire except for Conway Union
- Herefordshire Archives & Records Centre
  (herefordshire.gov.uk/archives)
- North East Wales Archives (www.newa.wales)
  Denbighshire and Flintshire
- Pembrokeshire Archives
  (www.culture4pembrokeshire.co.uk/content.asp?nav=3)
- Powys Archives (en.powys.gov.uk/archives) Breconshire,
  Montgomeryshire, Radnorshire
- Shropshire Archives (www.shropshirearchives.org.uk)
- Stockport Archives
  (www.stockport.gov.uk/heritage-library-archives)
- Wirral Archives (www.wirral.gov.uk/archives)
  Wirral and Birkenhead Unions

A growing number of local workhouse records, particularly those relating to inmates, are now available online, as images and/or transcriptions. Most active in this area are the commercial genealogy companies such as Ancestry (ancestry.co.uk), whose offerings include records for West Glamorgan unions, and Findmypast (findmypast.co.uk), which have some Cheshire and Monmouthshire records.

Many family history societies have transcribed Poor Law records relating to their area and made them available for purchase in print or on CD via suppliers such as Genfair (genfair.co.uk), or online to their members. Free online access to such records is less common. Shropshire Archives has begun to digitise some of its Poor Law Union records with a view to making them available online. The free FamilySearch website (familysearch.org) has online records for Cheshire workhouses.

CENTRAL AUTHORITY RECORDS

The central authority overseeing Poor Law administration after 1834 was successively the Poor Law Commissioners (1834–47), the Poor Law Board (1847–71), the Local Government Board (1871–1919), and the Ministry of Health (1919–48). The main repository of records from these bodies is the UK National Archives (TNA – nationalarchives.gov.uk). The TNA's Poor Law holdings are mostly filed in their MH (Ministry of Health) series of records. Some of the most useful sections are:

- MH9: Registers of staff appointments/departures at each workhouse (with dates, salaries, reasons for leaving)
- MH12: The voluminous correspondence between each Poor Law Union and the central authority – some now digitised including those for the Cardiff Union (1834–53) and Llanfyllin Union (1834–56)
- MH14: Architectural plans for many workhouses (1861–1918)

A useful online guide to these records is available at nationalarchives.gov.uk/help-with-your-research/research-guides/poverty-poor-laws.

The central authority's annual reports, etc. contain a vast amount of material about the poor relief system, including much about individual unions and their workhouses. These publications form part of the UK Parliamentary Papers, which are now accessible online (see page 270).

OTHER RECORDS

- Civil registration of births and deaths (1837 onwards) – indexes are widely available online, e.g. findmypast.co.uk, thegenealogist.co.uk, ancestry.co.uk and bmdindex.co.uk
- Census returns – widely available online, e.g. ukcensusonline.com, genesreunited.co.uk, archives.com and other commercial providers
- Baptism records – workhouse baptisms often took place in the local parish church and form part of its records
- Burial records – pauper burial details are occasionally found in the records of parish churches or municipal cemeteries

19

Useful

Websites

Access to the websites listed below is free of charge except for those marked (£). Some non-free sites may be accessible without payment via local libraries or record offices, or by members of educational or other institutions that hold subscriptions.

General Resources

workhouses.org.uk – a vast collection of information on the institutions run by the poor relief authorities across the British Isles.

british-history.ac.uk – a digital library of core printed sources for the history of the British Isles, e.g. volumes of the Victoria County History.

visionofbritain.org.uk – 'A vision of Britain between 1801 and 2001. Including maps, statistical trends and historical descriptions.'

parlipapers.proquest.com – UK Parliamentary Papers searchable online. Includes publications by the successive central Poor Law authorities. (Institutional subscription only.)

britishnewspaperarchive.co.uk – major archive of British newspapers 1700–2000. (£. Access also included with subscriptions to findmypast.co.uk.)

connectedhistories.org – search multiple online historical sources (1500–1900) including some of the above sites.

newspapers.library.wales – millions of articles from Welsh newspapers (1804–1919).

journals.library.wales – digitised copies of 450 Welsh historical journals.

nationalarchives.gov.uk – the official archive for the UK Government, and for England and Wales.

discover.libraryhub.jisc.ac.uk – catalogue of materials held by many UK national, academic and specialist libraries.

onlinebooks.library.upenn.edu – directory of free online book collections, e.g. locate copies of parliamentary reports, Victorian architectural journals such as *The Builder*, etc.

archive.org – archive of websites, books and other media. Particularly strong on pre-1900 texts.

hathitrust.org – major digital library (some facilities restricted to member institutions).

leicester.contentdm.oclc.org/digital/collection/p16445coll4 – large collection of historical trade directories of England and Wales 1760s–1910s. (The same content is now also available via ancestry.co.uk.)

MAPS

maps.nls.uk/os – historical Ordnance Survey maps of Great Britain.

digimap.edina.ac.uk/historic – historical Ordnance Survey maps of Great Britain. (Institutional subscriptions only.)

old-maps.co.uk – historical Ordnance Survey maps of Great Britain. (£ for full access.)

library.wales/discover/digital-gallery/maps – town, tithe and other maps of Wales.

maps.cheshireeast.gov.uk/tithemaps – tithe and other maps of Cheshire.

kypwest.org.uk – Ordnance Survey, tithe and other maps of Bristol and Gloucestershire.

thegenealogist.co.uk – comprehensive tithe maps of England and Wales (£).

20

PLACES TO VISIT

Many former workhouse buildings still exist, now converted to other uses. A few have become home to museums, where visitors can get an insight into their workhouse history, although some cover a much wider range of topics in their displays.

Llanfyllin Workhouse History Centre, Llanfyllin, Powys
the-workhouse.org.uk
Weaver Hall Museum and Workhouse, Northwich Cheshire
weaverhall.westcheshiremuseums.co.uk
The Workhouse, Southwell, Nottinghamshire
nationaltrust.org.uk/workhouse
Ripon Workhouse Museum and Garden
riponmuseums.co.uk/museums/workhouse_museum_gardens
Nidderdale Museum, Pateley Bridge, North Yorkshire
nidderdalemuseum.com
Thackray Medical Museum, Leeds, West Yorkshire
thackraymedicalmuseum.co.uk
Gressenhall Farm and Workhouse, near Dereham, Norfolk
museums.norfolk.gov.uk/gressenhall-farm-and-workhouse
Vestry House Museum, Walthamstow, London
walthamforest.gov.uk/vestry-house

The Cinema Museum, Kennington, London
cinemamuseum.org.uk
Guildford Spike, Guildford, Surrey
guildfordspike.co.uk
Red House Museum, Christchurch, Dorset
dorsetmuseums.co.uk/red-house-museum-and-garden

NOTES

ABBREVIATIONS

BMJ	British Medical Journal
CA	Cheshire Archives
GA	Gloucestershire Archives
HA	Herefordshire Archives
HEA	Historic England Archive (historicengland.org.uk/images-books/archive)
LGMD	Local Government Manual and Directory
NWC	North Wales Chronicle
OS	Ordnance Survey
PLC	Poor Law Commissioners
PP	House of Commons Parliamentary Papers
SA	Shropshire Archives
TNA	The National Archives

The dates given following web addresses indicate when each was accessed.

INTRODUCTION

1. 5 & 6 Edw. VI, c. 2.
2. 14 Eliz. I c. 5.
3. 18 Eliz. I c. 3.
4. 39 Eliz. I c. 3.
5. 39 Eliz. I c. 5.
6. 43 Eliz. I c. 2.
7. A local prison for idlers and vagrants.
8. Fletcher, 1911, p. viii; Owen H., 1808, p. 333.
9. Higginbotham, 2008, p. 14.
10. Car. II 1 & 14 c. 12.
11. Ibid.

12. british–history.ac.uk/vch/glos/vol5/pp173-195 (31/3/2020).
13. 9 Geo. I c. 7.
14. Davies, D., 1970, p. 116.
15. Rogers, 1928, pp. 371–2.
16. PP, 1834b, p. 73b.
17. Rogers, 1928, pp. 293–4 (slightly abridged).
18. PP, 1835, pp. 177–8.
19. Moss, 1967, p. 172.
20. 22 Geo. III c. 83.
21. Marshall, 1928, p. 160.
22. Gilbert, T. , 1775.
23. Ryland-Epton, 2020, pp. 171–4.
24. Abenhall, Arlingham, Awre, Cheltenham, Cirencester, Fairford, Flaxley, Littledean, Mitcheldean, Newent, Newland, Newnham, Painswick, Westbury-on-Trym and Winterbourne.
25. PP, 1804, pp. 712,716.
26. Ibid.
27. Ibid.
28. Davies, A.E., 1998, p. 326.
29. Walsh, 1974, p. 228.
30. Higginbotham, 2012, p. 305.
31. Higginbotham, 2007, pp. 12–13.
32. PP, 1834a, p. 170.
33. Quoted in Stewart & King, 2004, p. 76.
34. Ibid.
35. PP, 1834a, p. 659A-660A.
36. 4 & 5 Will. 4 c. 76.
37. Nicholls, 1854, p. 271.
38. Parker, 2004, pp. 170–3.
39. Thomas, B.B., 1934, pp. 180–1.
40. Flynn-Hughes, 1944, pp. 91–2.
41. Owen, B., 1990, p. 120.
42. Parker, 2004, pp. 185–6.
43. Davies, A.E., 1978, pp. 251–2.
44. PP, 1841, p. 251.
45. Davies, A.E., 1998, p. 333.
46. Davies, A.E., 1978, p. 253.
47. Jones, D., 1983, p. 81.
48. *Hereford Times*, 4/11/1837, p. 2. Fearnought was a stout woollen cloth, mainly used for bad weather clothing at sea. Linsey-Woolsey was a fabric with a linen or cotton warp and a wool weft. Grogram was a coarse fabric of silk, mohair or wool, often stiffened with gum.
49. PP, 1853, p. 5.
50. PP, 1842, p. 99.
51. PP, 1836, p. 90.
52. Ibid., p. 56.
53. Adapted from Draper, 2005, p. 73.
54. Flynn-Hughes, 1946, p. 93.

55. *Western Daily Press*, 21/7/1983, p. 2; Williams, D., 2012, p. 64; Morgan & Briffett, 1998, p. 11.
56. Higginbotham, 2008.
57. *Merthyr Telegraph*, 3/12/1864, p. 4. Joseph Rowntree of Leeds is not be confused with his York-based chocolate-making namesake.
58. Hollen Lees, 1998, p. 148.
59. BMJ, 16/11/1867, p. 459; workhouses.org.uk/BMJ1867 (5/6/2020).
60. PP, 1909, p. 170. The unnamed workhouse is identifiable as Pwllheli.
61. PP, 1869, pp. 41–51.
62. PP, 1866, p. 59.
63. Ibid., pp. 62–7.
64. PP, 1839b, p. 34.
65. PP, 1839a, p. 99.
66. *Chester Courant*, 21/12/1904, p. 6.
67. The LGB replaced the PLB in 1871.
68. PP, 1920, pp. 97,126.
69. *Cambrian News*, 23/2/1912, p. 5.
70. Gaston, 2009, p. 12.
71. NWC, 31/12/1864, p. 3.
72. *Potter's Electric News*, 24/7/1861, p. 2.
73. *Merthyr Telegraph*, 15/2/1868, p. 2.
74. *Cheshire Observer*, 16/7/1904, p. 3.
75. *Review of Reviews*, 1890, pp. 269, 381.
76. PP, 1890, p. xc.
77. *Pall Mall Gazette*, 19/10/1895, p. 9.
78. Morgan & Briffett, 1998, p. 19.
79. Morgan & Briffett, 1998, p. 17.
80. Williams, D., 2012, p. 22.
81. *Eddowes's Journal*, 9/7/1884, p. 7.
82. PP, 1777; PP, 1804; PP, 1818; PP, 1834b; PP, 1834c.

CHAPTER 1

1. NWC, 9/3/1867, p. 8.
2. NWC, 8/2/1868, p. 5.
3. TNA, MH14/1.
4. *Chester Courant*, 1/8/1906, p. 3.
5. Pigot & Co., 1828–29, p. 1157.
6. PP, 1834a, Part II, p. 173a; PP, 1834b, p. 635b.
7. Pigot & Co., 1835, p. 699.
8. NWC, 4/3/1852, p. 8.
9. NWC, 21/12/1867, p. 1.
10. *The Welsh Coast Pioneer*, 19/10/1900, p. 8.
11. *North Wales Express*, 11/11/1904, p. 3.
12. *Sheffield Evening Telegraph*, 11/6/1909, p. 4.

CHAPTER 2

1.   Jones, T., 1909, Volume I, p. 136.
2.   Hankins, 1997, p. 78.
3.   *Glamorgan, Monmouth and Brecon Gazette*, 17/12/1836, p. 2.
4.   *The Cambrian*, 4/5/1839, p. 3.
5.   *Hereford Times*, 10/12/1864, p. 11.
6.   *Brecon County Times*, 25/11/1904, p. 4.
7.   Parker, 2004, p. 193.
8.   TNA, MH14/6.
9.   *The Building News*, 18/6/1874, p. 707.
10. *Brecon & Radnor Express*, 2/1/1891.
11. *Brecon County Times*, 15/11/1904, p. 5.
12. *Brecon & Radnor Express*, 12/2/1914, p. 5.
13. *Brecon County Times*, 27/8/1914, p. 3; 16/3/1916, p. 5.
14. *Brecon County Times*, 12/11/1914, p. 4.
15. Hankins, 1997, p. 75.
16. Ibid., p. 79.
17. Ibid., p. 80.
18. 1871 census RG10/5583, f. 22, p. 5.
19. Williams, M., 2008, p. 7.
20. Hankins, 1999, p. 86.
21. PP, 1870, p. xxxv.
22. Williams, M., 2008, p. 36.
23. *Hereford Journal*, 4/1/1837, p. 3.
24. *Hereford Times*, 26/11/1864, p. 11.
25. PP, 1867, p. 240.
26. *Brecon County Times*, 4/11/1904, p. 8.

CHAPTER 3

1.   Davies, A.E., 1968, p. 16.
2.   Ibid.
3.   *Cambrian News and Merionethshire Standard*, 9/9/1887, p. 5.
4.   *Cambrian News and Merionethshire Standard*, 23/9/1898, p. 7.
5.   *The Welshman*, 29/3/1901, p. 6.
6.   *The Welshman*, 23/4/1841, p. 2. (Slightly abridged.) 'First class' inmates were the aged and infirm, 'second class' the able-bodied.
7.   *The Welshman*, 19/8/1842, p. 3.
8.   *Western Mail*, 21/9/1870, p. 4.
9.   BMJ, 1894; 2; 202.
10. *Cambrian News and Merionethshire Standard*, 16/12/1904, p. 6.
11. Davies, A.E., 1968, p. 13.
12. places.library.wales/search/?query=Llechryd AND workhouse (24/2/2020).
13. places.library.wales/search/?query= Meline AND poorhouse (24/2/2020).
14. Davies, A.E., 1978, p. 252.
15. glen-johnson.co.uk/albro-castle-cardigan-union-workhouse (10/5/2020).
16. *Welsh Gazette*, 3/11/1904, p. 2.
17. *Lancashire Evening Post*, 30 July 1910, p. 4.

18. Davies, A.E., 1978, p. 254.
19. peoplescollection.wales/items/8649 (7/7/2020).
20. *Cambrian News and Merionethshire Standard*, 18/11/1904, p. 2.
21. *Carmarthen Journal and South Wales Weekly Advertiser*, 7/11/1913, p. 5.
22. *Western Mail*, 28/11/1919, p. 8.
23. *Yorkshire Evening Post*, 5/2/1927, p. 7.
24. Davies, A.E., 1998, p. 331.
25. *The Welshman*, 13/3/1846, p. 3.
26. *Cambrian News and Merionethshire Standard*, 18/11/1904, p. 2.

CHAPTER 4

1.   Owen, G.D., 1941, p. 78.
2.   Howard, 1789, p. 214.
3.   Owen, G.D., 1941, p. 78.
4.   Spence, 1809, p. 97.
5.   *The Cambrian*, 5/10/1822, p. 3.
6.   Hankins, 1997, p. 60.
7.   *The Cambrian*, 1/10/1836, p. 2.
8.   Lewis, R.A., 1964, pp. 8–9.
9.   *The Welshman*, 19/9/1879, p. 4.
10. *Carmarthen Journal and South Wales Weekly Advertiser*, 29/9/1893, p. 4.
11. *The Welshman*, 25/1/1901, p. 4.
12. *The Welshman*, 20/1/1905.
13. *Evening Express*, 21/3/1906, p. 3.
14. *The Welshman*, 11/11/1904, p. 3.
15. Owen, G.D., 1941, p. 85.
16. Ibid., p. 79.
17. Hooker, 2013, p. 206.
18. Ibid., pp. 209–11.
19. Ibid., pp. 211–2.
20. *The Cambrian*, 28/7/1838, p. 3.
21. *South Wales Daily News*, 12/1/1899, p. 6.
22. *Nottingham Evening Post*, 18/4/1902, p. 6.
23. places.library.wales/search/?query=Llangennech AND poorhouse (4/6/2020).
24. *Evening Express*, 15/1/1892, p. 4.
25. *Western Mail*, 26/2/1892, p. 6.
26. *South Wales Daily News*, 23/7/1892, p. 7.
27. *The Llanelly Mercury and South Wales Advertiser*, 14/1/1897, p. 4.
28. *The Welshman*, 11/11/1904, p. 7.
29. *Western Mail*, 11/5/1928, p. 1.
30. Jones, K., 2011, p. 23.
31. Ibid., p. 30.
32. Ibid., p. 35.
33. Ibid., p. 78.
34. Ibid., p. 98.
35. Ibid., p. 151.
36. Ibid., pp. 174–8.

CHAPTER 5

1.	Flynn-Hughes, 1946, p. 89.
2.	Flynn-Hughes, 1944, p. 90.
3.	NWC, 7/10/1845, p. 2.
4.	Flynn-Hughes, 1946, p. 93.
5.	*South Wales Echo*, 28/12/1889, p. 3.
6.	Flynn-Hughes, 1946, p. 93.
7.	*North Wales Express*, 4/11/1904, p. 3.
8.	PP, 1909, pp. 169–70.
9.	*The Hospital*, 22/6/1912, p. 289.
10.	Dodd, A.H., 1968, p. 289.
11.	PLC, 1853, Volume 7, p. 150.
12.	NWC, 18/8/1855, p. 5.
13.	Ibid., 2/6/1855, p. 1.
14.	*North Wales Express*, 25/11/1904, p. 5.
15.	PP, 1909, pp. 168–9. The unnamed workhouse is identifiable as Carnarvon.
16.	Ibid.
17.	Draper, 2005, pp. 44–58.
18.	Ibid, pp. 171–3.
19.	PP, 1909, pp. 167–8. The unnamed workhouse is identifiable as Conway.
20.	*North Wales Weekly News*, 16/7/1909, p. 7.
21.	Jones, G., 1992, p. 5.
22.	Ibid.
23.	Flynn-Hughes, 1946, p. 94.
24.	Ibid., pp. 92–3. Lobscouse was potatoes boiled with a little chopped meat, then formed into a hash with onions and seasoning.
25.	Ibid., p. 96.
26.	*North Wales Express*, 23/12/1904, p. 5.
27.	PP, 1909, pp. 168–9. The unnamed workhouse is identifiable as Carnarvon.
28.	*Hull Daily Mail*, 19/1/1928, p. 1.
29.	*Gloucester Citizen*, 27/9/1928, p. 9.

CHAPTER 6

1.	NWC, 28/4/1846, p. 1.
2.	NWC, 20/6/1848, p. 1.
3.	*North Wales Express*, 4/1/1889, p. 4.
4.	PP, 1909, p. 166.
5.	*Carnarvon and Denbigh Herald*, 16/9/1910, p. 5.
6.	*Chester Chronicle*, 9/3/1838, p. 2.
7.	*Carnarvon and Denbigh Herald*, 17/6/1848, p. 2.
8.	*Carnarvon and Denbigh Herald*, 27/5/1848, p. 1.
9.	*Wrexham Guardian*, 22/6/1878, p. 6.
10.	NWC, 3/12/1878.
11.	*North Wales Times*, 26/1/1907, p. 3.
12.	PP, 1909, pp. 165–6.
13.	*Denbighshire Free Press*, 10/10/1914, p. 6.
14.	Palmer, 1893, pp. 160–1.

15. Dodd, A.H., 1926, p. 116.
16. Rogers, 1928, slightly abridged.
17. *The Cambrian*, 9 July 1814, p. 3.
18. workhouses.org.uk/Wrexham (23/2/2020).
19. Personal communication from Andrew Taylor.
20. Ibid. See also *Wrexham and Denbighshire Advertiser*, 4/7/1863, p. 4.
21. *Wrexham Advertiser*, 31/5/1873, p. 1.
22. *Wrexham and Denbighshire Advertiser*, 13/8/1887, p. 1.
23. *Wrexham Advertiser*, 8/3/1879, p. 1.
24. BMJ, 1894; 2; 264.
25. PP, 1909, p. 112.

CHAPTER 7

1. Willett, 1822, p. 112.
2. PP, 1834a, Part II, 170a.
3. Phoenix, 2011, p. 11.
4. *Chester Chronicle*, 23/9/1893, p. 5.
5. *Cheshire Observer*, 20/7/1895, p. 1.
6. *Wrexham Advertiser*, 23/5/1896, p. 5.
7. *South Wales Daily News*, 22/4/1895, p. 4.
8. *Cheshire Observer*, 16/7/1904, p. 3.
9. Jones T. , 1995, p. 2.
10. Ibid., p. 6.
11. TNA, MH14/15.
12. *Flintshire Observer*, 14/6/1867, p. 4, and 12/7/1867, p. 4.
13. *Flintshire Observer*, 8/2/1883, p. 4.
14. *Flintshire Observer*, 6/11/1913, p. 3.
15. Jones, T., 1995, p. 43.
16. Davies, Dawn et al, 2012, p. 5.
17. Parry-Jones, 1981, pp. 10–12.
18. Stanley, 1909, p. 11.
19. *Rhyl Record and Advertiser*, 27/9/1890, p. 4.
20. *Denbighshire Free Press*, 12/11/1904, p. 3.
21. *The Builder*, 6/6/1903.
22. PP, 1909, pp. 165–6. The unnamed workhouse is identifiable as St Asaph.
23. *Western Times*, 21/6/1912, p. 7.
24. *Western Mail*, 3/9/1923, p. 3.
25. *Flintshire Observer*, 1/5/1913; 1911 census.

CHAPTER 8

1. Hopkin-James, 1922, pp. 100–1.
2. Thomas & Wilkins, 1995, p. 18.
3. Ibid., p. 34.
4. Ibid., pp. 47–8.
5. *Western Mail*, 29/7/1903, p. 3.
6. *Glamorgan Gazette*, 8/4/1910, p. 4.

7.   *Western Mail*, 19/8/1876, p. 8.
8.   Grant, 1988, p. 43.
9.   Winstone, 1883, p. 66.
10. Glamorgan Archives, CL/MS/6/13.
11. llantrisant.net/index.php/landmarks/workhouse-landmarks (22/5/2020).
12. Stewart & King, 2004, p. 76.
13. Glamorgan Archives, P63/2.
14. RG11/5275, f. 153, p. 1.
15. *Cardiff Times*, 11/12/1858, p. 2.
16. *The Welshman*, 31/3/1848, p. 3.
17. *South Wales Daily News*, 14/11/1881, p. 4.
18. Owen-John, 2000, pp. 73–4.
19. Ibid.
20. *The Cambrian*, 11/11/1904, p. 8.
21. *The Cambrian*, 9/2/1833, p. 3.
22. Thomas, T., 1992, p. 167.
23. Ibid, pp. 120–2.
24. *Evening Express*, 4/7/1900, p. 4.
25. calmview.cardiff.gov.uk/Record.aspx?src=CalmView.Catalog&id=UM (25/5/2020).
26. Ibid.
27. *The Cambrian*, 7/10/1809, p. 1.
28. *The Cambrian*, 24/11/1838, p. 2.
29. TNA, MH14/25.
30. *Merthyr Telegraph*, 3/12/1864, p. 4.
31. Ibid; *Brecon County Times*, 7/11/1868, p. 8.
32. *Western Mail*, 6/10/1870, p. 3.
33. *The Cambrian*, 27/8/1875, p. 5
34. *Western Mail*, 26/7/1912, p. 6.
35. *Western Mail*, 27/11/1876, p. 6.
36. *Western Mail*, 17/11/1877, p. 1.
37. *South Wales Daily News*, 7/1/1880, p. 1.
38. *South Wales Daily News*, 30/8/1881, p. 1.
39. Thomas, J.E., 1974, p. 57.
40. *South Wales Daily Post*, 23/12/1910, p. 5.
41. *Cambria Daily Leader*, 23/1/1913, p. 4.
42. *Llais Lafur*, 22/7/1916. p. 3.
43. *Cardiff Times*, 29/1/1864, p. 4.
44. *Cardiff and Merthyr Guardian*, 17/11/1865, p. 4.
45. Jones, K., 2016, pp. 44–5.
46. *South Wales Daily News*, 1/10/1877, p. 1; 27/3/1884, p. 3.
47. *South Wales Daily News*, 11/10/1889, p. 1; 17/5/1890, p. 1.
48. *South Wales Daily News*, 17/6/1890, p. 1.
49. *South Wales Daily News*, 9/6/1892, p. 1.
50. Sockett, 1834, p. 4.
51. Ibid., p. 6.
52. Sockett, 1821, p. 20.
53. Ibid., pp. 33–4.
54. Grant, 1988, p. 47.
55. Jones, C., 2007, p. 56.
56. Lewis, B., 2003, pp. 36–8.

57.   *The Builder*, 29/10/1859, pp. 716–7; www.builderindex.org/?q=node/1798
      (22/5/2020).
58.   Lewis, B., 2003, p. 39.
59.   PP, 1867, p. 114.
60.   Kelly & Co., 1895, p. 685.
61.   *The Cambrian*, 22/1/1904, p. 7.
62.   Kelly & Co., 1895, p. 685.

CHAPTER 9

1.   NWC, 26/6/1838, p. 2.
2.   NWC, 5/11/1864, p. 2.
3.   PP, 1871, p. 446.
4.   *The Builder*, 31/7/1875, p. 686.
5.   *Cambrian News*, 2/10/1874.
6.   TNA, MH14/2.
7.   *North Wales Times*, 26/11/1904, p. 3.
8.   visitoruk.com/Llangollen/18th-century-T1892.html (6/2/2020).
9.   historicplacenames.rcahmw.gov.uk/placenames/recordedname/836b8abc-b450-443d-
      825c-5c22b1fe7ff2
10.   PP, 1834a, Part II, p. 173a.
11.   Larkin-Jones, J. & T., 1998.
12.   Ibid.
13.   NWC, 12/11/1864, p. 11.
14.   *Denbighshire Free Press*, 12/11/1904, p. 8.
15.   NWC,13/2/1858, p. 1.
16.   NWC, 12/11/1864, p. 11.
17.   *Y Goleuad*, 7/3/1874, p. 16.
18.   *Y Dydd*, 18/9/1903, p. 4.
19.   *Barmouth & County Advertiser*, 1/12/1904, p. 3.
20.   *Yr Adsain*, 19/8/1919, p. 5.
21.   *Western Mail*, 29/1/1923, p. 11.
22.   *Carnarvon and Denbigh Herald*, 21/4/1838, p. 1.
23.   *Cambrian News*, 23/4/1875, p. 6.
24.   BMJ, 1894; 2; p. 598–9.
25.   *Cambrian News*, 19/12/1902, p. 8.
26.   *Cambrian News*, 23/12/1904, p. 2.
27.   *Western Mail*, 15/4/1918, p. 2.

CHAPTER 10

1.   *Monmouthshire Merlin*, 8/9/1832, p. 3.
2.   Pigot & Co., 1835, p. 251.
3.   Powell E. , 1885, p. 71.
4.   *Monmouthshire Merlin*, 10/4/1830, p. 3.
5.   R G9/3997, f. 136, p. 65.
6.   Powell, E., 1885, p. 71.
7.   *Monmouthshire Beacon*, 29/9/1855, p. 1.

8.   *Monmouthshire Merlin*, 18/8/1871, p. 4.
9.   *Gloucestershire Echo*, 11/7/1914, p. 4; *Coventry Evening Telegraph*, 16/7/1914, p. 3.
10.   *Monmouthshire Merlin*, 4/5/1850, p. 2.
11.   *Evening Express*, 17/5/1906, p. 2.
12.   *Evening Express*, 2/4/1908, p. 2.
13.   *Weekly Mail*, 20/6/1908, p. 7.
14.   *Evening Express*, 21/1/1909, p. 3.
15.   *Monmouth Guardian*, 19/4/1918, p. 3.
16.   *Monmouthshire Merlin*, 12/12/1829, p. 3.
17.   *Monmouthshire Merlin*, 1/5/1830, p. 3.
18.   Cooper & Morrison, 2004, pp. 120–2.
19.   *Monmouthshire Merlin*, 16/5/1857, p. 1.
20.   *Western Mail*, 13/6/1877, p. 1.
21.   Kelly & Co., 1895, p. 40.
22.   *Western Mail*, 1/12/1894, p. 3.
23.   *Taunton Courier*, 22/5/198, p. 3.
24.   *Western Mail*, 21/7/1921, p. 5.
25.   Kissack, 1975, p. 182.
26.   PP, 1776, pp. 268–9.
27.   Eden, 1797, Volume 2, p. 448.
28.   british-history.ac.uk/vch/glos/vol5/pp101–117 (22/6/2020).
29.   british-history.ac.uk/vch/glos/vol5/pp117–138 (3/2/2020).
30.   Ryland-Epton, 2020, p. 164.
31.   *Monmouthshire Merlin*, 13/3/1830, p. 3.
32.   *Glamorgan Monmouth and Brecon Gazette and Merthyr Guardian*, 25/4/1835, p. 1.
33.   historicplacenames.rcahmw.gov.uk/placenames/recordedname/2a8f0a55-4e96-47df-9766-e6e9c9bb35a2 (6/2/2020).
34.   RG10/5301, f. 75, p. 4.
35.   PP, 1836, p. 365.
36.   Ibid.
37.   *Monmouthshire Merlin*, 19/11/1836, p. 1.
38.   *Monmouthshire Merlin*, 3/12/1836, p. 3.
39.   *County Observer and Monmouthshire Central Advertiser*, 7/3/1868, p. 1.
40.   *Post Office Directory of Monmouthshire & South Wales*, 1871, p. 52.
41.   *County Observer*, 12/11/1903, p. 5.
42.   *South Wales Gazette*, 14/9/1934, p. 5.
43.   Frost, 1821, p. 35.
44.   hdl.handle.net/10107/4669581 (4/5/2020).
45.   Pigot & Co., 1835, p. 262.
46.   caerleon.net/archive/literature/glh/27unions.htm (4/5/2020).
47.   PP, 1836, p. 365.
48.   Ibid.
49.   *Cardiff and Merthyr Guardian*, 20/8/1836, p. 1.
50.   *The Champion*, 19/5/1839, p. 4.
51.   PP, 1867, p. 239.
52.   *Hereford Times*, 4/5/1867, p. 4.
53.   *Cambrian News*, 4/11/1904, p. 3.
54.   Thomas, I., 1901.

55. caerleon.net/archive/literature/glh/29indust_schl.htm (17/4/2020).
56. PP, 1804, p. 310. 'Denwiston' has not been identified.
57. goytrelocalhistory.org.uk/goytre-poorhouse (7/8/2020).
58. Clark, 1958, p. 54.
59. *The Cambrian*, 16/8/1823, p. 3.
60. Pigot & Co., 1835, p. 264.
61. *Monmouthshire Merlin*, 17/9/1836, p. 2.
62. Foster, 1990, pp. 8–9
63. *Western Mail*, 16/7/1880, p. 1.
64. *Pontypool Free Press*, 19/4/1895, p. 5.
65. *South Wales Daily News*, 28/7/1897.
66. *Western Mail*, 7/8/1923, p. 1.
67. Foster, 1990, pp. 44–53.

CHAPTER 11

1. Thomas, Venerable Archdeacon, 1891, p. 6.
2. *Montgomeryshire Collections*, 1873, vol. 6, p. 334.
3. Hancock, 1873, pp. 335–6.
4. Owen, R., 1918, p. 177.
5. places.library.wales/search/?query=guilsfield AND workhouse (4/6/2020).
6. NWC, 2/5/1837, p. 1.
7. NWC, 6/3/1838, p. 1.
8. Hainsworth, 2004, p. 10.
9. Ward & Hainsworth, 2021, pp. 33–48.
10. *Montgomery County Times*, 30/6/1894, p. 4.
11. Hainsworth, 2004, p. 26.
12. Ward & Hainsworth, 2021, p. 99.
13. *Shrewsbury Chronicle*, 2/6/1854, p. 6.
14. NWC, 19/10/1861.
15. *Shrewsbury Chronicle,* 10/9/1858, p. 8.
16. *Aberystwyth Times*, 29/5/1869, p. 1.
17. *Aberystwyth Times*, 16/4/1870, p. 4.
18. *Montgomeryshire Echo*, 3/3/1894, p. 8.
19. *Montgomery County times*, 17/12/1898, p. 3.
20. *Y Negesydd*, 15/12/1904, p. 1.
21. *Cambrian News*, 17/3/1916, p. 5.
22. T. S. J., 1904, pp. 248–59.
23. Pearson, 1918, p. 145.
24. SA, PH/W/34/46.
25. MacLeod, 1906, p. 321.
26. 32 Geo. III c.96. Other members: Berriew, Llandyssil, Llanmerewig, Forden, Cletterwood, Hope, Leighton, Trelystan, Wolston Nyend [Trelystan], Aston, Castlewright, and Churchstoke.
27. Dodd, A.H., 1926, pp. 123–5.
28. Cathrall, 1828, p. 354.
29. Pryce, 1902, p. 267.
30. Ibid., pp. 279–80.

31.   Dodd, A.H., 1926, p. 123.
32.   Rowley-Morris, 1892, p. 94.
33.   Ibid., pp. 94–6.
34.   Ibid., p. 115–6.
35.   RG11/5480, f. 50, p. 18.
36.   *Shrewsbury Chronicle*, 7/7/1837, p. 2.
37.   Owen, B., 1990, p. 120.
38.   Ibid., p. 119–20.
39.   NWC, 17/12/1864, p. 11.

CHAPTER 12

1.   Pembrokeshire Archives, D-RTP/WCAP/7/26.
2.   BMJ, 1894; 1; 1422–3.
3.   *Haverfordwest and Milford Haven Telegraph*, 10/8/1898, p. 4.
4.   *County Echo*, 24/11/1904, p. 2.
5.   *The Welshman*, 1/2/1839, p. 2.
6.   TNA, MH14/25.
7.   John, 2004, pp. 47–8.
8.   CADW, 2015, p. 51.
9.   Cooper & Morrison, 2004, pp. 120–1.
10.   Hughes, C., 1989.
11.   Fustian was a coarse twilled cotton with a velvety pile.
12.   Hughes, C., 1989.
13.   Ibid.

CHAPTER 13

1.   Rogers, 1928, pp. 371–2.
2.   *Hereford Journal*, 17/5/1837, p. 3.
3.   places.library.wales/search/?query=Knighton (7/4/2020).
4.   *Eddowes' Journal*, 9/3/1870, p. 1.
5.   *Leominster News*, 15/10/1886, p. 5. At that time, a 'lavatory' was a washroom and a 'washhouse' was where clothes, etc. were washed.
6.   PP, 1885, pp. 20–1.
7.   *Wellington Journal*, 10/12/1904, p. 11.
8.   *Hereford Journal*, 21/12/1907, p. 3.
9.   *Brecon Radnor Express*, 28/6/1917, p. 7.
10.   Rogers, 1928, pp. 372–3.
11.   Parker, 2004, p. 173.
12.   *Hereford Journal*, 14/6/1837, p. 2.
13.   Parker, 2004, p. 185.
14.   *Hereford Times*, 14/11/1874.
15.   TNA, MH12/1674.
16.   *Hereford Journal*, 30/1/1839, p. 2.
17.   Parker, 2004, pp. 185–6.
18.   history.powys.org.uk/history/rhaeadr/poor11.html (7/6/2020).
19.   history.powys.org.uk/history/rhaeadr/poor12.html (7/6/2020).
20.   *Montgomeryshire Echo*, 1/4/1893, p. 1.

CHAPTER 14

1.   CA, ZCR/34/39.
2.   CA, P/119/6/1.
3.   CA, P/119/28/5.
4.   PP, 1804, p. 48.
5.   CA, P/119/24/50.
6.   Hitchcock, 1985, p. 61.
7.   Ingham, 1897, p. 168.
8.   Bagshaw, 1850, p. 339.
9.   CA, WMS 2530. For Warrington, then in Lancashire, see Higginbotham, 2006, p. 66.
10.   *Chester Chronicle*, 6/7/1838, p. 1.
11.   *Northwich Guardian*, 26/11/1881, p. 5.
12.   *The Builder*, 28/5/1904, p. 587.
13.   *Northwich Guardian*, 24/11/1894, p. 5.
14.   *LGMD*, 1929, p. 315.
15.   *Cheshire Observer*, 30/8/1862, p. 3.
16.   *Cheshire Observer*, 9/4/1864, p. 3.
17.   *Chester Observer*, 27/8/1864, p. 8; *Chester Chronicle*, 17/8/1867, p. 4.
18.   *LGMD*, 1908, p. 286.
19.   Hitchcock, 1985, p. 261.
20.   Burne, 1965, p. 45.
21.   Hemingway, 1831, pp. 192–3.
22.   *London Chronicle*, 28/2/1767.
23.   Rogers, 1928, p. 144 (slightly abridged).
24.   Hemingway, 1831, pp. 192–3.
25.   PP, 1834a, p. 275A.
26.   Charlesworth, 2010, p. 155.
27.   *Cheshire Observer*, 27/1/1917, p. 7.
28.   Semper, 1970, p. 85.
29.   Bagshaw, 1850, p. 423; Timmis Smith, 1970, p. 314.
30.   thestaffordshireknotgillowheath.co.uk/history (10/3/2020).
31.   Langley & Langley, 1993, pp. 4–5.
32.   Ibid.
33.   Ibid., pp. 9–10.
34.   *Congleton & Macclesfield Mercury*, 23/3/1872, p. 1.
35.   Langley & Langley, 1993, pp. 12, 70.
36.   *Chester Chronicle*, 2/10/1852, p. 8.
37.   *Chester Courant*, 20/5/1857, p. 4.
38.   Jones, J., 1999, pp. 4–5; Smith, D.B., 2017.
39.   Jones, J., 1999, pp. 28–9.
40.   PP, 1834a, p. 277A.
41.   Malmgreen, 1985, p. 100.
42.   Gawsworth Parish Council, 2019, p. 65.
43.   Knott, 1986, p. 89.
44.   Davies, C.S., 1961, p. 262.
45.   Ibid., p. 264.
46.   HEA, BF102007.
47.   Anonymous, 1888, p. 10.

48. HEA, BF102007.
49. Anonymous, 1888, p. 13.
50. *Pall Mall Gazette*, 19/10/1895, p. 9.
51. Hall, J., 1883, p. 209.
52. Ibid., p. 226.
53. Howard, 1789, p. 209.
54. PP, 1834a, p. 281A.
55. Garton, 1978, pp. 32–3.
56. Latham, 1973, pp. 58–9.
57. TNA, IR 29/5/145, plot 396.
58. OS 1881, 1:10560 Cheshire sheet LXV.
59. Tringham, 2013, p. 115.
60. RG09/2622, f. 82, p. 9.
61. HEA, BF102128.
62. *Gloucestershire Echo*, 30/4/1900. *Manchester Courier*, 17/12/1904.
63. Tringham, 2013, p. 115.
64. PP, 1834b, p. 73b.
65. *Chester Chronicle*, 9/6/1837, p. 1.
66. Hogg, 1998, p. 3.
67. Rochester, 1988.
68. *Chester Courant*, 29/6/1853, p. 1; Hogg, 1998, p. 7.
69. *Cheshire Observer*, 19/11/1859, p. 9. *Northwich Guardian*, 20/2/1875, p. 4.
70. *Northwich Guardian*, 23/8/1893, p. 4.
71. Hitchcock, 1985, p. 261.
72. PP, 1804, p. 48 (full list not given).
73. CA, WMS 2530.
74. PP, 1839a, p. 118.
75. *Chester Courant*, 8/3/1854, p. 5.
76. *Chester Courant*, 19/7/1854, p. 5.
77. *Chester Courant*, 28/2/1855, p. 1.
78. *Chester Courant*, 28/10/1857, p. 4.
79. *Cheshire Observer*, 22/8/1896, p. 8.
80. *Runcorn Guardian*, 4/4/1913, p. 5.
81. Anonymous, 1732, p. 98.
82. PP, 1834a, p. 278A.
83. Knott, 1986, pp. 171–2.
84. *Alderley & Wilmslow Advertiser*, 20/7/1894; *Manchester Courier*, 23/8/1848, p. 6.
85. OS 1:500 Stockport town map, 1875.
86. *Morning Chronicle*, 13/8/1842, p. 3.
87. BMJ, 6/12/1894, pp. 764–5.
88. *The Hospital*, 15/9/1906, pp. 428–430, 447–8.
89. *Chester Chronicle*, 5/8/1836, p. 4.
90. Yeoman, 1965, pp. 12–13; Handley, 2009, p. 121.
91. Yeoman, 1965, pp. 16–17.
92. Ibid., p. 16.
93. *Cheshire Observer*, 26/11/1927, p. 5.

CHAPTER 15

1. 7 & 8 Will. II, c.32.
2. Cary, 1700, pp. 11–15.
3. Ibid., pp. 16–17.
4. Anonymous, 1711, p. 3.
5. Rogers, 1928, p. 190.
6. PP, 1834c, p. 201g.
7. PP, 1834a, Part I, p. 512A.
8. BMJ, 26/10/1867, pp. 373–4.
9. HEA, BF101326.
10. *Western Daily Press*, 23/11/1904, p. 5.
11. Morrison, 1999, p. 9.
12. Lloyd, 1950, pp. 41–2.
13. historicengland.org.uk/listing/the-list/list-entry/1393302(23/6/2020).
14. *Cheltenham Chronicle*, 2/11/1809.
15. vchglosacademy.org/drafts/localgovt1738.pdf (22/6/2020).
16. GA, P78/1/VE/2/2.
17. british-history.ac.uk/vch/glos/vol7/pp174-183 (28/2/2020).
18. british-history.ac.uk/vch/glos/vol8/pp67-81 (30/3/2020).
19. Paget, 1988, p. 154.
20. Gilbert, C., 1987, p. 62.
21. *Cheltenham Chronicle*, 4/10/1838, p. 2; *Cheltenham Examiner*, 18/3/1840, p. 1.
22. *Cheltenham Chronicle*, 26/3/1844; *Cheltenham Examiner*, 13/11/1844, p. 2.
23. Cheltenham Old Town Survey, 1855–57.
24. *Cheltenham Chronicle*, 17/11/1874, p. 3.
25. *Cheltenham Chronicle*, 17/11/1885, p. 4.
26. *Cheltenham Chronicle*, 29/10/1904, p. 3.
27. Hall, L., 2011, p. 39.
28. southglos.gov.uk/documents/Heritage-Walks-Booklet-Final-Draft.pdf (25/6/2020).
29. GA, D9125/1/8956.
30. Bristol Archives P.FC/OP/2/29.
31. *Gloucestershire Chronicle*, 24/9/1836, p. 2.
32. Alcock, 1992, p. 38.
33. Anonymous, 1725, p. 105.
34. GA, P86/1/OV/2/1.
35. Ryland-Epton, Cirencester Workhouse under the Old Poor Law, 2017, p. 228.
36. vchglosacademy.org/drafts/ciren1825/social.pdf (27/6/2020).
37. Ryland-Epton, 2020, p. 171; british-history.ac.uk/vch/glos/vol7/pp69-86 (31/3/2020).
38. TNA, IR 29/13/32, plot 531.
39. HO107/354/13, f. 13, p. 14.
40. *Wilts and Gloucestershire Standard*, 3/2/1872, p. 1.
41. *Wilts and Gloucestershire Standard*, 5/12/1896, p. 1.
42. Brewer, 1890, pp. 652–3.
43. *Gloucestershire Echo*, 31/10/1904, p. 4.
44. GA, D674a/T206.
45. Rogers, 1928, pp. 191–2.
46. Ibid., p. 193.
47. Moss, 1967, pp. 153–63.

48. Ibid., p. 172.
49. GA, Q/RW/1.
50. PP, 1835, pp. 177–8.
51. BMJ, 26/10/1867, p. 374.
52. brh.org.uk/site/articles/eastville-workhouse-unmarked-graves-paupers-rosemary-green (4/4/2020).
53. BMJ, 20/10/1894, pp. 879–80.
54. *Western Daily Press*, 12/9/1902, p. 7.
55. Lindley, 1977, p. 162.
56. PP, 1834a, p. 882A.
57. GA, P230/OV/9/1; S230/2/1.
58. Lett, 1889, p. 18.
59. GA, D9125/1/11466.
60. bioeddie.co.uk/uley/theworkhouse.php (25/6/2020).
61. PP, 1834a, p. 886A.
62. historicengland.org.uk/listing/the-list/list-entry/1090893 (22/6/2020).
63. historicengland.org.uk/listing/the-list/list-entry/1090911 (22/6/2020).
64. GA, D2349/1.
65. GA, P193/OV/9/2; D3386/1.
66. *Gloucestershire Chronicle*, 7/5/1836.
67. Personal communication from Laura Baker.
68. british-history.ac.uk/vch/glos/vol4/pp141-152.
69. PP, 1776, pp. 256–7.
70. *The Cambrian*, 3/4/18390, p. 3.
71. Chandler, Herbert & Jurica, 2016, p. 213.
72. *Gloucestershire Chronicle*, 29/10/1836, p. 3; 4/2/1837, p. 2.
73. *Gloucestershire Chronicle*, 15//2/1873, p. 1.
74. Brewer, 1890, p. 654.
75. *Gloucester Journal*, 17/2/1912.
76. HEA, BF100594.
77. british-history.ac.uk/vch/glos/vol12/95-122 (22/6/2020).
78. PP, 1804, p. 172.
79. british-history.ac.uk/vch/glos/vol12/122-174 (30/3/2020).
80. *The Cambrian*, 16/3/1805, p. 4.
81. GA, P101/VE/2/1.
82. GA, P309/VE/2/1.
83. historicengland.org.uk/listing/the-list/list-entry/1156556 (24/6/2020).
84. Chandler, Herbert & Jurica, 2016, p. 104.
85. british-history.ac.uk/vch/glos/vol12/317-346 (27/3/2020).
86. *Gloucestershire Chronicle*, 20/2/1836, p. 2.
87. *Gloucester Citizen*, 15/8/1883, p. 2.
88. *Gloucester Citizen*, 27/7/1904, p. 3.
89. *Cheltenham Chronicle*, 15/4/1922, p. 4.
90. british-history.ac.uk/vch/glos/vol9/pp106-145 (1/4/2020).
91. british-history.ac.uk/vch/glos/vol7/pp5-13 (20/7/2020).
92. BMJ, 16/11/1867, p. 459.
93. *Gloucestershire Chronicle*, 24/10/1868, p. 2.
94. british-history.ac.uk/vch/glos/vol6/pp33-49 (31/3/2020).
95. british-history.ac.uk/vch/glos/vol6/pp27-33 (31/3/2020).
96. *Oxford Journal*, 28/5/1836, p. 4.

97. PP, 1861, p. 41.
98. *Oxford Journal*, 31/8/1872, p. 3.
99. Burgess, 2002, pp. 186–7.
100. british-history.ac.uk/vch/glos/vol11/pp134-136 (4/4/2020).
101. PP, 1804, pp. 170–1.
102. PP, 1834a, p. 884A.
103. british-history.ac.uk/vch/glos/vol11/pp181-182 (3/4/2020).
104. british-history.ac.uk/vch/glos/vol11/pp30-32 (3/4/2030).
105. british-history.ac.uk/vch/glos/vol11/pp200-201 (3/4/2020).
106. british-history.ac.uk/vch/glos/vol10/pp253-254 (2/3/2020).
107. *Gloucestershire Chronicle*, 16/7/1836, p. 4.
108. Baddeley, 1907, p. 224.
109. Ryland-Epton, 2020, p. 226.
110. british-history.ac.uk/vch/glos/vol11/p230 (3/4/2020).
111. british-history.ac.uk/vch/glos/vol11/p162 (3/4/2020).
112. GA, D1405/16/20, D2056/6. british-history.ac.uk/vch/glos/vol11/pp53-54 (30/3/2020).
113. british-history.ac.uk/vch/glos/vol10/p228(3/4/3030).
114. british-history.ac.uk/vch/glos/vol10/pp257-259 (3/4/2020).
115. british-history.ac.uk/vch/glos/vol10/p284 (4/4/2020).
116. RG13/2434, f. 36, p. 29.
117. *Cheltenham Chronicle*, 13/4/1837, p. 3.
118. Walmsley, 1993, pp. 8–10.
119. *Gloucester Citizen*, 12/11/1904, p. 4.
120. british-history.ac.uk/vch/glos/vol11/pp275-277 (4/3/2020).
121. *Gloucester Journal*, 18/3/1837, p. 2.
122. HEA, BF100642; *Stroud News*, 22/7/1904, p. 8.
123. british-history.ac.uk/vch/glos/vol8/pp146-153 (8/7/2020).
124. HEA, BF100625; historicengland.org.uk/listing/the-list/list-entry/1280322 (1/7/2020).
125. british-history.ac.uk/vch/glos/vol8/pp34-49 (30/3/2020).
126. Chandler, Herbert & Jurica, 2016, p. 321.
127. british-history.ac.uk/vch/glos/vol8/pp196-208 (30/3/2020).
128. *Hereford Journal*, 15/5/1839, p. 3.
129. *Gloucester Journal*, 21/1/1905, p. 7.
130. Personal communication.
131. GA, D2658/22.
132. thornburyroots.co.uk/sms/workhouse (24/6/2020).
133. GA, Q/SR/1791/B; Q/SR/1791/D; GDR/T1/21.
134. *Gloucester Journal*, 20/8/1804, p. 3.
135. GA, GDR/T1/21.
136. GA, P42/OV/2/10.
137. historicengland.org.uk/listing/the-list/list-entry/1128931 (5/7/2020).
138. Cherry, 2011, p. 16.
139. *Bristol Mercury*, 1/4/1848, p. 4.
140. *Gloucester Journal*, 19/2/1881, p. 4.
141. *Gloucestershire Chronicle*, 21/7/1888, p. 1.
142. *Western Daily Press*, 2/9/1899, p. 4.
143. british-history.ac.uk/vch/glos/vol12/233-254
144. british-history.ac.uk/vch/glos/vol10/pp97-98 (5/7/2020).

145. GA, P228/VE/2/1.
146. british-history.ac.uk/vch/glos/vol10/pp44–46
147. british-history.ac.uk/vch/glos/vol5/pp173-195 (31/3/2020).
148. Ryland-Epton, 2020, p. 164.
149. GA, P30a/VE/2/1.
150. *Hereford Times*, 19/4/1851, p. 1.
151. GA, P110/VE//2/1.
152. Ryland-Epton, 2020, p. 164.
153. GA, G/WE/32.
154. *Hereford Times*, 14/10/1882, p. 11.
155. *Gloucester Citizen,* 16/8/1898, p. 2.
156. *Gloucestershire Chronicle*, 2611/1904, p. 3.
157. british-history.ac.uk/vch/glos/vol10/pp134-135 (2/4/2020).
158. british-history.ac.uk/vch/glos/vol10/p152 (2/4/2020).
159. Ryland-Epton, 2020, p. 164; redlionarlingham.co.uk/media/2843/arlinghamlflt.pdf (7/6/2020).
160. *Gloucestershire Chronicle*, 18/6/1836, p. 1.
161. *Wilts and Gloucestershire Standard*, 8/9/1866, p. 4.
162. GA, P/368/1/OV/7/2.
163. Dent, 1877, p. 307.
164. Ibid., p. 149.
165. Aldred, 2009, pp. 94–5.
166. Morrison, 1999, p. 77; Knight & Co., 1848, p. 103.
167. *Cheltenham Chronicle*, 5/7/1913, p. 6.
168. *Western Daily Press*, 1/8/1915, p. 4.

CHAPTER 16

1. HA, R27/10937, E38/73, E38/29.
2. Davies, D., 1970, p. 116.
3. HA, BO92/55; N37/34.
4. RG12/2070, f. 47, p. 23.
5. HA, N5/1.
6. HA, A01/8.
7. HA, BK52/29.
8. HA, AC16/27.
9. RH11/2596, f. 53, p. 2.
10. Elliot, 1985, p. 1.
11. Ibid., p. 2.
12. Ibid., p. 17.
13. Ibid., p. 9.
14. 9 & 10 William 3 c.34.
15. Law Commission, 2012, p. 216.
16. HA, AH70/234.
17. Allen, 1821, p. 25.
18. Eden, 1797, Volume 2, pp. 269–70.
19. *Hereford Journal*, 9/9/1807, p. 2.
20. Morrill, 1974, p. 244.
21. HA, A95/IV/10.

22. HA, L3/184.
23. *Hereford Journal*, 3/10/1798, p. 3.
24. Morrill, 1974, p. 245.
25. *Hereford Journal*, 5/12/1849, p. 2.
26. *Hereford Times*, 7/12/1850
27. *Gloucestershire Chronicle*, 7/6/1879, p. 8.
28. *Hereford Journal*, 10/10/1903, p. 2.
29. *Hereford Journal*, 19/12/1904, p. 2.
30. HA, G73/1.
31. PP, 1834c, p. 54g.
32. HA, AG55/56.
33. *Hereford Journal*, 28/12/1836.
34. *Kington Times*, 15/12/1917, p. 2.
35. *Kington Times*, 22/3/1930.
36. HA, D24/1.
37. herefordshire.gov.uk/herefordshires-past/the-post-medieval-period/institutions/ workhouses/herefordshire-workhouses/ledbury-church-lane-workhouse (27/2/2020).
38. Powell, J., 2008, pp. 33–41.
39. HA, E3/371-391, bundle 144.
40. RG10/2681 f. 109, p. 19.
41. Powell, J., 2008, p. 49.
42. Ibid., pp. 53–5.
43. Ibid., p. 61.
44. *Evesham Standard*, 17/12/1904, p. 3.
45. Hitchcock, 1985, p. 265.
46. Reeves, 1980, pp. 88–9.
47. Ibid., p. 38.
48. HA, N31/33.
49. RG10/2716, f. 15, p. 24.
50. HA, A58/6.
51. Powell J. , 2008, pp. 137–40.
52. PP, 1909, pp. 133–5 (slightly abridged). The unnamed workhouse is identifiable as Ross.
53. *Kington Times*, 16/10/1920, p. 2.
54. Morgan & Briffett, 1998, p. 3.
55. PP, 1834c, p. 55g.
56. HA, AC84/86, AC84/87.
57. british-history.ac.uk/vch/glos/vol5/pp231-247 (22/6/2020).
58. *Hereford Journal*, 24/7/1811.
59. HA, AA33/23.
60. HA, L24/ii/i/iii.
61. *Hereford Journal*, 22/9/1824, p. 1.
62. RG11/2586, f. 88, p. 22.
63. HA, W43/111.
64. discovery.nationalarchives.gov.uk/details/r/C2301836 (17/3/2020).
65. Morgan & Briffett, 1998, p. 4.
66. PP, 1867, p. 239.
67. HEA, BF100521.
68. Morgan & Briffett, 1998, p. 23.
69. *Ross Gazette*, 3/11/1904, p. 3.

70. Morgan & Briffett, 1998, p. 19.
71. Reeves, 1980, pp. 156–7.
72. herefordshire.gov.uk/herefordshires-past/the-post-medieval-period/institutions/workhouses/herefordshire-workhouses/almeley-woonton-workhouse (27/2/2020).
73. *Hereford Journal*, 1/6/1836, p. 2.
74. *Hereford Journal*, 5/10/1836, p. 3.
75. *Hereford Journal*, 12/11/1836, p. 2.
76. Personal communication from Sharyn Exelby.
77. *Hereford Journal*, 10/8/1867, p. 4.
78. HEA, BF100472.
79. *Tenbury Wells Advertiser*, 2/6/1908, p. 5.

CHAPTER 17

1. Gaydon, 1968, p. 283; SA PH/P/15/53.
2. search.shropshirehistory.org.uk/collections/getrecord/CCS_MSA2934 (5/6/2020); location suggested by 1901 census RG13/2531 f. 69, p. 15.
3. Gaydon, 1968, p. 24.
4. Ibid., p. 69.
5. Ibid., p. 326.
6. Phillimore, 1902, p. 448.
7. Gaydon, 1968, p. 189.
8. Ibid., p. 213.
9. historicengland.org.uk/images-books/photos/item/IOE01/08875/09 (2/3/2020).
10. Smith L. , 2007, p. 37.
11. Wroxeter, Berrington, Cound, Eaton Constantine, Kenley, Leighton, Uffington, Upton Magna and the chapelry of Cressage.
12. Crofton, 2002, p. 9.
13. Ibid., p. 13.
14. Ibid.
15. Ibid., pp. 14–16.
16. PP, 1909, pp. 131–2. The unnamed workhouse is identifiable as Atcham.
17. Anonymous, 1732, p. 159.
18. PP, 1834a, p. 661A.
19. Bagshaw, 1851, p. 467.
20. historicengland.org.uk/listing/the-list/list-entry/1188341 (20/3/2020).
21. Smith L. , 2007, p. 81.
22. SA P59/C/1.
23. Whitmore, 1837, p. 6; Smith L. , 2007, p. 82.
24. e.g. see *Eddowes's Journal*, 28/6/1848, p. 3.
25. Ibid., p. 88.
26. british-history.ac.uk/vch/salop/vol10/pp22-44 (4/4/2020).
27. historicengland.org.uk/listing/the-list/list-entry/1383315 (4/4/020).
28. Smith, L., 2007, p. 88.
29. Ibid.
30. Ibid.
31. PP, 1867, p. 254.
32. Fletcher, 1909, p. 312.
33. Fletcher, 1920, p. 132 of Neen Savage section.

34. Fletcher, 1915, p. 13.
35. Fletcher, 1920, p. 156 of Kinlet section.
36. Blakeway, J.B., 1908, p. 87.
37. HO107/1985, f. 157, p. 34.
38. Smith L. , 2007, p. 91.
39. SA, PL6/321.
40. Rogers, 1928, pp. 293–4. (Slightly abridged.)
41. historicengland.org.uk/listing/the-list/list-entry/1054539 (21/3/2020).
42. HO107/919/1, f. 38, p. 1; HO107/919/ 10, f. 46, p. 1.
43. Goff, 2004, pp. 31–2.
44. Goff, 2005, p. 7
45. SA, P61/L/2/1.
46. Smith, L., 2007, p. 99.
47. Ibid.
48. Peele & Clease, 1903, p. 113.
49. www.british-history.ac.uk/rchme/heref/vol3/pp127-133 (18/11/2021).
50. PP, 1831, p. 328.
51. Smith, L., 2007, p. 102.
52. HEA, BF100981.
53. HEA, BF100984.
54. PP, 1909, p. 131. The unnamed workhouse is identifiable as Drayton.
55. Smith, L., 2007, pp. 39–40.
56. Bagshaw, 1851, p. 223.
57. Rogers, 1928, pp. 294–5.
58. Smith, L., 2007, p. 42.
59. SA, 6000/17612.
60. PP, 1834c, p. 196g.
61. PP, 1834a., Part II, pp. 171a–172a.
62. *Wrexham Advertiser*, 19/6/1869, p. 8.
63. Stephen, 1899, Volume 59, p. 11.
64. Howard, 1789, p. 175.
65. Wright, 1826, p. 178.
66. *Hereford Journal*, 9/11/1831, p. 3.
67. Pigot & Co., 1835, p. 363.
68. herefordshire.gov.uk/herefordshires-past/the-post-medieval-period/institutions/workhouses/herefordshire-workhouses/leintwardine-workhouse (27/2/2020).
69. Williams, D., 2012, p. 9; Peele & Clease, 1903, p. 152.
70. Smith, L., 2007, pp. 105–7.
71. Williams, D., 2012, pp. 10–11.
72. Ibid., pp. 38, 71–3.
73. *Eddowes's Journal, and General Advertiser*, 9/5/1883, p. 8.
74. british-history.ac.uk/vch/salop/vol10/pp399-447 (11/4/2020).
75. Smith, L., 2007, p. 57.
76. Ibid., p. 60.
77. PP, 1849, p. 309.
78. Jones, K., 2009, pp. 113–4.
79. PP, 1867, p. 256.
80. HEA, BF100985.
81. *Wellington Journal*, 9/71898, p. 5.
82. *Wellington Journal*, 12/11/1904, p. 11.

83.   british-history.ac.uk/vch/salop/vol11/pp232-236 (21/3/2020).
84.   SA, P207/L/8/4.
85.   Smith, L., 2007, pp. 64–5.
86.   Fletcher, 1913, p. 155.
87.   Wakeman, 1892, pp. 101–2.
88.   HO107/905/2 f. 20, p. 19.
89.   Fletcher, 1913, p. 109; sambrook.info/History.html (17/3/2020).
90.   gnosallhistory.co.uk/workhouse.htm (5/4/2020).
91.   Fletcher, 1913, Tibberton section, p. 54.
92.   Smith, L., 2007, p. 65.
93.   Ibid., p. 66.
94.   PP, 1856, p. 64.
95.   Ibid., pp. 68–9; HEA, BF101304.
96.   *Wellington Journal*, 5/2/1898, p. 7.
97.   PP, 1902, p. 135.
98.   Phillimore, 1905, p. 258.
99.   Dodd, A.H., *The Old Poor Law in North Wales*, 1926, p. 115.
100. llansilin.org/newsletter/NL88.pdf (6/2/2020).
101. Rowley, 1983, p. 20.
102. Lloyd Kenyon, 1902, p. 375.
103. Phillimore, 1906, pp. 384–5.
104. Oswestry Parish and Town, St Martins, Selattyn, Whittington, West Felton, Ruyton, Kinnerley, Knockin, Llanyblodwel, and part of Llanymynech.
105. 31 Geo. III c.24.
106. Knight & Co., 1848, p. 145.
107. *Border Counties Advertiser*, 15/11/1876, 13/10/1876.
108. Rowley, 1983, pp. 21–3.
109. *Worcester Journal*, 16/12/1819 p. 3.
110. *Aberdeen Press and Journal*, 15/3/1907, p. 5.
111. SA, D641/3/E/6/13/57.
112. *Bye-gones*, January 1902, p. 298.
113. Smith, L., 2007, pp. 69–70.
114. search.shropshirehistory.org.uk/collections/getrecord/CCS_MSA37306/ (7/7/2020).
115. Smith, L., 2007, p. 71.
116. Ibid., p. 72.
117. Knight & Co., 1848, p. 145.
118. Owen, H., 1808, p. 333.
119. Fletcher, 1911, p. viii.
120. Owen, H. , 1808, p. 333.
121. Tomkins, 1999, p. 211.
122. 24 Geo. III s.2 c.15.
123. Abridged from Rogers, 1928, pp. 297–9.
124. PP, 1836, p. 361.
125. 7 Geo. IV c.141.
126. british-history.ac.uk/vch/salop/vol11/pp232-236 (20/3/2020).
127. PP, 1834b, p. 395b.
128. british-history.ac.uk/vch/salop/vol11/pp316-317 (20/3/2020).
129. archelou.co.uk/ercall_burials/1750.htm (11/4/2020).
130. Smith, L., 2007, p. 76.

131. Knight & Co., 1848, p. 145.
132. HEA, BF100979.
133. *LGMD*, 1920, p. 302, and 1929, p. 340.
134. Fletcher, 1908, p. 465.
135. SA, P221/L/9/7.
136. Smith, L., 2007, p. 110.
137. Knight & Co., 1848, p. 145.
138. PP, 1867, p. 258.
139. *Shrewsbury Chronicle*, 4/11/1904, p. 8.
140. *LGMD*, 1934, p. 142.
141. CA, D/6487.
142. SA, X6000/42/9/12078.
143. 32 Geo. III c.85.
144. Smith, L., 2007, p. 49.
145. Morrison, 1999, p. 130.
146. PP, 1849, p. 288.
147. *Wolverhampton Chronicle and Staffordshire Advertiser*, 12/9/1849, p. 2.
148. Hill, 1868, pp. 75–6.

BIBLIOGRAPHY

Alcock, P., *Whispers from the Workhouse: The story of 'The Spike'* (Bristol, 1992).

Aldred, D. H., *A History of Bishop's Cleeve and Woodmancote* (Amberley Publishing, 2009).

Allen, J., *Bibliotheca Herefordiensis* (J. Allen, 1821).

Anonymous, 'Some Considerations offer'd to the Citizens of Bristol, relating to the Corporation for the Poor in the said City' (1711).

Anonymous, *An Account of Several Work-houses for Employing and Maintaining the Poor* (Joseph Downing, 1725).

Anonymous, *An Account of Several Work-houses for Employing and Maintaining the Poor* (Joseph Downing, 1732).

Anonymous, *A Walk through the Public Institutions of Macclesfield: Macclesfield Courier and Herald* (1888).

Anonymous, *A Short History of the Clatterbridge Hospitals* (Central Wirral Hospital Management Committee booklet, 1966).

Baddeley, W. S., *Cotteswold Manor: Being the History of Painswick* (1907).

Bagshaw, S., *History, Gazetteer & Directory of the County Palatine of Chester* (1850).

Bagshaw, S., *History, Gazetteer & Directory of Shropshire* (1851).

Ball, R., Parkin, D., and Mills, S., *100 Fishponds Road: Life and Death in a Victorian Workhouse*, 2nd ed. (Bristol Radical History Group, 2016).

Blakeway, J. B., 'History of Pontesbury', *Transactions of the Shropshire Archaeological and Natural History Society*, Series 2, Vol. V, pp.229–252 (1893).

Blakeway, J. B., 'Notes on Kinlet', *Transactions of the Shropshire Archaeological and Natural History Society*, Series 3, Vol. VIII, 83–150 (1908).

Brewer, E., 'Workhouse Life in Town and Country: Cirencester and Gloucester', *Sunday at Home*, pp. 652–4 (1890).

Brown, R. L., *Parish and Pauper: A History of the Administration of the Poor Law in the Parish of Castle Caereinion, Montgomeryshire* (Gwasg Eglwys y Trallwng, 1999).

Burgess, P., 'The Mystery of the Whistling Sewermen: How Cecil Sharp Discovered Gloucestershire Morris Dancing', *Folk Music Journal*, 8(2), pp.178–94 (2002).

Burne, R. V., 'The Treatment of the Poor in the Eighteenth Century in Chester', *Journal of the Chester and North Wales Architectural, Archaeological and Historic Society*, 52, pp.33–48 (1965).

CADW. *Pembroke: Understanding Urban Character* (2015).

Cary, J., *An Account of the Proceedings of the Corporation of Bristol in Execution of the Act of Parliament for the better Employing and Maintaining the Poor of that City* (Bristol, 1700).

Cathrall, W., *The History of North Wales*, Volume II (J. Gleave and Sons, 1828).

Chandler, J., Herbert, N. M., & Jurica, A. R., *A History of the County of Gloucester (Vol. XIII)* (Oxford University Press, 2016).

Charlesworth, L., *Welfare's Forgotten Past: A Socio-Legal History of the Poor Law* (Routledge, 2010).

Cherry, T., *I'm a pauper, get me out of here: Thornbury Workhouse, 1836–1871* (Thornbury and District Heritage Trust, 2011).

Clark, A., *The Story of Pontypool* (Pontypool, 1958).

Cooper, N., & Morrison, K., 'The English and Welsh Workhouses of George Wilkinson', *The Georgian Group Journal* XIV, pp. 104–130 (2004).

Crofton, C., *The Making of a Workhouse: The History of Cross Houses Hospital* (2002).

Davies, A. E., 'Some Aspects of the Old Poor Law in Cardiganshire 1750–1834', *Journal of the Cardiganshire Antiquarian Society*, VI, pp. 1–44 (1968).

Davies, A. E., 'The New Poor Law in a Rural Area', *Ceredigion* VIII(3), pp. 245–90 (1978).

Davies, A. E., 'Poor Law Administration in Cardiganshire' (G. H. Jenkins, & I. G. Jones, Eds.) *Cardiganshire County History* 3, 323–41 (1998).

Davies, C. S., *A History of Macclesfield* (Manchester University Press, 1961).

Davies, D., 'Care of the Poor in Winslow Township, 1753–1812', in J. G. Hillaby, *Bromyard: a Local History* (pp. 113–121), (1970).

Davies, Dawn et. al., *A History of H.M. Stanley Hospital, St Asaph, Denbighshire 1838–2012: A site record* (Betsi Cadwaladr University, 2012).

Dent, E., *Annals of Winchcombe and Sudeley*, (John Murray, 1877).

Dodd, A. H., 'The Old Poor Law in North Wales', *Archaeologica Cambrensis*, VI, 111–32 (1926).

Dodd, A. H., *A History of Wrexham, Denbighshire* (Bridge Books, 1957).

Dodd, A. H., *A History of Caernarvonshire 1284–1900* (Caernarvonshire Historical Society, 1968).

Draper, C., *Paupers, Bastards and Lunatics: The Story of Conwy Workhouse* (Gwasg Carreg Gwalch, 2005).

Eden, F. M., *The State of the Poor: Or, an History of the Labouring Classes in England* (London, 1797).

Eden, FM, Rogers, A. G. (Ed.), *The State of the Poor: A History of the Labouring Classes in England* (Routledge, 1928).

Elliot, N., *Dore Workhouse in Victorian Times* (Ewyas Harold Branch of the W.E.A, 1985).

Fletcher, W. G. (Ed.), *Shropshire Parish Registers: Diocese of Lichfield Vol. IX* (Shropshire Parish Register Society, 1908).

Fletcher, W. G. (Ed.), *Shropshire Parish Registers: Diocese of Hereford Vol. IX* (Shropshire Parish Register Society, 1909).

Fletcher, W. G. (Ed.), *Shropshire Parish Registers: Diocese of Lichfield Vol. XII* (Shropshire Parish Register Society, 1911).

Fletcher, W. G. (Ed.), *Shropshire Parish Registers: Diocese of Lichfield Vol. XIII* (Shropshire Parish Register Society, 1913).

Fletcher, W. G. (Ed.), *Shropshire Parish Registers: Diocese of Hereford Vol. XVI* (Shropshire Parish Register Society, 1915).

Fletcher, W. G. (Ed.), *Shropshire Parish Registers: Diocese of Hereford Vol. XVII* (Shropshire Parish Register Society, 1920).

Flynn–Hughes, C., 'The Bangor Workhouse', *Transactions of the Caernarvonshire Historical Society,* 5, pp.88–100 (1944).

Flynn–Hughes, C., 'The Workhouses of Caernarvonshire 1760–1914', *Transactions of the Caernarvonshire Historical Society, 7, pp. 88–100 (*1946).

Foster, B., *A History of Pontypool Union Workhouse 1838–1930* (1990).

Frost, J., *A Letter to Sir Charles Morgan, of Tredegar, etc.* (Samuel Etheridge, 1821).

Garton, E., *Nantwich in the 18th Century* (Cheshire Libraries and Museums, 1978).

Gaston, H., *A Lingering Fear: West Sussex Hospitals and the Workhouse Legacy* (Southern Editorial Services, 2009).

Gawsworth Parish Council, 'Gawsworth Neighbourhood Plan' (2019).

Gaydon, A. T. (Ed.), *Victoria County History of Shropshire* (Vol. VIII) (Oxford University Press, 1968).

Gilbert, C., 'Workhouse Furniture', *Regional Furniture*, 1, pp.61–70 (1987).

Gilbert, T., *A Bill, Intended to be Offered to Parliament, for the Better Relief and Employment of the Poor* (1775).

Goff, A., 'The Clun Poor Law Union - Part 1: From Poor-house to Workhouse 1836 –1845', *South West Shropshire Historical and Archaeological Society Journal*, 15, pp.25–35 (2004).

Goff, A., 'The Clun Poor Law Union - Part 2: The Victorian Workhouse 1845–1900', *South West Shropshire Historical and Archaeological Society Journal*, 16, pp.6–15 (2005).

Grant, R., *On the Parish: An Illustrated Source Book on the Care of the Poor under the Old Poor Law* (Glamorgan Archive Service, 1988).

Hainsworth, J, *The Llanfyllin Union Workhouse* (The Llanfyllin Dolydd Building Preservation Trust, 2004).

Hall, J., *A History of the Town and Parish of Nantwich* (E.J. Morton, 1883).

Hall, L., 'Down the Garden Path', *Glevensis*, 44, pp.35–45 (2011).

Hancock, T. W., 'Llanrhaiadr-yn-Mochnant, Its Parochial History and Antiquities', *Montgomeryshire Collections*, VI, pp.319–340 (1873).

Handley, M. D., 'The Great Boughton Poor Law Union, 1837–71', *Transactions of the Historic Society of Lancashire and Cheshire*, 158, pp.169–92 (2009).

Handley, M. D., 'The Wirral Poor Law Union 1836–61', *Transactions of the Lancashire and Cheshire Antiquarian Society*, 104, pp.119–135 (2009).

Hankins, F., 'From Parish Pauper to Union Workhouse Inmate (Part 1)', *Brycheiniog*, XXIX, pp.53–86 (1997).

Hankins, F., 'From Parish Pauper to Workhouse Inmate (Part 2)', *Brycheiniog*, XXXI, pp.65–108 (1999).

Hemingway, J., *History of the City of Chester* (Vol. II) (J. Fletcher, 1831).

Herrod, D., *The County Hospital Hereford* (The Press, 1980).

Higginbotham, P., *Workhouses of the North* (The History Press, 2006).

Higginbotham, P., *Workhouses of the Midlands* (The History Press, 2007).

Higginbotham, P., *The Workhouse Cookbook* (The History Press, 2008).

Higginbotham, P., *The Workhouse Encyclopedia* (The History Press, 2012).

Hill, F., Children of the State (Macmillan, 1868).

Hitchcock, T. V., *The English Workhouse: a study in institutional poor relief in selected counties 1695–1750* (DPhil thesis, University of Oxford, 1985).

Hogg, S., *Cold Comfort at the Northwich Union Workhouse* (Northwich & District Heritage Society, 1998).

Hollen Lees, L., *The Solidarities of Strangers: The English Poor Laws and the People 1700–1948* (Cambridge University Press, 1998).

Hooker, G., *Llandilofawr Poor Law Union 1836–1886: 'The most difficult union in Wales'* (University of Leicester PhD Thesis) (2013).

Hopkin-James, L. J., *Old Cowbridge: Borough, Church and School* (Educational Pub. Co.,1922).

Howard, J., *An Account of the Principal Lazarettos in Europe* (Warrington, 1789).

Hughes, C., 'The 150th Anniversary of Riverside, Pembroke', Commemorative Brochure (1989).

Hughes, D., 'Poor Law History In Monmouthshire Since 1834', *Presenting Monmouthshire*, 27 (1969).

Ingham, A., *Altrincham and Bowdon: with Historical Reminiscences of Ashton-on-Mersey, Sale, and Surrounding Townships* (1897).

John, M., 'A Sacking Matter in Narberth', *Journal of the Pembrokeshire Historical Society*, XIII, pp.43–56 (2004).

Jones, C., *Musings of a Middleton Boy: Growing up on the Gower Coast* (Bertrams Print on Demand, 2007).

Jones, D., 'Pauperism in the Aberystwyth Poor Law Union 1870–1914', *Ceredigion: Journal of the Cardiganshire Antiquarian Society*, 9, 78–101 (1983).'

Jones, D. L., 'The Fate of the Paupers: Life in the Bangor and Beaumaris Union Workhouse 1845–71', *Caernarvonshire Historical Society Transactions*, 66 (2005).

Jones, G., *Carchar, Nid Cartref: Hanes Cynnar Wyrcws Pwllheli, 1840–1890* (Clwb y Bont,1992).

Jones, J., P. Brigg (Ed.), *Macclesfield Workhouse* (Graveyard Press, 1999).

Jones, K., *Pit Men, Poachers and Preachers: Life and the Poor Law in the Madeley Union of Parishes 1700–1930* (Dog Rose Press, 2009).

Jones, K., *Newcastle-in-Emlyn Union and Workhouse* (Summerhill Press, 2011).

Jones, K., *A Lingering Fear: The Story of Pontypridd Union Workhouse* (2016).

Jones, P., and King, S., *Pauper Voices, Public Opinion and Workhouse Reform in Mid-Victorian England* (Palgrave Macmillan, 2020).

Jones, T., *A History of the County of Brecknock* (Blissett, Davies, 1909).

Jones, T., *The Holywell Workhouses* (1995).

Jones, T. D., 'Poor Law Administration in Merthyr Tydfil Union 1834–1894', *Morgannwg*, 8, pp.35–62 (1964).

Kain, R. J. P., Oliver, R. R., *The Tithe Maps of England and Wales: A Cartographic Analysis and County-by-County Catalogue* (Cambridge University Press, 1995).

Kelly & Co., *Kelly's Directory of Monmouthshire and South Wales* (1895).

King, S. S., 'The History of the Poor Law in Wales: Under-Researched, Full of Potential', *Archives*, 36, pp.134–48 (2001).

Kissack, K., *Monmouth: the Making of a Country Town* (Phillimore, 1975).

Knight & Co., *The Union and Parish Officers' Pocket Almanac and Guide* (1852).

Knott, J., *Popular Opposition to the 1834 Poor Law* (Croon Helm, 1986).

Langley, M., & Langley, G., *At the Crossroads: A History of Arclid Workhouse and Hospital* (1993).

Large, D., *Bristol and the New Poor Law* (Bristol Branch of the Historical Association booklet, 1995).

Larkin-Jones, J. & T., *Items of Interest from the History of the 'Old Corwen Workhouse'* (Local leaflet,1998).

Latham, F. A., *Tarporley: the History of a Cheshire Village* (Tarporley Local History Group, 1973).

Law Commission, *Statute Law Repeals: Nineteenth Report, draft Statute Law (Repeals) Bill* (2012).

Lett, W. R., 'Notes on Mediaeval Dursley', *Transactions of the Bristol and Gloucestershire Archaeological Society*, 13, 16–18 (1889).

Lewis, B., *Swansea and the Workhouse: The Poor Law in 19th Century Swansea* (West Glamorgan Archive Service, 2003).

Lewis, D., *The History of Llantrisant* (Beddau Centenary Committee, 1966).

Lewis, R. A., 'William Day and the Poor Law Commissioners', *University of Birmingham Historical Journal*, IX, 172–87 (1964).

Lindley, E. S., *Wotton Under Edge: Men and Affairs of a Cotswold Wool Town* (Sutton, 1977).

Lindsay, J., 'The Problems of the Caernarfon Union Workhouse from 1846–1930', *Caernarvonshire Historical Society Transactions*, pp.52–3 (1991–2).

Lindsay, J., 'Poor Relief in North Wales and East Lothian: A Comparison of the East Lothian', *Transactions of the East Lothian Antiquarian and Field Naturalists Society*, XXIV, pp.41–66 (2000).

Lloyd Kenyon, R., 'Township of Felton', *Transactions of the Shropshire Archaeological and Natural History Society*, Series 3, Vol. II, pp.359–380 (1902).

Lloyd, A., *Quaker Social History 1669–1738* (1950).

MacLeod, F. A., 'The History of Chirbury', *Transactions of the Shropshire Archaeological and Natural History Society*, Series 3, Vol. VI, pp.227–376 (1906).

Malmgreen, G., *Silk town: Industry and Culture in Macclesfield, 1750–1835* (Hull University Press, 1985).

Marshall, D., *The English Poor in the Eighteenth Century* (1928).

Morgan, C. A., & Briffett, J. M., *The Ross Union Workhouse 1836–1914* (Ross-on-Wye and District Civic Society, 1998).

Morrill, S., 'Poor Law in Hereford 1836–51', *The Woolhope Naturalists' Field Club*, 41, pp.239–52 (1974).

Morrison, K., *The Workhouse: a Study of Poor-Law Buildings in England* (Royal Commission on the Historical Monuments of England, 1999).

Moss, M. S., 'The Building of, and the Subsequent Running of, the Westbury-on-Trym Workhouse, near Bristol', *Transactions of the Bristol and Gloucestershire Archaeological Society*, 86, pp.151–72 (1967).

Newent Local History Society, *Chapters in Newent's History* (Newent Local History Society, 2003).

Nicholls, G., *A History of the English Poor Law* (London, 1854).

Owen, B., 'The Newtown and Llanidloes Poor Law Union Workhouse, Caersws, 1837–1847', *Montgomeryshire Collections*, 78, pp.115–60 (1990).

Owen, G. D., 'The Poor Law System in Carmarthenshire During the Eighteenth and Early Nineteenth Centuries', *Transactions of the Honourable Society of Cymmrodorion*, pp.71–86 (1941).

Owen, H., *Some Account of the Ancient and Present State of Shrewsbury* (E. J. Morton, 1808).

Owen, R., 'Welshpool Landmarks: An Account of the Old Houses of Pool Town and its Suburbs', *Collections Historical & Archaeological Relating to Montgomeryshire*, 38, pp.153–84 (1918).

Owen-John, F., 'The Gower Union and Penmaen Workhouse', *Gower*, 51, pp.71–79 (2000).

Paget, M., *A History of Charlton* Kings (Charlton Kings Local History Society, 1988).

Palmer, A. N., *History of the Town of Wrexham* (1893).

Parker, K., 'Radnorshire and the New Poor Law to Circa 1850', *Radnorshire Society Transactions*, 74, pp.169–98 (2004).

Parry, G., *Trallodfa'r Tlawd Y Wyrcws Yng Ngorllewin Meirionnydd Yn Y Bedwaredd Ganrif Ar Bymtheg* (Aberystwyth Canolfan Uwchefrydiau Cymreig a Cheltaidd Prifysgol Cymru, 1996).

Parry-Jones, E., *From Workhouse to Hospital: The Story of H.M. Stanley Hospital, St Asaph 1840–1980* (Clwyd Area Health Authority, 1981).

Pearson, J. M., 'A Threatened Welshpool Landmark', *Collections Historical & Archaeological Relating to Montgomeryshire*, 38, pp.145–6 (1918).

Peele, E. C., and Clease, R. S. (Eds.), *Shropshire Parish Documents* (W.B. Walker, 1903).

Peeling, B., and Knight, C., *The Royal Gwent and St. Woolos Hospitals: A Century of Service in Newport* (The Old Bakehouse, 2004).

Phillimore, W. P. (Ed), Shropshire Parish Registers: Diocese of Hereford Vol. VII (Shropshire Parish Register Society, 1902).

Phillimore, W. P. (Ed.), Shropshire Parish Registers: Diocese of Lichfield Vol. V (Shropshire Parish Register Society, 1905).

Phillimore, W. P. (Ed.), Shropshire Parish Registers: Diocese of St Asaph Vol. I (Shropshire Parish Register Society, 1906).

Phoenix, R., *Life in the Hawarden Union Workhouse 1855–1930* (2011).

Pigot & Co., *Pigot & Co.'s National Commercial Directory* (1828–9).

Pigot & Co., *Pigot & Co.'s National Commercial Directory* (1835).

PLC, Official Circulars of Public Documents and Information (1853).

Powell, E., *History of Tredegar* (South Wales Printing Works, 1885).

Powell, J., *Hard Times in Herefordshire: the effects of the workhouse and the New Poor Law* (Logaston Press, 2008).

PP, Reports on the Relief and Settlement of the Poor [as reprinted in PP, 1803, pp. 249–96] (1776).

PP, Report on the Returns made by the Overseers of the Poor [as reprinted in PP, 1803, pp. 297–539] (1777).

PP, Reports from Committees of the House of Commons 1774–1802 (Vol. IX) (1803).

PP, Abstract of Returns Relative to the Expence and Maintenance of the Poor (1804).

PP, Abstract of the Answers and Returns Relative to the Expence and Maintenance of the Poor in England (1818).

PP, Twenty-Fourth Report of the Charity Commissioners (1831).

PP, Report into the Administration and Practical Operation of the Poor Laws: Appendix A (Reports) (1834a).

PP, Report into the Administration and Practical Operation of the Poor Laws, Appendix B (Answers to Rural Queries) (1834b).

PP, Report into the Administration and Practical Operation of the Poor Laws, Appendix B2 (Answers to Town Queries) (1834c).

PP, First Annual Report of the Poor Law Commissioners (1835).

PP, Second Annual Report of the Poor Law Commissioners (1836).

PP, Eighth Annual Report of the Poor Law Commissioners (1842).

PP, Thirteenth Annual Report of the Poor Law Commissioners (1847).

PP, Minutes of the Committee of Council on Education 1847–8–9 (1849).

PP, Married Couples over 60 Relieved in Workhouses (1853).

PP, Minutes of the Committee of Council on Education 1855–6 (1856).

PP, Paupers in Workhouses (1861).

PP, Reports on Vagrancy (1866).

PP, Poor Law (Workhouse Inspection) (1867).

PP, Twenty-First Annual Report of the Poor Law Board (1869).

PP, Twenty-Second Annual Report of the Poor Law Board (1870).

PP, Twenty-Third Annual Report of the Poor Law Board (1871).

PP, Workhouses (Consumption of Spirits &c.) (1885).

PP, Twentieth Annual Report of the Local Government Board (1890).

PP, Thirtieth Annual Report of the Local Government Board (1902).

PP, Royal Commission on the Poor Laws and Relief of Distress, Appendix 28: Reports of Visits (1909).

PP, First Annual Report of the Ministry of Health (1920).

PP, Official Circulars of Public Documents and Information 1840–51, vols. VII–X (1970).

Pryce, T., 'History of the Parish of Llandysilio', *Collections, Historical & Archaeological Relating to Montgomeryshire*, Part IV, 32, pp.227–294, (1902).

Reeves, N. C., *The Leon Valley: Three Herefordshire Villages, Kingsland, Monkland & Eardisland* (Phillimore, 1980).

Rochester, M., *The Northwich Poor Law Union and Workhouse* (Salt Museum leaflet, 1988).

Rowley, S.V., *Poor Relief in the Parish of Kinnerley, Shropshire c. 1700–1840* (1983).

Rowley-Morris, E., History of the Parish of Kerry. Montgomeryshire Collections, XXVI, 83–116 (1892).

Ryland-Epton, L., 'Cirencester Workhouse under the Old Poor Law', *Transactions of the Bristol & Gloucestershire Archaeological Society*, 135, 225–36 (2017).

Ryland-Epton, L., *Social Policy, Welfare Innovation & Governance in England: The Creation and Implementation of Gilbert's Act 1782* (PhD Thesis, Open University, 2020).

Semper, W. H., 'Local Government and Politics Since 1700', In W. B. Stephens (Ed.), *History of Congleton* (pp. 82–120) (Manchester University Press, 1970).

Smith, D. B., *No Ordinary Surgeon: the Life of William Binley Dickinson* (Amberley, 2017).

Smith, L., 'Refuges of Last Resort: Shropshire Workhouses and the People who Built and Ran Them', *Transactions of the Shropshire Archaeological and Historical Society*, LXXXII, pp. 1–125 (2007).

Sockett, H., *The Substance of Three Reports Made to the Inhabitants of the Town and Franchise of Swansea Respecting the Management of the Poor in that District in the Years 1818–1819–1820* (T&J Allman, 1821).

Sockett, H., *A Concise Account of the Origin of the House of Industry, and the Management of the Poor in the Town and Franchise of Swansea, for the Years 1818 and 1832, Both Inclusive* (1834).

Spence, E. I., *Summer Excursions* (Vol. II) (1809).

Stanley, H. M., *The Autobiography of Sir Henry Morton Stanley* (D. Stanley, Ed.) (Cambridge University Press, 1909).

Stephen, L., *Dictionary of National Biography* (Oxford University Press, 1899).

Stewart, J., & King, S., Death in Llantrisant: 'Henry Williams and the New Poor Law in Wales', *Rural History*, 15(1), 69–87 (2004).

Summers, M., & Bowman, S., *Of Poor Law, Patients and Professionals... A History of Bristol's Southmead Hospital* (Bristol, 1995).

T. S. J., Welshpool Parish Book (Pool Middle) 1765–84. Montgomeryshire Collections, XXXIII, 247–360 (1904).

Thomas, B. B., The Old Poor Law in Ardudwy Uwch-Artro. Bulletin of the Board of Celtic Studies, 7, 153–91 (1934).

Thomas, I., *Newport Union: a Retrospective* [Typescript, Gwent Archives] (1901).

Thomas, J. E., 'The Poor Law in West Glamorgan 1834 to 1930', *Morgannwg Transactions of the Glamorgan Local History Society*, 1, 45–69 (1974).

Thomas, J. H., & Wilkins, W. E., *The Bridgend-Cowbridge Union Workhouse and Guardians* (D. Brown and Sons, 1995).

Thomas, T., *Poor Relief in Merthyr Tydfil Union in Victorian Times* (Glamorgan Archive Service, 1992).

Thomas, Venerable Archdeacon, *Meifod Parish Notes. Montgomeryshire Collections*, XXV, 5–8 (1891).

Timmis Smith, P., 'Congleton's Secular Buildings', in W. B. Stephens (Ed.), *History of Congleton*, pp. 309–317 (Manchester University Press 1970).

Tomkins, A., 'Paupers and the Infirmary in Mid-Eighteenth-Century Shrewsbury', *Medical History*, 43, 208–227 (1999).

Tringham, N. J., *A History of the County of Stafford: Audley, Keele and Trentham* (Boydell & Brewer, 2013).

Wakeman, O., 'Some Leaves from the Records of the Court of Quarter Sessions, for the County of Salop, Part III', *Transactions of the Shropshire Archaeological and Natural History Society*, Series 2, Vol. IV, pp.65–114 (1892).

Walmsley, P., 'The Shocking Occurrence at Stroud Workhouse, 1849', *Gloucestershire History* (7), pp.8–10 (1993).

Walsh, V. J., 'Old and New Poor Laws in Shropshire, 1820–70', *Midland History*, 2(4), pp.225–43 (1974).

Whitmore, W. W., *Report of the Bridgnorth Union* (1837).

Willett, R., *A Memoir of Hawarden Parish, Flintshire* (1822).

Williams, D., *The Story of Ludlow Workhouse 1839–1929* (Logaston Press, 2012).

Williams, M., *Crickhowell Union Workhouse: The Spike* (2008).

Winstone, J., 'Reminiscences of Old Cardiff', *Cardiff Naturalists' Society Reports and Transactions*, XV, 60–75 (1883).

Wright, T., *The History & Antiquities of the Town of Ludlow* (Procter & Jones, 1826).

Yeoman, J. B., Some Poor History and the Wirrall Union (Central Wirral Hospital Management Committee booklet, 1965).

INDEX OF PLACES

Abbey Dore 219
Aberayron 22, 37, 38
Abergavenny 28, 121
Aberystruth 121–3, 132
Aberystwyth 23, 40, 58
Adlington 166
Albrighton 255
Alderbury 232
Aldsworth 201
Alkington 210
Almeley 229
Almondsbury 210
Altrincham 31
Angle 146
Arclid 163
Ashperton 223
Ashton–upon–Mersey 156
Astley 232
Atcham 16, 36–7, 39
Audlem 169
Aust 209
Avening 204
Awre 211

Baddiley 169
Bala 113
Bangor (Caernarvonshire) 15, 21, 27–8,
  37, 39, 75, 77

Bangor (Flintshire) 86
Baschurch 243
Bassaleg 129
Bausley 232
Bedwas 129
Bedwellty 37, 122–3
Begelley 144
Benthall 248
Berrington 13, 231–2
Betchton 163
Betws-yn-Rhos 91
Biddulph 162
Birkenhead 31, 36, 39, 157, 177
Bishop's Castle 13, 35, 41, 239
Bishop's Castle 35
Bishop's Cleeve 215
Bisley 204
Blaina 121
Bledington 202
Bollington 156, 166
Bostock 13, 171
Bourton-on-the-Water 202
Brecon 49
Bridgend 36, 37, 95
Bridgnorth 234
Bridstow 227
Brimpsfield 189
Bristol (Quakers), 184

Bristol (Southmead), 32, 37, 39
Bristol (St George), 191
Bristol (St Peter's), 10, 30, 36, 179
Bristol (St Philip & St Jacob), 190
Bristol (Stapleton), 37, 181, 191
Bromborough 198
Bromyard 216
Broseley 247
Broughton 89
Bryncoch 105
Buildwas 248
Builth 23, 27, 37, 50
Burghill 220
Buttonbridge 238

Caerphilly 97
Caersws 22, 28, 138, 141
Cam 195
Camrose 143
Cardeston 232
Cardiff 33, 35, 36, 97
Cardington 237
Carew 146
Carmarthen 37, 65
Carnarvon 37
Carrington 156
Chapel Hill 125
Charlton Kings 185
Cheltenham 13, 35, 37, 40, 184
Chepstow 28, 125
Chester 10, 13, 37, 39, 159
Cheswardine 241
Chetton 235
Chetwynd 251
Child's Ercall 241
Chipping Sodbury 27, 187
Chirbury 139
Chirk 253
Chorley 166
Church Stretton 235
Cirencester 13, 189
Clatterbridge 177
Claverley 234
Cleobury Mortimer 28, 39, 238
Clifford 54

Clifton 14, 192
Cloddiau 141
Clun 239
Coaley 195
Coberley 184
Cockett 111
Coleford 127
Colwall 223
Condover 231
Congleton 13, 27, 33, 161
Conway 29
Corfton 246
Corwen 39, 114
Cound 232
Cowbridge 95
Cradley 216
Crickhowell 23, 53
Cross Houses 232
Cwmdu 53

Dawley 249
Deerhurst 208
Dihewyd 57
Dilwyn 229
Dingestow 128, 132
Dolgelley 38, 116
Donnington 251
Dore 37
Dorrington 241
Dorstone 54
Dowlais 103
Drayton 241–2
Dunham 156
Dursley 195
Dutton 172
Dymock 199

Eardisland 229
Eastington 213
Eaton 169
Eaton-under-Heywood 237
Edgmond 250
Eglwys-Fach (Eglwysbach) 83
Eglwysilan 97
Elberton 210

Ellesmere 13, 16, 243
English Bicknor 127
Ewenny 95

Faddiley 169
Fairford 189
Farlow 238
Forden 16, 139
Forthampton 209
Forton 250
Frampton Cotterell 187
Frampton-on-Severn 213

Garway 128
Gawsworth 166
Gloucester 10, 27, 37, 39, 196
Gnosall 250, 251
Goetre 132
Goodrich 227
Goostrey-cum-Barnshaw 171
Grappenhall 172
Great Boughton 27, 164
Great Sutton 176
Guilsfield 135

Halton 172
Ham and Stone 210
Hartpury 199
Hatton (Cheshire) 172
Hatton (Shropshire) 237
Haverfordwest 39, 143
Hawarden 13, 88, 90
Hawkesbury Upton 187
Hay-on-Wye 25, 54
Heaton Norris 175
Hereford 10, 23, 28, 219, 220
High Ercall 259
High Leigh 156
High Offley 250
Higher Clase 110
Higher Llanrhidian 110
Higher Penderry 110
Hinton, Breadstone and Hamfallow 210
Hoarwithy 227
Hodgeston 146
Hodnet 241

Holyhead 46
Holywell 90
Hope-under-Dinsmore 225
Horsley 203
Hoylake 178
Hubberston 143
Hull and Appleton 172
Huntley 199

Ightfield 260
Iron Acton 187
Itton 125
Ivington 225

Jeffreyston 144

Kentchurch 217
Kerry 141
Kimbolton 225
King's Stanley 204
Kingsland 225
Kingswood 195
Kington 20, 151, 222
Kinlet 238
Kinnerley 253
Knighton 13, 20, 37, 149–52
Knutsford 13, 155

Lampeter Velfrey 144
Lampeter 23, 62
Lampha 95
Laugharne 65
Lawrenny 146
Ledbury 13, 37, 216, 223
Leighton 232
Leintwardine 246
Leominster 224
Leonard Stanley 205
Letterston 143
Lilleshall 251
Little Brampton 151
Little Sutton 176
Little Wenlock 13, 248
Littledean 212
Littleton-upon-Severn 210
Llandaff 97

Llandderfel 113
Llandefeilog 66
Llandeilo Talybont 110
Llandetty 49, 53
Llandilo Fawr 68
Llandingat 70
Llandovery 22, 70
Llanelly (Breconshire) 53
Llanelly (Carmarthenshire) 71
Llanerchymedd 44
Llanfabon 102
Llanfair Caereinion 22
Llanfair Waterdine 149
Llanfyllin 135
Llangarrow 227
Llangathen 68
Llangattock 53
Llangeler 67
Llangendeirne 65
Llangennech 71
Llangenny 53
Llanglydwen 144
Llangollen 114
Llangynidr 53
Llanidloes 141
Llanover 132
Llanrhaiadr-yn-Mochnant 135
Llanrug 77
Llanrwst 83
Llansanffraid-Glan-Conwy 79
Llansilin 252, 253
Llanstadwell 147
Llantilio Crosseny 128
Llantilio Pertholey 121
Llantrisant 15, 18, 97
Llantwit Fardre 97, 108
Llantwit Major 95
Llanwenarth 132
Llanwnda 143
Llechryd 61
Llwynypia 109
Llys-y-fran 144
Longhope 211
Loveston 144
Lower Clase 110
Ludchurch 144

Ludlow 9, 13, 30, 35, 41, 149, 245
Lugwardine 220
Lydbury North 239
Lydham 239
Lymm 13, 155, 156

Macclesfield 9, 22, 28, 35, 41, 165, 167
Machynlleth 38, 137, 138
Madeley 32, 248
Madley 217
Maentwrog 21
Malpas 262
Manorbier 146
Marchwiel 86
Market Drayton 241–2
Marple 175
Marston 171
Matherne 125
Meifod 135
Merthyr Tydfil 31, 35, 37, 40, 102
Middlewich 13, 171
Millington 156
Milson 238
Minchinhampton 204
Miserden 204
Mitcheldean 12, 211
Mobberley 156
Monkland 225
Monkswood 132
Monmouth 127
Monythusloine (Mynyddislwyn) 129
Moore 172
Morda 253
Much Wenlock 13, 247
Mydroilyn 12, 57

Nantwich 9, 169
Narberth 22, 144
Nash 151
Neath 27, 31, 36–7, 104
Neen Savage 238
Nevern 61
Newcastle (in) Emlyn 38, 73
Newent 38, 198
Newhall 170
Newland 127

Newnham 211
Newport (Monmouthshire) 31–3, 37, 129, 130
Newport (Shropshire) 13, 250–1
Newton Nottage 95
Newton 171
Newtown 141
North Nibley 195
North Rode 166
Northleach 25, 37, 201
Northwich 25, 171
Norton (Cheshire) 172
Norton (Gloucestershire) 196

Olveston 210
Oswestry 16, 253
Over 171
Overbury 208
Overton 244
Oystermouth 110

Painswick 204
Panteg 132
Partington 156
Pembridge 222
Pembroke 25, 146
Penally 146
Pencoed 95
Penmaen 100
Pennard 110
Penperlleni 132
Penrhyndeudraeth 118
Peterstow 227
Pickhill 86
Pontardawe 37, 106
Pontesbury 231
Pontsarn 103
Pontypool 37, 132
Pontypridd 37, 107
Poole 169
Port Eynon 110
Portskewett 125
Pott Shrigley 166
Pownal Fee 155
Prees 260
Prestbury 185

Presteigne 20, 23, 151
Pwllheli 23, 28, 31, 81

Quatt 35, 235, 265

Ragland 128
Rainow 166
Randwick 204
Rangeworthy 210
Redberth 146
Redmarley D'Abitot 199
Redwith and Northwick 210
Rhayader 20, 22–3, 151, 153
Rhossili 110
Roath 97
Rock 238
Rodborough 204
Rodd 151
Rogerstone 129
Ross-on-Wye 27, 30, 37, 41, 227
Rostherne 155
Ruardean 227
Ruckley 232
Runcorn 172
Ruthin 37, 85
Ruyton-of-the-Eleven-Towns 252

Sale 156
Sandbach 162
Selattyn 253
Sesswick 86
Sheriffhales 255
Shifnal 13, 254
Shipton Moyne 207
Shobdon 225
Shrewsbury 9, 16–17, 234, 258
Slimbridge 195
Soudley 237
Southerndown 95
Southmead 194
Southwell 17
Spoonley 241
St Asaph 37, 91
St Athan 95
St Brides Major 95
St Dogmaels 61

St Edrens 143
St Florence 146
St Issells 144
Stanford Bishop 216
Stapleton 181, 191
Staunton 199
Stockport 13, 31, 37, 175
Stoke-upon-Tern 241
Stonehouse 205, 212
Stow-on-the-Wold 202
Stroud 13, 37, 203, 205
Sudbrook 127
Sutton Lane Ends 166
Swansea 15, 27, 36, 109

Tarporley 13, 169
Taynton 199
Tetbury 25, 37, 39, 207
Thelwall 172
Thornbury 25, 209–10
Tibberton (Gloucestershire) 199
Tibberton (Shropshire) 251
Timperley 156
Trecynon 103
Tredegar 121, 123
Tregaron 23, 38, 64
Tuffley 197
Tytherington 209

Uley 195
Upton Bishop 227
Upton Crews 227
Upton Magna 232
Utkinton 169

Vowchurch 217

Walford 227
Warburton 156
Warrington 156, 172
Weaver 171
Wellington 13, 27, 35, 37, 231, 258
Welshpool 135, 138
Wem 260
Weobley 229
West Felton 253
West Walton 143
Westbury 231
Westbury-on-Severn 211
Westbury-on-Trym 14, 191
Westerleigh 187
Weston 169
Weston-under-Penyard 227
Whitchurch (Shropshire) 16, 42, 262
Whitchurch (Glamorgan) 97
Whitebrook 128
Whittington 253
Wickwar 187
Wilmslow 155
Wincham 171
Winchcombe 25, 215
Winslow 13, 216
Wistanstow 237
Witton-cum-Twambrook 171
Woodmancote 215
Woonton 229
Worfield 234
Worthen 139
Wotton-under-Edge 195
Wrexham 34, 37, 86
Wrinehill 169, 171
Wrockwardine 13

Yate 187